THINGS MY MOTHER
NEVER TOLD ME

BLAKE MORRISON

# Things My Mother Never Told Me

**Granta Books**
New York·London

Granta Books USA, 1755 Broadway, 5th Floor, New York, NY 10019
www.granta.com

First published in hardcover in the United States of America by
Granta Books 2003
First published in Great Britain by Chatto & Windus 2002

2 4 6 8 10 9 7 5 3 1

ISBN 1-86207-702-9

Designed by Peter Ward
Printed in the United States of America on acid-free paper
April 2004

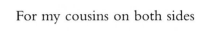

For my cousins on both sides

Many things that I would not care to tell any
    individual man I tell to the public.

MONTAIGNE

Behind the corpse in the reservoir, behind the ghost on
    the links,
Behind the lady who dances and the man who madly
    drinks,
Under the look of fatigue, the attack of migraine and
    the sigh
There is always another story, there is more than meets
    the eye.

AUDEN

# CONTENTS

Crownhill, Plymouth
20.I.43

Dear Agnes (Gennie in future),

Just a line to let you know that the shocking type is still alive. I am sorry you couldn't turn up at the station to see him off. It was really very selfish of him to suggest it, wasn't it? He (I in future) would have left a poor defenceless Gennie in the dark in the city of Manchester.

How are you? Still busy I suppose. I have been very busy since getting back here and look like being an hell of a sight busier shortly. They are going to make me take a sick parade six miles away from here at 08.30. I shall probably be the sick one.

I have only had one night out since I got back so I think I am behaving very well, don't you? I suppose you, on the other hand, are carrying on as usual.

Love, Arthur

Hope Hospital, Pendleton, Salford 6
27.I.43

Dear Arthur,

Thanks so much for your letter received last week. Was rather surprised to hear from you in spite of the fact that you did say you would write some time!

Life here has been peaceful since you left – everyone being very respectable. I did not like the crack in your letter about my 'carrying on as usual' – I have not even been 'smoking and drinking'. Actually you are one up on me by having had a night out – it is probably more than that now.

I was in Lancaster yesterday, at the Assizes, but did not have to

go in the witness box – they all pleaded guilty and the abortionist got
6 months . . .

   If you think my effort deserves an answer do write again.

   Agnes.

ONE MINUTE SHE'S posing in her gown and mortar board,
the next she's on the boat. It's what you do if you're young
and Irish: get away as quickly as you can. America was her first
thought. But, with her schooling and her medical degree, she
needn't go that far. England's crisis is her opportunity. With so
many of their own called up, they're crying out for doctors –
even Irish girl doctors like Agnes O'Shea. It was the name of the
place that drew her: Hope. Never mind that it's in Salford, which
people say is grim. Her friend Mary Galvin will be following in
a couple of months. Several other girls she knows from Dublin
are also heading across. It's a brain drain approved by De Valera's

government: over in England these doctors can learn about air-raid casualties, useful experience should Ireland, despite its neutrality, be attacked. But returning, armed with knowledge, isn't on her agenda. If things work out she'll be staying in England till the war ends, maybe longer. There's a boy back in Kerry, a family friend called Tom, with chestnut eyes; and another, Billy Rattigan, who tempted her with a car as an engagement present. But no one's going to keep her from the boat.

Summer of '42. My mother – not yet my mother – is on her way. She stands by the rail, as millions have before: dreamer, chancer, economic migrant. Dun Laoghaire grows tiny in her wake. Herring gulls wheel above like smudgy angels. On the far side of the water lies Hope.

# CHAPTER ONE

# How Many Children?

NOT LONG BEFORE she died, my mother gave me quite a turn. I was visiting her at a nursing home called Cromwell's, in the same Yorkshire village where she'd lived for forty years. For most of my childhood, Cromwell's had been the Manor House Hotel, a business that failed to prosper no matter how often it changed hands. She hated the greystone gauntness of the building, and when it became a nursing home said she'd rather take an overdose than 'end up there'. In the event, when she became too ill to manage at home, it seemed the only sensible option. She resented the indignity but accepted the logic. Friends and neighbours could drop by. My sister lived just across the road.

The rooms in Cromwell's are named after English poets, and when my mother was admitted they put her in Larkin, not a good omen. The room was far from unpleasant but this was a place for the elderly and dying, and I wondered what Larkin, the laureate of death, would have made of being commemorated in this way. In time, my mother switched rooms. The staff could see she wasn't thriving, and moved her to Byron, near the main entrance, where there was always someone passing by. She wasn't going to recover — a fungal infection, aspergillus, had taken over her lungs — but it was thought her spirits might improve in a busier part of the home, Larkin being a gloomy backwater. The move paid off. A month of Byron and she seemed much brighter. The last time I'd visited, on a day-trip from London, she'd talked so long and hard that I left feeling exhausted, as though it was me who needed nursing, while she burned invincibly on.

This time I'd been in Hull, for a conference, as it happened, on Larkin's poetry, an excuse to see my mother on the way home: Hull to Skipton is no small hop but at least they're up the same end of the country. Around eleven o'clock on Sunday morning, sweaty from two trains and a minicab, I walked in on her without knocking – then halted and began to retreat. I'd got the wrong room, I thought. But Byron was the name on the door. Well, then, they'd put the wrong woman in it – the tiny figure with thin white hair under the sheets couldn't be my mother. But it was, *she* was: I recognised the mohair cardigan on the bedside chair and the radio she'd brought over from the house. 'Mum,' I said, several times, until the old lady stirred from foetal sleep and greeted me. I pulled the curtains wide and helped her sit upright, only then seeing the bruise down one side of her face from where she'd fallen three nights before. There were little white slivers of sticking plaster round her eye – like the wrinkles you get after reading without sunglasses on a summer's day. The bruise and plasters gave her a comic look, like a black and white minstrel, but she seemed oblivious to it. We talked on, long past lunch. Later my sister Gill came over. By the time I left, my mum was indisputably my mum again. But I felt shocked at having failed to recognise her.

She was old and frail that day – 'not herself', and about to become so for ever. And yet my error seemed symptomatic. It was as though I didn't really know her. As though she'd always been someone else.

✻　✻　✻

THREE WEEKS LATER, in mid-July, I was back again, the sun pouring in from distant hills. Her house had been empty since she went into Cromwell's. But now the doors stood open in the heat and the lawn was crowded with relations. 'A proper family do', my father would have called it, though the do was really the end of family. Ragged robin and cow parsley lined the drive. Puffs of cloud drifted over the sun, as though to cast the odd shadow, out of respect. From the end of the garden came a swish and pock that to me, that day, sounded like a mallet striking bone. The British Open golf championship had just been on, and the children, unearthing an ancient wooden driver in the garage, were hitting shots into the lush green meadow. The meadow grass was thick, and already the supply of golf balls had dwindled from twenty to four. Soon the last of them would be lost forever in the rough.

For my father's funeral five years before, the village church had been packed. Today we'd wondered would anyone turn up. I could feel my mother willing the place to be empty, so she could slip away unnoticed, without a fuss. That was how she was, or how she'd been: quiet, self-contained, not one to draw attention to herself. Though a doctor just like him, a family GP, she'd been a woman of her generation, deferential to her husband and uncomfortable in a crowd. The low voice, the soft grey eyes, the muted colours all said the same: 'Why would anyone be interested in *me*?' And yet the church, when we reached it, looked as crowded for her as it had been for him. Not that my sister and I, in our front pews, were best placed to count heads. And not that numbers are a judgment on a life. But it was consoling to feel the press of friends and patients at our backs.

Among them was Auntie Beaty, a woman with whom my father had been 'obsessed' (his word) for nearly a decade. Beaty, not an aunt at all, but the other woman. Beaty, source of my mother's midlife suffering, but later her confidante and closest friend. Beaty, whose relationship with him they talked about in the aftermath of his death, clinging to what they had in common: that they had loved him. All of it – reconciliation as well as pain – was water under the bridge now. And here was Beaty in my parents' house again, having come back with her husband Sam from church. Once, her presence at a family occasion might have caused awkwardness with my father's relations, those who'd *heard*. Today Beaty was welcome. She'd been having treatment for cancer. A less scarlet woman was impossible to imagine.

'It's the drugs,' she said, patting her waist, as though I'd accused her of putting on weight. 'When your mum last saw me she said, "I didn't mind delivering Josephine thirty years ago, but you can forget this one".' She laughed. 'I'd have taken offence with anyone else.'

'Let me top you up,' I said.

'Whooah, I'm supposed to be driving.' She looked round. 'A good turnout.'

'Yes. No one from her side, but . . .'

'Did you get in touch with them?'

'Everybody I could find in the address book,' I said. 'But it's a long way to come. And her brothers and sisters are all dead. Eileen was the last. She died a few weeks ago. I'm not sure Mum even knew.'

'There were ten of them, weren't there?'

'Something like that. A lot, anyway.'

I moved on with my wine, refilling glasses. A mottled hand reached out to clasp mine, an eye or two detained me. They were sorry for my trouble – sorry for their own, too, since by the law of averages their turn was coming soon. My parents, my godparents, the other halves of those present today were floating somewhere in oblivion. On the mantelpiece was a photo of my parents' wedding. From the row of grinning faces, the only survivor was Uncle Ron – husband of my father's sister Mary (herself dead for over a decade). Even Ron, with his trim moustache and dentist's precision, had lately gone downhill. Today he sat alone in an armchair, away from the company. The recent operation for mouth cancer made it hard for him to speak, and he dabbed at his mouth with paper tissues. At least, I told myself, he had driven here, was self-sufficient, could do the *Telegraph* crossword and listen to music. It was possible to be an octogenarian and alive.

I glanced at my sister Gill, who was carrying a plate of sausage rolls. We were orphans now, too old for that to mean what it means in Dickens's novels, too human for it not to count. Don't think of it, I thought. Remember the good times. Keep smiling and pouring the drinks. Easier said than done. My father had died quickly, and we could recall him in stubborn health only weeks before his wake. My mother had been dying slowly ever since his death – a widow and forlorn, with all the nameless agues of ageing, until along came aspergillus, a white fungus that filled her lungs. It was hard to recall her looking healthy. But on her birthday three months back we'd brought her over from Cromwell's, and given her cake and champagne, and she'd sat in this house fraily smiling from an armchair with two badges pinned to her cardigan, 'Eighty Years Young' and 'Frankly My Dear I Don't Give a Damn'. The big Eight-O: she was amazed to have made it, her husband and siblings having fallen short. Now she too had run down to zero, was oh, nothing but ashes in a jar. But in April she'd been smiling. And that day was what we talked of now, and how she had sat here counting her blessings while preparing, after the party, to die.

*A good life . . . no more suffering . . . all for the best.* Her friends shook hands and drifted off, their tail-lights dwindling in the dusk. I collected a stack of plates, their willow pattern flaked with the remains of *vol au vents*, and took them to my sister at the sink.

So the wake was over and none of my mother's family had come. Yet she was fond of her nieces and nephews, and in their lifetimes her siblings had tried to keep in touch. Uncle Joe, who used to call while over from Ireland on business and drink whisky with my father; Auntie Kitty, gaunt, nasal, shining-eyed, who also visited several times; Auntie Eileen, who'd developed Alzheimer's but whose wit was unimpaired when last we met; Auntie Sheila, of course, a teacher in the Midlands, lonely and unmarried, who for years had stayed with us during school holidays; and then one more – I'd no name or face, but hadn't my mother once spoken of giving morphine to a dying brother? With her, that made six.

'I thought there were eight,' my sister said.

'Really?'

'She had a brother called Patrick, didn't she?'

'He must have been the one she gave morphine to.'

'And wasn't there an older sister called Criss?' said Gill.

'Not that I know of.'

'She more or less brought Mum up, I think.'

'So she must have been a *lot* older.'

'I suppose.'

Gill didn't know, or didn't want to know. Talk seemed to afflict her, though the real affliction was grief. I was feeling it too. But perhaps she felt it more deeply. She had her own troubles as well – serious problems with her eyesight. It was a lot to live with, on top of death. And now me, with my pointless questions.

Later that night Gill and I got maudlin-drunk together – on white wine, the milk of amnesia. We were quiet at first but then things turned nasty. Newly orphaned, we both felt a need for mayhem. If there'd been someone to fight or fuck, that would have been perfect, but we only had each other, so we rowed. Gill said of course I knew, didn't I, that she, Mum, had loved her, Gillian, more than she had ever loved me – a remark which went in as intended. I didn't doubt my mother loved Gill: I could still hear her scream from forty years back when the wardrobe toppled upstairs and she ran like the wind to get there and drag Gill free. But I didn't doubt my mother had loved me too. It was demeaning to get into this – children squabbling over a corpse. I told Gill she was malicious. She called me a bastard. Ancient grudges were fetched out: the time I'd run into her in my pedal car, the time stepping off the fishing boat when she nearly slipped into the water because I on the quayside wouldn't offer my hand. Round and round we went, like caged animals, till exhaustion or reason got the better of us, and we made peace, and sat by the television, dozing in the embers of our rage. At some point her two children came in from the garden and took themselves off to bed. And at some point her husband Wynn returned from the pub. But Gill slept safely on. She was still sleeping when I slipped out through the darkness, walked over to my mother's, and climbed into her bed.

✻   ✻   ✻

I was used to sleeping in it. On trips up to see her in Cromwell's, I'd often stayed overnight and, as the one bed in the house already made up, it seemed the most convenient place.

Now my mother, five days cold, had become a ghost, but I'd no reason to feel unnerved. She wasn't the haunting type, and would be pleased to know the bed was getting an airing. The only discomfort was her mattress – the layer of lumpy sponge which, despite her back pain, she'd never bothered to replace. I thrashed about on it, angry at the thrift which had denied her comfort and was now denying me. The scents from her pillow were soothing as cough medicine but I couldn't get off to sleep. Nameless guilts lay with me on the mattress, growling out of the dark, *You could have done more.*

I turned the light on to reassure myself the room was empty. It was – too much so. The dip in the mattress was like a print of her absence, its hollow her length and shape. When my father died, it had been simple: he was there, then missing, and I grieved for the life – the spark, the energy, the intractable spirit – that had filled the vacancy. With my mother, it was more complex. She herself had been more complex, harder to pin down. In the framed photo on the windowsill, her eyes seemed to cloud over, her features to recede. I was tired. It had been a long day. I need-ed to sleep. Adrift on the hollow mattress, I tried counting her siblings. Six? Eight? What did it matter? But equally, why didn't I know? Not to know was certainly a failing – and that night of the funeral felt strange.

My mother had gone cold on me. Who was she? Or, to get the tense right, who had she been?

✶    ✶    ✶

SHE'D GROWN UP in Ireland, I knew that much. But for years when people asked me *where* in Ireland, my answers varied. Kerry or Limerick, Kenmare or Killarney, Kilkenny or Ennis-kerry or Kildare: I'd been told, more than once, but I forgot. When I was five, we spent a holiday in Ireland – our first and last. I could remember, or had photographs to remember for me, horses, bare feet, a wooden shack, a long sandy beach, a hole in the earth with new-born pups, a grocer's shop with a bench and dog outside.

I'd met aunts, uncles and cousins on that trip. But it wasn't an experience we repeated. Occasionally my mother would take the boat from Liverpool or Holyhead, and go back for a funeral or a few days' break. But she didn't allow us to join her. My father's family – his parents, his sister Mary and her four kids – lived less than an hour away. We spent every Christmas with them; most holidays, too. My cousins on that side – the Astles, my *real* cousins – were almost like brothers and sisters. Family meant Lancashire, and a web of my father's relations. Ireland seemed a continent away, and my mother's family as remote as an Amazonian tribe.

The remoteness was increased by the lack of photos. There were none dating from my mother's childhood. What did her parents look like? I'd no idea, and wasn't encouraged to ask. After her death, I came across a crumpled photo of a man and woman, she posed demurely with a posy, he perched above her with a moustache, centre parting and dandyish tie. I didn't recognise the couple. They hadn't the look of Morrisons. It was only later, meeting my cousins and seeing other photos, that I confirmed they were my mother's parents. The photo had been buried among wallets of my father's photos, dying not to be noticed. Did she take it out in secret sometimes? I'd no idea.

Once, in the early 1990s, when she was ill, I made a point of interviewing my mother about her childhood, fearful this was my last chance to find out. Though confined to bed, she did her best to escape.

'My childhood? Ach, it's so boring,' she said, and sent me off to do this or fetch that, anything but answer my questions. In the end I just sat there with my notebook, the son turned investigative reporter.

'My father's name was Patrick O'Shea,' she sighed. 'My mother's name was Margaret – Margaret Lyons till she married him.'

'And where was it you grew up again?'

'Killorglin. K-I-double-L-O-R-G-L-I-N. Near Killarney, in County Kerry. The house was in the middle of town, on Langford Street. We visited when you were little. Don't you remember?'

'Not really. And what was it your father did?'

I felt embarrassed asking. What someone's father did was a question you might ask of a newish friend, or of the exchange student arriving to spend a week with your teenage child. It wasn't something to ask your ageing mother.

'He was a wool merchant. He'd go out to markets three or four times a week and buy wool, then sell it, and ship it, to Bradford, where he'd trained, or sometimes to America. He had a large storehouse to keep it in. Did have. One night it burned down, with all his wool in it ready for export. I suppose I must have been about ten. I can't remember much except a great hoo-ha in the house, and shouting and tears because he wasn't insured, and a smell of burnt wool that hung around the town for months. Still, we did all right – he also owned the shop next door and the pub across the road.'

That night of the funeral, alone in her bed, I couldn't remember the rest of the conversation. But when I got back to London, I fished out the notebook – and found she'd also talked about her mother: 'More a lady of leisure than a housewife. Didn't even know how to boil an egg. Never had to. Employed a maid and kept her at it from dawn till midnight.'

There were also the names of four more brothers, none of whom I'd met: Paul ('the black sheep of the family'), William ('read Law at Trinity but later ran the family pub'), Peter ('much older, my mother's favourite, he wore plus-fours, and was very tall, unlike the rest of us – he died at twenty-three') and Dan ('much older, too, I've even vaguer memories of him, but I know he had TB, and went to Switzerland, or was it California, anyway the cure didn't work – he died round the time Peter did').

How many siblings did that make? Nine? Ten? And what about Criss, whom Gill had mentioned: where did she fit in? I thought of a famous essay by L. C. Knights which I'd read as a student, 'How Many Children Had Lady Macbeth?' Its point, I vaguely recalled, was that Shakespeare's text contradicted itself ('I have given suck,' says Lady M, 'and know/ How tender 'tis to love the babe that milks me', but nothing else in the play indicates that she had children). With my mother's family there was confusion, too: how many siblings had Agnes O'Shea?

\* \* \*

IT WAS AUTUMN before I went back to Yorkshire. Heavy rain had flooded the fields by the Aire. There were matters to discuss with the solicitor. There were also belongings to divide up, some for Gill and some for me. Long before her death, my mother had made us agree a list of articles we wanted, 'to stop any squabbling'. Which worked, but didn't make the process any less painful. I felt empty and leaden – not just orphaned but bereft of my oldest confidante. Yet I couldn't pretend to feel as I had when my father died. It wasn't that I loved my mother any less; in many ways I had been closer to her. But she had given us plenty of time to get used to her departure. And now she had gone, the emotions I experienced were familiar, and the condolences people sent had the same hollow ring. 'After the first death there is no other,' wrote Dylan Thomas, hinting at eternal life but also describing grief, which isn't as rawly shocking second time round. Some things hit me harder: clearing the house, for instance (she wasn't there to help), or sitting by my dumbstruck telephone (she wasn't going to call). But beyond the loss was another feeling: that I'd never found her in the first place.

It was a feeling that grew when, under the frayed green leather lid of her writing bureau, I came upon a letter from a woman called Margaret, who said she was my mother's great-niece: 'my grandmother was your sister Madge.' Margaret lived in the Midlands. She was tracing her family tree, and wondered if my mother could help. The letter dated back to 1994, and there was no sign my mother had answered it. I sat down and replied, telling Margaret what I knew and asking had she made any progress; what I didn't say was that my mother had never mentioned a sister called Madge. Her reply came a few weeks later. She enclosed a family tree. There were a few question marks and a couple of dates I knew to be wrong. But her tree included a Christine – Criss, presumably – and also a Jenny. I was dubious about Jenny: the name didn't sound very Irish. Even so, my mother's family was expanding.

Why had she never mentioned a Madge or Criss to me? In her last years, she'd sometimes been confused. There'd been the time she thought I was my father. There'd been the time she thought crowds of people were in the room with her. There'd been the time I phoned and she said to hang on while she called upstairs for Kathy, my wife; Kathy was at home with me, but before I could say anything I heard my mother calling 'Kathy', and she continued to call for several minutes, until at last giving up and apologising – very mysterious, but Kathy must have gone out. At times like this I thought 'Alzheimer's', and assumed she must be losing her wits, and worried they'd be lost completely (and that I'd lose her) before she died. Though no doctor could be sure what caused her bouts of confusion, there was no shortage of possibilities: she didn't eat properly, didn't sleep well, muddled up her pills, drank gin on top of medication, and may have suffered mini-strokes.

At Cromwell's, though, properly cared for, she was more lucid than she'd been for a couple of years. She'd also seemed lucid that day I asked her about her siblings, when she omitted at least two names. What was it all about?

✳    ✳    ✳

Killorglin
13.9.44

Dear Arthur,

You suggest I spend three months at home here. No thanks, and if you lived in a dump like this you wouldn't stay three months either. It is only a small town – more a village, I suppose, where there's nothing to do but gossip, and if I don't go around and say hello to everyone they'll say I've got big ideas since I went away. You have to live in place like this to know what it's like. Two weeks is more than enough for me. Any longer and I'd go nuts.

Looking for answers, or just a holiday, I wrote to my cousin Marguerite, who I knew not only lived in Killorglin but rented out holiday lodges there. I booked a week in late October, the autumn mid-term break, and arrived with my family off the overnight Swansea-Cork ferry. The sun came out as we drove in over the River Laune. Marguerite's lodges overlooked the water and we parked outside. The riverweed shook its tresses. Swans dipped to behead themselves in the current. Four women went past in a scull, a cox in a motorboat urging them on. Marguerite welcomed us with butter, bread and milk, and talked of the other relations I must meet. Her sister Gina had the shop – a florists now – in Langford Street. Another cousin, Rhetta, ran the pub over the road, still called O'Shea's, and her sister Ann helped out. I could see something of Uncle Joe in Marguerite – also a bit of Auntie Sheila and my sister Gill. Killorglin was familiar and familial, a place poking up out of the mist like the sudden mountain we could see, the tallest in Ireland, Carrauntoohil. Was this ancestral memory rising up in me? That my mother had grown up here? Or that I'd been here myself as a child? Whichever, it felt like a kind of homecoming. I'd have to be careful. I was going to get sentimental if I didn't watch out.

Next day, on the tourist run round the Ring of Kerry, I wondered at each stop-off point if my mother as a child had stopped there too. I stood by the Torc waterfall, and a fine mist blew off it, and my eyes were damp thinking of her climbing the rocks with schoolfriends, or (later) with 'pals' from medical college, one of whom might have longed (as I did now) for some response from her, the brush of her cold lips, the touch of her frozen hand. We drove on. Did she ever sit by Iskanamacteery Lake? Or walk the Gap of Dunloe? Or take the Ballaghbeama Pass? How often did she visit Cahersiveen, where Daniel O'Connell, the great liberator, was born? Would she have gone in summer to the college at Ballinskelligs, where children are taught to speak Irish? If so, why did she fail to teach a single word of Irish to me? A poet called Michael McKenna once dedicated a book to her: 'To my love, Agnes, with all my heart.' How whole-hearted, really, was his love? Had she loved him back? Did poetry move her? Or did she find poetry enough in the place-names here: Sneem, Tahilla, Barfinnihy, Parknasilla, Innisfallen, Knocknabula, Coomaglaslaw, Cahernageeha, Coomcalee? This was the westerly edge of Europe, and I felt grandiosely elegiac for the civilisation that had been here once, or the people who had, or maybe just the one person. Moochingly revisiting old places, I felt like Thomas Hardy in mourning for his wife.

Our last stop was the strand at Ross Beigh. It was here, I knew, that my mother and her numberless siblings would come by donkey-cart each June. Patrick O'Shea had taken a twenty-one-year lease on two adjoining houses down on the beach, and the family would stay there till school resumed in September. It was a mere ten miles from Killorglin, but to them then (to me now) another country, another season. High dunes of marram grass. Long white sands. The dark mound of Seefin behind. And the view across Dingle Bay. I must have seen these when I was five – as my mother had, when she was five. But I couldn't remember it, and didn't know how to remember her. I'd never known the girl from County Kerry, only the Yorkshire lady doctor and mother of two. So what? Why shouldn't she keep her childhood from me if she chose? Didn't I keep things from my children? Don't all of us have secret places for ourselves? The kids ran on, leaving virgin footsteps in the dunes. Why should this place feel special, just because my mother had once played here? Origins are a thing of the past. Roots are no earthly use to men and women. What made my mother had nothing to do with me.

That night we went to the pub with Marguerite, her husband Sean and mother Bridie – not the family pub, O'Shea's, a no-nonsense drinking-place (long bar, television, a handful of regulars with their pints of Guinness), but Bianconis, which was noisy and upmarket and served meals. We ordered seafood salad all round. At seventy-something, Bridie – my Auntie Bridie – looked robust. As Uncle Joe's widow, she was the last link to my mother's generation, the keeper of their stories. Perhaps she'd have things to tell me. This pub wasn't the place but I arranged to talk to her next day.

She lived in the original Langford Street house, next door to her daughter Gina's flower shop. On my way in, I chatted to Gina – pretty, blonde, smiley – as she snipped carnations, a bright flourish of wedding bouquets behind her, a pink and white funeral wreath saying 'Mam' to one side. Bridie had a pot of tea ready. She also had three handwritten sheets of paper for me, copied, she said, from my grandfather Patrick O'Shea's personal notebook which, on his death, had come into the hands of Uncle Joe. It was his list of the O'Shea children, neatly numbered, with the names of their parents above.

Patrick ('Paddy') J. O'Shea (b 1867), wool merchant
married
Margaret Lyons (b 1874), Jan 20 1894

1 Child (son), born Dec 6 1894, died same day
2 John, b 22 Jan 1896
3 Mary Christine (Criss) O'Shea, b Dec 3 1896
4 Child (daughter) b Nov 29 1897, died same day
5 Margaret (Madge), b 15 April 1899
6 Daniel, b April 30 1900
7 James Joseph, b 14 May 1901, died 7 Feb 1902
8 Johanna, b 7 Sept 1902, died July 2 1903
9 Michael, b 7 Nov 1903, died
10 Gerald, b 26 Dec 1904, died
11 Patrick, b 15 Jan 1906
12 Peter, b 13 Oct 1907
13 Eileen, b 27 Dec 1908
14 Child (stillborn son), b August 1909 (caused through assault by pension officer)
15 William, b 23 May 1910
16 Julia (Sheila), b 15 Aug 1912
17 Joseph, b 23 March 1914
18 Paul, b 26 April 1915
19 Agnes, b 18 April 1917
20 Kitty, b 8 Sept 1918.

Bridie said I could keep what she'd written out. More care-fully than if they'd been pages from the Book of Kells, I slipped the three sheets inside my notebook. I hadn't really taken in their contents yet. Nor could I laugh with Bridie over the idea of a family so large – hadn't she come from a large family, too, and hadn't she and Joe, in later, more contraceptive-minded times, had seven or eight children of their own? We chatted instead about the wool business, which Joe had run from the yard outside her window: though the house itself was modest, the yard stretched deep and long, with room for several sheds and outbuildings. Bridie didn't say so, but I grasped now the implausibility of Joe having the business at all. John, eighteen years his senior, must originally have been due to inherit, but he had died in 1918, at twenty-four. The next son, Daniel, died in 1931, of TB; Peter, too, died that year, of peritonitis, after a ruptured appendix. By then, the next two sons had ruled them-selves out: Patrick, a year older than Peter, had trained to be a doctor, William, three years younger, to practise law (the one who later ran the pub). The others sons had died at birth or shortly after. Which was why the family wool business had ended, in the hands of my Uncle Joe, the seventeenth child and eleventh-born son.

Back at the cottage, I looked again at Bridie's three hand-written sheets, and felt oddly comforted by the profusion, or transfusion, of O'Sheas – the new blood in my blood. All those names and numbers: a near-alphabet, an A–Z or at any rate an A–T. Twenty children in twenty-four years: by any standards, that was going it some. Nearly a quarter of a century of pregnancies and births: how could my mother have called her mother a lady of leisure? Some of the gaps between children were less than a year, scarcely long enough for a woman to have recovered from the last labour before embarking on the next. The second and third children, John and Criss, came barely ten months apart. Was Margaret O'Shea (née Lyons) one of those women whose children 'just popped out'? In legends and dirty jokes, women as procreative as she was expire, worn out, before they're forty. But she lived to be seventy-two. She'd had two generations' worth of children, almost: a Victorian-Edwardian period, followed by an Edwardian-Georgian. How differently those two generations fared, though. Of those in the first half, six died as infants, two more before they were thirty; only Criss and Madge lived on. 1901 to 1904 was the worst patch: four children dead, one for every year. Miniature coffins became the family furniture. My grandparents — *my grandparents*: since I never knew them, it still seemed odd to say it — must have thought of stopping then: ten births in ten years, but only four survivors. Luckily (lucky for my mother, lucky for me), they persevered. And how. Ten more children, nine of whom lived on to adulthood, eight to a good age. Only that stillborn son to mar the years 1906–18. The note my grandfather had written about the stillbirth — 'caused through assault by pension officer' — suggested he still felt bitter, though by then he was hardly short of heirs. What caused the assault? Some dispute between him and the tax authorities? Was he the victim of injustice or persecution? Or was his bitterness partly guilt that some fault or crooked dealing on his part had precipitated the incident? Worse was to come in 1918: in the year of the birth of Kitty, last of the line, the death of John, the oldest surviving son. Just twenty-four years old. Lined up to run the family business until . . . what? The trenches? The Troubles? I reminded myself to ask next time I saw Bridie. ('It was the flu,' she said later — he was one of twenty million who died in the great epidemic that year.) No more children after that. They'd surely have stopped anyway. Margaret was forty-four and, in the modest accommodation they had, must have felt like Old Mother Hubbard. I'd been told that the children slept on opposite sides of Langford Street: the boys at the pub, the girls above the shop, a double-dormitory arrangement. There wasn't room for them in the one shoe.

So there were twenty. Only thirteen had lived beyond infancy, and three had died before being given names. Even so, it was odd that my mother, whose speciality was paediatrics and who talked of how upset she felt whenever she delivered a dead baby, had never mentioned these other siblings, or siblings that failed to be. Before her time though they were, she must have known about them. Why the silence? Why not say she was one of twenty, or at least one of thirteen? Perhaps the awkwardness was that such numbers advertised her Irishness. Many others in the diaspora had likewise fudged their origins. Back then, in England at least, Irishness carried a taint – of peasant ignorance, poverty or gun-running – which emigrants did well to lose. These days things were different. The Celtic Tiger was roaring, and calling home its brood. To be Irish and one of many was chic: hadn't *Angela's Ashes* (a story involving poverty, child death and TB in Limerick) struck a chord around the world? We were all Irish now, or hoped to be. When, later that day, my last in Killorglin, I went to the town cemetery in search of the family grave, I couldn't help but notice the GB registration plate on a car parked by the gates: Brits like me on the Celtic ancestral trail.

There were so many O'Sheas buried there, I'd begun to despair of finding the right headstone when I spotted the square, grey slab 'in loving memory of Patrick J. (Paddy) O'Shea', with Margaret and four of their children – Johnny, Daniel, Peter and Sheila – chiselled beneath. The slab sat on an oblong of gravel, fenced off by iron railings from the common grass. Other relations and cousins were buried nearby. What I felt standing among them wasn't glamour or belonging but smallness. My mother was one of a score, and I was a scion among scores of other scions. It was as well I hadn't come here to feel special.

*       *       *

MOODILY FERRIED BACK home, I tried to suppress a sense of betrayal. Why couldn't she have talked more about her past? I had no history of abuse or neglect to tax her with. On the contrary, I'd thought of my childhood as happy. 'No man is a wonder to his family,' wrote Montaigne, yet my family had made me feel uniquely loved. Had my mother felt the same, when she was young? How uniquely loved can you feel, as the nineteenth of twenty?

Our family had been the classic Fifties–Sixties set-up: dad, mum, boy, girl, car, television and dog. The Killorglin set-up was a classic of its era, too, though on the large side even in southern

Ireland (in 1909 the *News of the World* thought it sufficiently newsworthy to print a photo of an Irish family with five sons and nine daughters; the O'Sheas were in the same league). There are advantages in large families, it's said: good for character-building, the little ones entertain each other, safety in numbers, etc. But how close can such children get to their parents? In his notebook Patrick O'Shea had misremembered my mother's birth-date, getting it wrong by two days. (The records at University College Dublin repeat the error.) With the best will in the world, my grandparents could have had little time for my mother, or for her alone. Was this why she told my sister she'd been brought up by Criss, already twenty when she was born? It would make sense. Madge, Eileen and even Sheila, her big sisters, could have helped too. But Criss, her biggest sister, would have had other reasons for wanting to mother her. At sixteen or seventeen she had got pregnant, by a soldier so it was said. Her parents hushed it up, and sent her away to have the baby – a boy – in secret (a termination would have been out of the question). Her baby handed over for adoption, Criss came back to Langford Street, where my mother was born, a child she could look after as her own – until she met Patrick Joy, a farmer eight years older than her, whom she married and had a son with. Did Patrick know about her earlier child? He might not have minded too much if he did, since he had an inducement to marry Criss: the gift from her parents of a substantial farm, an 'estate' even, called Mount Rivers. Certainly William, Criss's son by Patrick, grew up in ignorance of his half-brother: it was a shock to him when the child she'd had adopted, a man of seventy by then, turned up in Killorglin a few years back, in search of relations. Criss seems to have been one for secrets. No doubt her first baby was a secret kept from her youngest sisters. There might have been whispers in bed at Langford Street. But my mother was too young to have understood.

There was much she might not have known, but there was also what she did know and had withheld. How to react to this? Anger seemed inappropriate: I missed her too much, and some fudging of her family history was hardly a crime. Many people feel ashamed of their backgrounds. If my mother, making a career for herself among the English middle classes, had been reluctant to describe herself as the nineteenth child of twenty, that was surely understandable. She'd reinvented herself – and done it so thoroughly that she failed to set the record straight with her own children. Perhaps with her husband, too: had she told him how many O'Sheas there'd been? It didn't matter. It was easy to forgive. There was nothing *to* forgive. It wasn't as if she'd killed anyone, or committed bigamy. I felt petulant all the same, like a jilted lover.

At least the jilted lover has his memories. But how was I to remember my mother? She'd been taciturn, chameleon-like, self-erasing. My cousin Kela, looking at old photos of her, said: 'She was distant. Like a page in a fashion magazine. Not there even when she was there, if you know what I mean.' I did. Her graduation photos show a dark-haired beauty, eyes looking into the middle distance, mortar board at a jaunty angle, a generous sweep of curl down her back. In photos from her thirties she looks as slim and young as a first-year student, not a mother-of-two GP. Yet there was the distance Kela spoke of, too, and the shape-shifting. Absent even when present: that was it. Friends described her as 'deep'. Now it seemed there were depths concealed even from those close to her. One day when I was ten she'd come downstairs with her suitcase packed, a blank look on her face, saying she was going away for a few days and not to worry. Worried silly, I'd not known what to make of it. Later, I put it down to a crisis (or ultimatum) involving my father and Beaty. But had it been something else, the disjunction between the life she'd left and the life she'd made? In my head, I began to rewrite history. Hadn't she always been evasive? What about that holiday in Ireland which I'd proposed a year or so after my father died? She'd had a camper van, then, a Hymer. We could have gone together, toured the old places, looked up relations. But she had pleaded a broken arm – said could we wait till she felt stronger, fitter, better able to travel. The broken arm hadn't stopped her going out with friends at home. I should have been more insistent. In my father's lifetime she had been compliant, a quiet shadow at the edge of his glaring sun. On his death she had inherited all his stubbornness, his I'll-damn-well-do-what-I-like. Just what you'd expect of a chameleon. But I hadn't seen the chameleon. I thought she was her, Kim, the gentle doctor, the wife and widow, my mum.

*   *   *

IN THE LONG night of an English winter, I found myself getting on at her. Surely, Mum, near the end, when there was nothing to lose, you could have opened up a bit. It might have helped if you had talked − helped you as well as me. Was it my fault I couldn't be there more often? Tell me, please. And tell me if you can, from wherever you are, what Criss was like, and about your brother Paul, and all you can recall of your first years.

'Oh, you're not quizzing me,' she'd come back, just like the old days. 'What's it matter? It was all so long ago. *I* was all so long ago.'

'I'd just like to see the past more clearly.'

'You can't. It's gone.'

'Tell me about these brothers and sisters of yours − the ones I didn't know.'

'I hardly knew them, either. What's the point?'

'I think it would help.'

'Nothing helps. It's just your grief. Let be.'

She was right, as usual. Nothing helped. Still, I did want to understand her better. There'd been a life Before She Had Me and I had inklings of it now: Langford Street, holidays at Ross Beigh, boarding school at Killarney, her friend Mary Galvin suggesting that they train as chemists and my mother, bolder, more ambitious, saying 'Why not doctors?' Then University College, Dublin, to which she went, precocious, at sixteen, paying annual fees that varied from four guineas to over thirty (with an extra six guineas for dissections in 1938). Then graduation in 1942. Then England in wartime. Then my father. Then marriage. Then children. But what had made her bury, or renounce, her past? At school, taught English by an Irishman called Paddy Rogers, I'd thrilled to Stephen Dedalus in James Joyce's *Portrait*

25

*of the Artist as a Young Man* flying by the nets of family, religion and nation. A remote and impossibly dangerous enterprise, it seemed. But hadn't my mother made this flight too?

✻    ✻    ✻

I THOUGHT THERE were no answers to my questions. Then I remembered the letters. In truth, I'd never really forgotten them. In his study, under a blanket, beneath a makeshift table next to the drinks cabinet, my father had kept a stack of plastic carrier bags. In the bags were brown paper parcels, and in the parcels foolscap envelopes, and in the envelopes neat stacks of letters. I'd no idea how many letters there were, or what they said, and in his lifetime I wasn't all that interested. After he died, clearing cupboards and drawers, my mother had talked of getting rid of them.

'No,' I said, suddenly superstitious. 'Don't chuck them out. You never know.'

'Who'd want to read a lot of old letters?' she grumbled.

'I think he meant them to be kept,' I protested.

'No, he just couldn't bear to throw anything away.'

It was true. Anything that had once been something he kept for possible reincarnation – which meant a house (and garage, and barn, and assorted outbuildings) full of useless objects. The heap of envelopes might be useless, too. I'd no reason to suppose different. Except the careful way he'd laid a blanket over them. And a memory of him saying they were letters from the war. In his aftermath, I felt pious. While he'd dissolved, these had been preserved. Each time I went back, I became more conscious of their presence. It was her house, and her right, but I dreaded my mother shredding or burning them. As my visits increased, with her fractures and illnesses, I'd make a point of checking they were still there under the blanket. When she went into Cromwell's, four months before her death, I transferred the carrier bags into a wardrobe. Her cleaner, I reasoned, might mistake them for rubbish and throw them out. My real fear was that my mother, close to death, might ask for them to be destroyed. Well, she'd have to ask me then, because only I knew the hiding-place. Luckily she didn't. I felt sneaky enough already. Grief-struck, too: I was about to lose her, and was damned if I'd lose the letters as well.

About a month before she died, taking no chances, I carried the letters with me back to London. It was a shit's trick, no denying it, but at least I left the envelopes alone, not daring to touch them while she was alive. When she died, it still felt wrong – too soon, too depressing a prospect. It was the idea of them I'd wanted so badly. They were my legacy, along with the china, Lowry prints and bits of furniture. But now I'd got them I couldn't bear to look. All that winter and autumn they sat there, untouched.

In the bitter cold of the new year, I steeled myself and opened a parcel at random. The letters dated from 1944. I'd stumbled into the archive of my parents' courtship.

*Arthur to Agnes, 30.4.44*

Your last letter to me was delayed because the 'M' looked like an 'H' and was delivered to a Harrison in another section. You'll have to be less of a medical professional with your writing in future. Any mail delays are frustrating. But one day we'll be able to whisper things to one another for the rest of our lives.

*Agnes to Arthur, 19.5.44*

How I wish I could lie in your arms (here or at Auntie's) and tell you how much I love you. Why did we fall in love like this, darling? I don't ever really wish we hadn't met, but it would have been the wisest thing. It all feels so hopeless. If you were here now you'd see me doing something you've always wanted to see me do – cry. It's taken me ages to write this – the interruptions coming not from others this time but from myself.

*Arthur to Agnes, 6.6.44*

Well, the second front has opened. Just heard it on the 3pm overseas bulletin in the Mess: 11,000 planes, 4,000 large ships, successful landings. I hope it continues to go well, and that there hasn't been too great a leakage of gen. Please be careful, darling, I feel so blasted helpless out here, in this calm, cloudy heat. Did I tell you that the new S/Ldr never got here, having been killed en route?

*Agnes to Arthur, 6.6.44*

Terrific news, isn't it – first Rome, then this. Heard hundreds of planes going over about 5am, but never thought of the second front. It does seem strange just sitting here as usual with all this excitement going on – it makes me wish I were doing something, so I wonder how you feel. But I'm glad you are where you are.

*Arthur to Agnes, 7.6.44*

Yes, darling, you have committed yourself to saying 'I love you' quite a bit, at least on paper. I'll save all the evidence so that when you are in some particularly nattering mood one day (after a tiresome day with the three kids) I can produce them and tell you to shut up and read them. Then you'll come over, put your arms round my neck and say 'I do, you know'.


'I'll save all the evidence,' he promised. And so he had. There were thousands – gossipy letters, lonely letters, angry letters, fearful letters, letters about how they might, or might not, build a life together after the war. I took all spring to get through them. My basement office was cold, but the letters were like a glow of hot bricks. Explaining myself to anyone would have been hard: 'Read the new Updike yet?' 'Nah, I'm reading my mum and dad.' Even to me, it seemed odd. The therapist in my head told me I was in denial, that this was just a hopeless yearning to see my parents alive again. I thanked the therapist for the observation but decided it was glib. Why, if I wanted them back, didn't I pore over the reminders of my time with them, in their middle and later years – the bric a brac, day-planners and photo albums? Instead of which I was absorbed in two people younger than me, at a time when I wasn't around. I knew there were similar letter collections in attics and suitcases all over the world. Some would be written by Holocaust survivors, members of the Resistance, generals in the desert, witnesses to momentous events – people with dramatic stories to tell. But that didn't make my parents' letters any less special. To have a record of what they were doing and thinking on particular days half a century ago seemed extraordinary. They were doctors, not writers, but they'd written – and hung on to every word.

Of course I felt transgressive. This might be a trove my father had kept for his heirs but, like most treasures, it had been sealed up. I felt especially sacrilegious reading my mother's letters, thin blue sheets of air-mail paper held by rusty, sixty-year-old pins. I could imagine my father hurriedly tearing open the envelope, reading his lover's words over and over, then tenderly stabbing these pins through. He'd stored the letters in batches of fifty or so, to be re-read at leisure and (as he says in that letter of 7 June 1944) to be used as weapons after the war. I'd no idea whether my parents had ever read their letters again in peacetime. But here was I reading them – having first, to make it easier, removed the pins. The letters weren't grenades. And my parents couldn't explode at me. It felt dangerous handling them all the same.

Frustratingly, the only letters apart from theirs were all from *his* friends and relations. My mother wasn't the hoarding type, and nothing on her side had survived. Yet the more I read (and re-read, and researched, and asked around), the more I understood there was a story here. My parents weren't the only protagonists; others, too, played their part, not least Mary, my father's sister and mother's closest wartime friend. It wasn't a tale of derring-do or epic grandeur. There were no weekends at Chequers with Churchill or plots to assassinate Hitler. But in its quiet way – *her* quiet way – it touched on what touches everyone: love, identity, family, gender, work, nationhood and faith. It was a story that explained a lot. A story full of things she'd never told me.

# CHAPTER TWO

# Oonagh, Agnes, Gennie, Kim

*Agnes to Arthur, 27.1.43*

. . . Reswick and I had a flare-up last week – he was being particularly nasty for a few days. I went to Brown and told him I wanted to leave. I think he suspected what it was all about and spoke to Reswick, who later apologised to me and said he had been worrying about his exam results and that things would be better from now on. I spoke to Brown again and said I still wanted to leave but he said we had a gentleman's agreement that I'd stay at least six months. Of course when he put it like that I felt I had no alternative. Reswick continues to be sociable and let me do a Caesar on Sunday, but I'm sure it won't last long.

I saw that naval type in Sissons one afternoon lately – he was alone as usual. I think that is all the local gossip.

S HE HAS A FEEL for obstetrics, everyone says so. Or rather the women say so, the nurses, midwives and mothers at Hope. The doctors, being men, are condescending, spelling out the basics as they would to a halfwit from the bogs. Perhaps it's her youthfulness: though twenty-five, she could pass for seventeen and they treat her accordingly, as though she didn't know a foetus from a femur. Perhaps it's her sex: the joke among the boys is that the brains of 'hen doctors' aren't big enough for the job. Or perhaps it's because she's pretty and therefore dumb – not that she thinks herself pretty but men, especially married men, have a habit of telling her so. At least Reswick, who's young, single and foul-tempered, isn't that type. And the work keeps her occupied. It's the off-duty hours she finds the worst, the endless time to kill. Once Mary Galvin comes, whom she has known since childhood, she'll have a friend to do things with (or do nothing with). But till then there's only her sister Sheila, who's teaching in London, too far to get to on rare days off. A kindred spirit or two would help. The nurses are friendly enough but Mider – the midwifery and maternity department – is no place for soul-mates, let alone men. She begins to feel stranded, as though on an isolation ward. Then in October she's told of a party and jumps at the invitation. There are doctors on other wards she'd like to meet.

Instead of which she meets Arthur Morrison, back on a weekend's leave (a '48') from Plymouth, where he's a doctor with the RAF. She has heard the nurses talk about an Arthur: a wild one, they say – a drinker, prankster and flirt. Can this be the same man? The winged blue uniform's not bad, but she'd imagined someone tall and dashing. Glass in one hand, cigarette in the other, he reminds of her someone – her father, she realises with a sinking heart. 'Ye Gods, they've appointed a woman,' he says when introduced. She guesses the rudeness is a put-on, though with the English, especially Englishmen in uniform, you can't be sure: the more stripes, the greater their arrogance, as though a woman – *any* woman – would be desperate to have them. 'I hear in Ireland you can qualify in six months,' he teases. 'Three months,' she replies, 'if you're a girl.' It comes back to her now: Arthur Morrison's handwriting on the case notes to a patient she saw last week – very lucid handwriting, by doctors' standards, but the diagnosis he made was dodgy, to say the least. If he doesn't watch his step, she'll tell him so. But by now he's attentive – buys her a drink, offers a ciggie, flirts, and asks for a dance. His feet are all over the place, either from beer or unfamiliarity with the foxtrot. His hands on her waist are uncertain, too, which reassures her: she has been warned about English wolves. In any case, the dancing's quickly over, an air-raid siren (the usual false alarm) bringing the evening to a premature close. They say goodnight casually. No kiss. No great loss, either, if he thinks as little of women doctors as he makes out.

Next morning he turns up on her ward. 'Just passing through,' he says, but she doubts it, all the more so when he invites her for coffee. They sit in the bleak canteen, exchanging gossip and war news. Grimmy — resident surgeon — has been doing a number with nurse Ross. Monty has just defeated Rommel at Alamein — the beginning of the end, so the papers say. Their own war is only just starting: he has been in Coastal Command, and she at her English hospital, for under three months.

'Why Plymouth?' she asks.

'For training,' he says. 'Till I'm posted overseas.'

'When will that be?'

'In a few weeks.'

'I thought it must be tomorrow,' she says, eyeing his uniform.

'Nothing like being prepared.'

'And where will they send you?'

'They've not said,' he says, but talks of where he'd like to go, she — in a teasing send-up of a send-off — polishing his brass buttons for him while he speaks. Anyone watching would say the two of them had taken a shine to each other. They linger over their undrunk coffees, past the hour of Reswick's ward-round. What's it like to fly, she asks? Fun in small doses, he says, but as an MO he has been taught only the basics, in case of emergency ('the crew all dead and Muggins here asked to bring the plane home'). Pilot heroics he leaves to Michael, his sister Mary's husband, a DFC; for himself, he says, he's 'far too windy'. She smiles at the admission. Most men in uniform like to brag; this one's endearingly fallible. They're on the verge of arranging to meet again, but then Mike Winstanley walks in ('Up to your old tricks, Arthur?'), and the moment passes, and she rushes off to join Reswick on his ward-round.

And as the weeks pass, with Mider being so busy and her social life picking up and no word from Plymouth, doesn't give Arthur a second thought.

Just before Christmas, there's another party — a bigger one this time, in the canteen at Hope. Two young Irish nurses insist she accompany them, 'to save us from the wolves', and they share a bottle of sherry in her room. One's from Dublin, the other from Galway, and as they perch on the bed, swigging from tea-cups, they bemoan the hopelessness of the men at Hope, not a patch on those back home. The sound of a band hits them long before they reach the party:

In shady shoals, English soles do it.
Goldfish, in the privacy of bowls, do it.
Let's do it, let's fall in love.


Her head spins with noise and sherry. Cleared of tables, sprigged with holly and mistletoe, the canteen is almost festive, though no one has the nerve to dance. At the makeshift bar stand a trio of blue and khaki uniforms – forces doctors home on leave. She doesn't recognise him at first. But the small one, barrel-chested, pint in hand, is undeniably Arthur.

'Ah, the Irishwoman,' he says.

'Irish*women*,' she corrects him. 'We're taking over.'

'Arthur Morrison,' he nods to her two companions. 'I used to work here.'

'But why are you here tonight?' she says, more rudely than she means.

'They're still mucking about with my posting.'

'You're too important to risk, eh?'

'Too useless to bother with, more like. Fancy a drink?'

He gets one in, which she knows is a mistake. 'My head's not made for gin,' she tells him, as he buys a second and third. Somehow her glass is always full. Does that mean she's drinking or not drinking? Slow down, she tells herself. But everything seems to happen so fast. Suddenly Mike Winstanley's there, with another doctor, and together they drag off the two nurses.

'I bet Mike's been flirting with you,' says Arthur.

'I'm a woman, aren't I? There'd be something wrong if he didn't.'

'I've been flirting, too. A girl in Plymouth called Terry. Nothing serious yet, but she's a stunner.'

Nothing serious, but she finds she's annoyed with him. And

33

at the way he watches how she'll react. And at his smile, when he sees her displeasure. Well, it looks like a smile. Her vision's all skew-whiff. It could be a frown.

'Ter-ry,' she says, hovering on the syllables, 'funny name for a girl.'

'Jealous?' he asks.

'Why would I be jealous?'

'She's hoping we'll get engaged.'

'That'll be nice for you.'

'But I'm holding out.'

'Why, if she's a stunner?'

'Fancy a dance?'

'I don't feel like it.'

'I'll have to make do with a sister then,' he says, and rushes off. From his look when she refused him, she'd say he was keen on her. Or is he merely playing games? She can't decide. Stuff him – he can have his Terry, and the nurses, what does she care? Turning her back on the dance-floor, she talks to Guffy, the Hope anaesthetist, whose halitosis is legendary – they say he puts patients under by breathing on them. Amazed at her attentions, he buys her another – no, no, she mustn't but she does. Next thing, she's dancing with him. Grateful for the support, she rests her hand on his arm, then drapes herself on his shoulder. The band sing of trouble ahead, but meanwhile there's moonlight and music. The two Irish nurses smile encouragingly as she drifts past. Over his shoulder, she grimaces back. Love and romance? With Guffy? They've got to be joking.

Back at the bar, short of dance partners, Arthur is pretending not to watch. Though he hardly knows her, he can tell she's been drinking too much. Guffy! He's tempted to leave her to it. But when Moriarty, or is it Coward, says 'Arthur, you should rescue her', he walks across and cuts in, brusque as an old stag: 'Care for a dance?' Unprotesting, she slips into his arms. The song's more upbeat, though you wouldn't know it from the way she leans on him. 'Oh, I love to climb a mountain,' she mouths, but he doesn't seem to know the words. She'd let him kiss her, if he tried. Why doesn't he try? They're cheek to cheek, nothing could be more natural. But when she draws back and catches his eye, it slips away from her, as though embarrassed. By what? Her wooziness? Other people watching? It's a relief when the smoochy numbers stop and the music turns loud and fast. Everyone takes the floor now – even the fishes, the boozers who never leave the bar. Despite what he thinks, she's feeling quite sober, enough to know she'll suffer for this come morning. They uncouple and join a wider circle for the finale – left leg in, right leg in, a whole crowd of them hokey-cokeying: 'That's what it's all about.' There are cries for more when the band stops and the band is happy to oblige. But she's tired, and the rumbustiousness is too much for her. Together, they sit out the encore, he with a pint of best, she with a glass of lukewarm water.

At midnight the lights come on. She should be off now, the two nurses are waiting, but he won't let her go. They stand there playing for time while everyone drifts out, distant doors slamming under the stars. 'You're cold,' he says, taking her hand in his. 'Shall we find a fire?' Strong black coffee would be more like it, but they head for the doctors' sitting room, which is warm, tatty and (as they'd hoped) completely empty. From the battered sofa they stare into the flickering coals. And what might have ended in nothing becomes what this is about.

✳   ✳   ✳

*Arthur to Agnes, 24.8.44*

Have I ever really impressed on you just what effect your cleaning my buttons had one morning in October 42? How I then forgot about you (almost) till next time I came on leave? And how I nonchalantly approached you? And that first night when everyone left us and you sat on the couch with me in front of a dying fire, and then kissed me for devilment despite what you had heard?

So HE WOULD recall it for her later. The fateful first kiss. The night from which everything followed. But I shouldn't overdo it.

The buttons, the fire, the kiss, the sofa and (as he'd keep reminding her) the alcohol: they mean a lot to me because without them I'd never have been born. But in the sum of things this wasn't a cataclysmic event. The two of them might have met other people. They might have had other children. For them life would have been different, and for me it wouldn't have happened, but none of us would have known what we were missing and the century would have panned out much the same.

Still, let me ask the question. What were the odds of my parents meeting? Quite short odds: both were doctors, and about the same age, and medicine, like most professions, is a small world. Quite long odds: they came from different countries, and there was a war on. They met through work, at a hospital – but not really, because he left before she arrived and only returned for a brief visit. They met at a party, and were attracted to each other – but he was half-engaged to a woman in Plymouth, and she had various admirers, one a family friend. He was too short and boozy for her taste; she wasn't blonde or bosomy enough for his. She felt ambivalent about England and didn't know how long she'd stay. He felt ambivalent about female doctors – liked having pretty girls around, but was more relaxed with nurses. Both had things going for them – the promise of careers ahead. But wherever it was they were going, chances were it wouldn't be the same place.

What were the odds they'd meet again that Christmas (which they did, several times, mostly in pubs) after kissing on the sofa? So-so. He was home for ten days, and wanted to see her, but recoiled at the memory of her staggering about the dance floor with Guffy. She liked the way he kissed but thought him priggish (she hadn't been *that* drunk) and anyway he'd soon be overseas. And when they said goodbye in the new year and promised to write, what were the odds they'd keep that promise? Fifty-fifty at best. It was an 'I'll call you', no more. Even if honoured, it might have come to nothing soon enough. They weren't in love, and in the first flush of 1943 neither knew where they stood. In late January, none the less, they did exchange letters – he mildly teasing her about failing to see him off from the station in

Manchester, she regaling him with recent trials she had endured (including a court trial in Lancaster, that of an abortionist). The letters were circumspect. But there were phone calls, too, late at night, after a drink or two. He had broken things off with Terry, he told her. 'What you get up to in Plymouth is your business,' she said: for all she knew, he and Terry could be going stronger than ever. Still, his telling her it was over seemed significant – even more so when, in early February (his posting delayed), he invited her to meet his parents the following weekend.

What were the odds of him inviting her home, just weeks after they'd met? Most Englishmen, she had found, saw their homes as fortresses – dark castles to retreat inside, not (as in Ireland) open hearths for drink and *craic*. In six months at Hope, no one had asked her back even for tea. So she was flattered by the invitation. But worried by it too. What did it mean, in England, to be taken to meet a man's parents? Was it the prelude to something else? Would it be casual? What should she wear? What if his family took against her? What were his parents expecting? Did they even know of her existence? The more she thought about it, the more she fretted. She'd have liked to discuss it with someone. But who?

What were the chances of them meeting, dancing, kissing and – within weeks – going home to his parents? And the relationship then lasting, despite them being separated? And them lasting, when friends and relations were being killed? And all their differences being resolved, so they could marry? Infinitesimal. And yet the thing was inevitable. As love does, for any two people, it happened inexorably, against all odds.

\*   \*   \*

HIS HOME'S A redbrick villa pitched on an escarpment in Worsley, overlooking the Bridgewater Estate. Windyridge, they call it. Five bedrooms, central heating, bay window, sloping front lawn, garage and apple orchard out back – it's a house built for a Mancunian businessman, handy for town but also solid and *elevated*. Kathleen, Arthur's mother, seems as tiny in it as a pea

under a mattress. Bright-eyed and curly-haired, she's so small that when she inspects the chicken roasting in the top oven of the Aga, she barely needs to bend down. Agnes thinks her sweet, not least for giving them time to be alone. Arthur shows her round like an excited boy, rushing her from room to room, though it's not the house he seems proudest of, nor the weed-strewn, red-shale tennis court beyond the orchard, but his red MG sports car (under repair) in the wooden shed. She likes the spaciousness of Windyridge but finds it alien: so many rooms, and so few people living in them. With Mary married, and Arthur away in Plymouth, and their father Ernest out all day at work, she wonders how poor Kathleen copes.

At 1.30, Ernest returns from the bowls club. He does his best to be friendly, pumping Agnes's hand and offering sherry, but she finds him terribly forbidding. He's not a tall man, but with his chest, his jowls, his balding hair, his booming voice, his absolute conviction, he reminds her of Winston Churchill. He works in town, in John Dalton Street, running Dorning & Morrison, the business he inherited from his father. Mines, railways, canals, reservoirs, large estates, you name it, he'll do the surveys and valuations. Lately, with the war, business has shrunk a little. 'But the nation still needs coal and trains,' he says. 'We battle on.' Kathleen – Mummy, as he calls her – is also from a family of engineers: Blakemore & Co. were once the biggest manufacturer of nuts and bolts in all of Lancashire – it was they who supplied the 1,000 tons of bolts that hold the Mersey Tunnel together. 'We're nuts and bolts people,' he says as they go into the dining room, where Kathleen is waiting for him to carve. 'You must take us as you find us. No standing on ceremony here.'

But to Agnes lunch at Windyridge is ceremonial in the extreme. Willow pattern plates, bone-handled cutlery, white lace napkins, the mantelpiece clock ticking through every conversational gap – it's very English middle-class. If a guest held a knife the wrong way – the handle vulgarly angled upward between forefinger and thumb rather than neatly tucked under – the offence would be silently noted and the appropriate social inference drawn. She's glad to have been taught table manners at home, and to be able to say, when Ernest asks her what her father does, 'He's a wool merchant', which sounds a respectable occupation.

'And where did you qualify?'

'University College, Dublin.'

'So your roots are . . .'

'I'm from County Kerry. That's down . . .'

'In the south, I know.'

She knew they'd work it out, whether or not Arthur forewarned them. Though the accent has softened since she came to England, her Kerry lilt is still there. She feels uncomfortable, all the same. The way Ernest said 'roots' makes her sound like a turnip or something. And is she being paranoid or was there an edge to that 'south'? He stares at her through steel-rim spectacles, not unkindly but inscrutable. Would he have preferred her to come from Belfast? The sound of knives scraping plates sends a cold shiver through her. The conversation moves on, to Monty, Hitler and Goebbels, to Krauts and Eyeties and Japs. By the time Kathleen serves them sago pudding, Agnes has begun to feel uncomfortable. Ernest has decided views, having served in the last war as a Lance-Corporal with the Artists' Rifles and thus 'learned a thing or two about the Hun'. What he has learned makes him doubt that hostilities will soon be over.

'We're on top,' says Arthur, 'Hitler knows he's had it.'

'But that won't stop him fighting to the bitter end,' says Ernest. 'From here on every life lost is a wasted life.'

'I feel for the mothers,' says Kathleen, her hand on the ladle in the Pyrex dish. 'Mrs Strachan, Mrs Plowright, Mrs Craughton . . .'

'We don't intend you to join them, pet.'

'I'll be fine, Mummy,' says Arthur.

'That's what your cousin Dan said in 1940.'

'He was unlucky. But at least he did his bit.'

'Just lie low and look after number one,' Ernest tells Arthur, 'that's my advice.'

'Be a coward, you mean.'

'Better a living coward than a dead hero. The only cowards in this war are the nations that won't get involved. The bloody neutrals.'

Is she imagining this, she wonders, or did Ernest just avoid her eyes?

'Friendly neutrality they call it,' he goes on. 'What the hell's friendly about standing by when people are having their throats slit?'

'Individuals can get involved even if their countries don't,' says Arthur, catching the drift. 'There's a Swede in our Mess.'

'But why do their damned leaders funk it? How can they sit on the fence when their closest neighbour is being torn apart?'

'Of course, *Ireland's* neutral,' says Agnes, as though Ernest must have been thinking of another country entirely. 'But many people in Ireland disagree with De Valera.'

'I'm glad to hear it,' says Ernest.

'The Irish might still come in,' says Arthur.

'It's too late now even if they do,' snaps Ernest. 'Think of all our ships torpedoed by the Hun in Irish waters. And all our planes that have crashed because they've run out of fuel and aren't allowed to land on Irish airfields. And meanwhile hundreds of German spies are hiding out in hotels in the south.'

Since arriving in England, Agnes has heard a lot about the spies boosting Kerry's tourist trade. Maybe it's true, but she can't say she has ever come across one. There are other stories: about trawlermen in Dingle Bay selling fish and cigarettes to German U-boat crews; about the IRA helping Hitler to bomb Belfast; about the censoring of newspapers by the Irish government, to prevent any criticism of the Nazis. Ernest has heard these stories too. But there are other reasons for his animosity, as she later finds out. In 1939, an IRA bomb went off in Manchester, not far from his work, and a fish porter was killed. Those bog-trotting Irish swine. Nest of troublemakers. Never trust them. Lily-livered and work-shy at the best of times. Always making out they're victims of history. Spoilt children, more like. The country was all peat-bogs till the English planters came. A bit of gratitude would be in order, not guns and whining. And now they're letting the Nazis use them as a back door. Whose side do they think they're on? If de Valera had any sense, he'd offer England all the help he can and in return Churchill would probably give him Ulster. But nothing can get dirty Dev into the war. Not the Americans coming in after Pearl Harbor. Not even those Luftwaffe raids on Belfast and (in error) Dublin, when hundreds were killed. Cowards and rats, they are. We should stop sending them food and coal, and starve the bastards . . . But for Agnes's presence, Ernest would have plenty more to say on the subject, as his family knows from experience. It's why they try to defuse him. 'Let's go through to the lounge for tea,' Kathleen suggests, and in the same breath Arthur says, 'Two of Agnes's brothers are in the forces.'

'Patrick's an officer in Africa,' she confirms. 'He's in his late thirties. Paul's just a bit older than me, and he's with the army in France.'

'You must be proud of them,' says Ernest.

'My brother-in-law Jerry's in the army too.'

'Jerry? Let's hope he kills a few.'

'And I've other relations in khaki.'

'But I suppose when they go home they're forced to wear civilian clothes, because de Valera won't admit there's a war on, only an "Emergency".'

'There'll be an emergency here if you don't go through,' says Kathleen, clucking everyone from their seats.

In the lounge, the subject is dropped. 'Daddy's just like that, it's nothing personal,' Arthur will later tell Agnes, squeezing her hand, and she'll try to believe him. It's not as if such sentiments are new to her: she's heard how people talk, she reads the papers, she knows her history. She bristles none the less. Irish neutrality is a complex issue. Can't Ernest grasp what it's about – a newly sovereign nation trying to show some independence and self-respect? Is it fair to speak of 'funk' when tens of thousands of Irishmen are fighting for the Allies of their own free will? If it were up to her, Ireland would do more to help. But oh, this self-righteousness. Haven't the English been Nazis to the Irish, in the past? Sure, the Irish should harp on history less, but the English should think of it more.

Quietly, po-*lie*-tly, she sips her tea. She has no taste for conflict, and in a new country, feeling her way through the labyrinths of etiquette, she's unsure of her ground. To argue with Ernest would be like taking on Churchill. Perhaps in time she'll feel able to answer back – if things with Arthur haven't petered out by then. Who knows what will happen? She drinks her tea in the fading winter light, and listens to Ernest's battle-plan for Sicily. She puts up and shuts up and becomes as un-Irish as she can.

✳    ✳    ✳

Cherry Trees, St Mary's Ave, Northwood
6.3.43

Dear Gennie,

I'm pretty prompt in writing, aren't I. You'll see the reason shortly . . .

AGNES, I'VE BEEN calling her. But Arthur uses a different name. 'Gennie' is how he thinks of her and it's with 'Dear Gennie' that his letters begin. Another woman might be troubled that he can't bring himself to use her Christian name. But she has told him she loathes it as much as he does. A third-century virgin martyr, traditionally depicted holding a lamb: to *this* Agnes, the associations are undesirable. Lambs mean sheep, and sheep mean the skins heaped up in her father's wool-yard – the world she has left behind. So although she signs herself Agnes, religiously, and won't adopt Gennie (not even when his sister Mary calls her it too), she's prepared to contemplate a change. In May 1943 she offers him Oonagh: 'I just remembered it the other day – it's the Irish for Agnes (pronounced Una here, but in Ireland Oona). What do you think?' Not much it seems: he doesn't take it up, nor does she feel enough of an Oonagh to insist.

They are still trying to deliver and baptise her nine months later. 'We forgot the christening, didn't we,' she writes in February 1944 after a weekend together. 'Have you thought of it since?' He has, he replies, but 'can't think of the right name yet. Don't like Sherry. Haven't you some suggestions? Something short and catchy but not too boyish like Bobby, which doesn't fit you? What about Billie? Quite sweet. Anyway, your turn now, pet.' In a PS, he adds: 'What about Kim for a nickname? KIM.' Bobby, Billie, Kim: does she notice that these names are also men's names? If so, doesn't she find his androgyny odd? Is the laddish 'Terry' (his sweetheart in Plymouth) a coinage too, his version of Teresa? No less perturbing is his use of 'pet', which is what his Daddy calls his Mummy and what he (his father's son) calls his new love. Yet she doesn't react to his names and endearments, except to complain 'the christening is going very badly . . . Wish I had been given a decent name.' Eventually she signs off with a '?' in place of Agnes, as though uncertain who she is. Ten days later, after another weekend together, accepting his suggestion, she ends her letter 'Kim'. Kim it is, then. Reborn, rechristened, reinvented, she will be Kim for the rest of her life.

Was this my mother's first mistake, a capitulation that set the trend for several more? It's *Pygmalion* revisited, Eliza transformed

by Henry Higgins so she can take her place in the English bour-
geoisie. Not that I mind whether she's Oonagh, Agnes, Gennie
or Kim, but why did she let him decide? In time the accent
faded too. (With an Irish gardener she employed later in life, Mr
Kelly, she would sometimes revert to Kerry brogue. And after my
father died, friends said the brogue became stronger. But
throughout her middle years no one would have known where
she came from.) Arthur was being a bully – why couldn't he
accept her as she was? Yet there's nothing in the letters to suggest
he minded her accent, and she was under no compulsion to
change her name. If she'd told him, 'Get lost – it's Agnes or
nothing,' he'd have moaned and nagged but finally come round.
Her acceptance of the rechristening plan proves she was ready to
ditch her identity. It was part of cutting the cord with Ireland.
He saw this and encouraged it. But the impulse was already
there.

Names are important. Once married and no longer an
O'Shea, she became Dr A. Morrison, which was confusing,
indeed effacing, since my father's title was the same. He tried
to help out, by calling himself Dr A. B. Morrison. But for simplicity's sake patients preferred to know her as the Lady Doctor,
and a few even called her the Mrs Doctor, to distinguish her
from the Mr. At home there were confusions too. She'd grown
up calling her parents Mammie and Daddie. But he called
his Mummy and Daddy, and it was this 'normal' *English* use that
triumphed when they had children of their own. To us she was
Mummy, whether she liked it or not (after a time *I* didn't like it,
preferring Mum or the prolier 'our Mam'). By us I mean not
just Gill and me but my father, who called her Mummy even
when we weren't there – and even when his own mother was
still alive. From the start he seems to have thought of them as
doubles – equivalents in his affection, at least. 'When I write
home to Windyridge, I put K. M. Morrison on the envelope,' he
informed her in 1944 (K. M. stood for Kathleen Mildred). 'Add
an "I" and I'll be writing to my future wife.'

His wife he knew as Mummy, his mistress Beaty he called
Auntie, while Terry was the name he gave our family labrador. A

psychoanalyst might want to make something of this. But it's my mother that interests me here – the slipperiness of her names and her desire to be someone new.

✧   ✧   ✧

*Arthur to Kim, Northwood, 6.3.43*

I'm pretty prompt in writing, aren't I. You'll see the reason shortly.

I arrived in London by 7pm, and at Northwood by 8. Transport (with two WAAFs) to Cherry Trees, owned by a W/Cdr Truss (easily remembered name), who is overseas. Mrs Truss is very pleasant, as is her daughter (18, attractive – pity I'm not staying long). Continued to HQ, about a mile away, where I learnt from Air/Cdr Biggs (Principal Medical Officer) that I was to go to Iceland for at least a year – flying soon. Had a few beers and a game of snooker.

Now to the point. I think I ought to be able to get Sunday off. Will you come down? You see I mightn't see you for a very long time after that and shan't be here next time you have a weekend off. I should finish at 7pm so could be in London . . .

HELL.

I was just called down then – I am leaving now, well in 3 hours, for a couple of weeks in Belfast, so have to pack again. This is too bad. I will ring from Belfast. Look after yourself, pet.

*Kim to Arthur, Hope Hospital, 8.3.43*

I went out to see Mary yesterday. Your Dad said 'Do you know where Arthur is? In Belfast.' I asked how they knew and your Mammie said the operator had told them on Monday night. I had to pretend to be surprised and felt a h- of a hypocrite. When they had left, Mary said 'I suppose you knew where he was', so I told her the whole story and she was quite amused.

I stayed till 9.15, then walked from Windyridge to Worsley Court House and all the way down I wondered what I was missing and then I realised there was no one to rush me onto the bus.

Funny that you don't remember Saturday morning's (2.30am)

45

phone call. Maybe it's just as well. You were rather insistent that it would be A if I were in Belfast. I was equally insistent that it would be B – which of course it would have been anywhere – but you took a dim view of that.

FOILED OF THE chance to see Arthur, she spends the day with his sister instead. Mary has just turned twenty-three, though the joke is she's only five, since her birthday, 29 February, comes round only every four years. 'Teeny' they call her, though she isn't, least of all now, eight months' pregnant with her first child.

Despite her slowness (swollen stomach, swollen feet), she fills Windyridge like a life-force. Her voice doesn't boom like Ernest's but she knows how to get a point over, how to *underline* the words which matter by *pausing* just before them then *driving them home* (and if need be adding an exclamation mark!). Taking Gennie by the arm conspiratorially, she says she hopes that *he*, Daddy, isn't making things difficult for her. He did for Michael, till they married, which seemed to shut him up. Michael's not around this weekend. He had planned to come with her, from Oakington, near Cambridge, where his base is, but couldn't be spared from bombing duties. Over lunch – roast beef and Yorkshire pudding, a special-occasion meal to celebrate her birthday – Mary talks a lot about Michael's flying: the nightly raids, the white silk scarf he wears for luck, the piece of fuselage he once gave her as a memento (from a German plane, a Heinkel, shot down in the North Sea). Agnes feels grateful for the babble. It's so different from the last time she was here, when the tensions and scraping dinner-plates made her shiver. Oh, Mary and Ernest crackle and spit at each other, but it's only fatherly-daughterly feuding. It feels like a real family. Like home.

After lunch, she and Mary go for a walk. They've met only the once before, over Christmas, and never really talked, but it's as though she has known Mary all her life. Whatever happened to English reserve? Out it comes, the whole CV.

Mary seeing Michael on a tram when she was just *fourteen*. His bagging her for every dance at the Christmas 1937 Inter-Varsity Ball. The letters he wrote her from Bolton School. The letters he wrote her after joining the family leather-and-tanning business. The letters he wrote her from RAF stations in Chippenham, Doncaster and Upper Heyford, with their promise 'I am going to have you, and soon'. So he did. At the wedding in 1940, Arthur was best man. Agnes has already seen the photographs, showing Michael with his nerveless eyes and film-star looks. She has also seen the letter Michael wrote Arthur when his cousin went for a burton in 1940: 'Although I know you will be very cut up about Dan, I do hope you will be able to see everything "balanced out" in the very near future.' Laconic, unruffled, urbane: was ever a man more classically RAF than Michael

Thwaites? Before they married, Mary tells her, she'd been *bored* (her one brief job was at a bank in Manchester). But the past two years have been bliss – the off-duty bits, anyway, when they can swim, dance, play tennis, go walking, be alone together.

A low plane hurtling from nowhere scares the hell out of them both. Mary puts a hand to her stomach, as though to protect her unborn child. If only she could protect Michael, too, but she doesn't mind admitting she's scared. These aren't the anxieties she had before they married – was he feckless? would he be faithful? how good were his prospects in the leather trade? – but the stress of him flying so many ops. How long can he be the rubber ball of the squadron, the one who keeps bouncing back? Why this need to go on proving himself? He likes to make light of his bombing sorties. The *crumpf, crumpf* of enemy flak is 'rather cosy', he says, and tracer fire climbing upward is 'like bubbles in a glass of champagne'. Chin up, press on regardless: that's his motto. But it isn't easy, never knowing if he'll come back. 'It won't happen to me,' he says, but what if it did? On one raid the flare path was in a difficult direction: he hit the tree-tops on take-off and had a huge bough sticking to his undercarriage when he came down. Another time he flew to Hamburg and after dropping his bombs – the flaring triumph as gasworks, factories and hospitals went to blazes – he was pinned like a moth in the glare of forty searchlights, and (having escaped them) he wandered off course, narrowly missed an air balloon, and then pranged and caught fire on landing, all his crew luckily surviving though the wireless operator had frostbite because the set was duff and he'd had to bang two wires together all the way home. Stories like that aren't good for Mary's nerves but it's best to be under no illusions. Lately Michael has been flying missions to the Ruhr, the Crump Dump, and has grown ever more laconic, speaking of 'flaps' and 'fun and games' and 'hot spots' and 'flak you could get out and walk on'. Oh, she knows why he's sparing her the detail – there's the baby's health to think of – but she fears him underestimating the dangers. 'I'm just trying in some dumb way to make England a fit place for my nearest and dearest,' he once wrote. Admirable sentiments. But what's the use of building a better England if you aren't around to enjoy it? Once this tour's over, she wants him to move to something less front-line.

The baby is another worry. Of course she wants to have the birth cheaply – why should a perfectly *natural* process cost a lot of money? But are ordinary clinics only for poor people or can women of her class go too? She would have the baby at home if it weren't such an upheaval for Mummy. In some parts of the country there are maternity places for Officers' Wives, but she doubts whether the rates are affordable. No, it will have to be a nursing home. If she'd known Agnes earlier, perhaps she could have gone to Hope. But Ernest has heard of a place called Doriscourt, at Whalley Range, and provisionally booked her in. It will mean being away from Michael for a few days, but he'll be flying missions anyway. 'What do women *wear* for birth?' she asks Agnes, as they tread their slow way back to Windyridge. She has asked Arthur to get her one of those gowns that nurses have in theatre – the ones that cover you completely except for a bit at the back. She's shy about being examined, you see, and wouldn't like to give birth undressed. She also wonders can she endure the pain. And she can't think of a name, either. Mark Morrison Thwaites? Lawrence Blakemore Thwaites? The idea is to keep her parents' surnames alive but so far nothing sounds quite right. 'Any suggestions?'

Agnes doesn't have any. It's enough trying to keep afloat in the torrent of Mary's frets. What an odd couple they must look inching forward, Mary so swollen and she so gaunt. Yet Mary's the tense one, while her role is to offer reassurance. What's in a name? Robert Maurice Thwaites? Edgar Blakeson Thwaites? If they knew each other better, she'd tell Mary to spare herself and wait. But the fretting has little to do with baptism. It's an outlet for other fears, the ones Mary buries again – putting on her bright daughterly face – as they turn into the drive of Windyridge.

✳   ✳   ✳

*Arthur to Kim, Station Sick Quarters, Reykjavik, 22.4.43*

How are you, pet? Have you decided to love me yet? I feel pretty lonely up here at present with no chance of ringing you up in the evenings. I'd give an hell of a lot to be able to go to sleep with my back to you.

I was on my way two hours after being on the phone to you. We were rather overloaded with baggage and bombs, and it was pitch-dark and raining. They wanted us to take off on the short runway but the pilot refused to – a damn good job because we only just got off as it was. We started looking for subs at dawn around a convoy but the weather was shocking and we didn't find anything. The journey after that was uneventful apart from the fact that we went through [CENSORED] at good speed. We sighted Iceland at 3pm – miles and miles of marshy, bleak, uninteresting land with a background of snow-covered mountains. The roads – if you can call them roads – were a mass of puddles and I got bounced to hell in the transport.

It's rather like November at home. But we're comfortable in the mess and billets. The blokes are a decent crowd and I've no doubt I shall enjoy myself when I settle down. I arrived the evening before a party (a rare event, with women present) but was too tired (and too drunk by the time the women arrived) to appreciate it.

Write long chatty letters please, pet, and then I shall have something to reply to without running foul of the censors. Don't refer to the contents of this letter – it's not careless talk but I doubt it would pass the censor. I will make a rule to write short letters like this at least once a week rather than long ones about every two months.

PS Don't forget to keep going to our house and to look after them for me.

*Kim to Arthur, Hope Hospital, 25.4.43*

Just thought I'd drop you a line before I leave – I'm on my way back to Dublin tonight. Heard from Kitty yesterday that Mammie hasn't been feeling too well lately and has gone to Dublin to see a specialist. I said I'd come right away and told her to get the police at home to send me a telegram – otherwise I could not get my passport. In the meantime Daddie sent me a telegram from Dublin saying Mammie was better and there was no need to come, but by then I'd made my mind up.

I went to Liverpool with my old friend from home, Mary Galvin. When we got to the passport office it was 1.15, and it officially closed at 1pm, but it was open and I went in. They told me they could not possibly get one ready because it took hours or even days. But having looked through my old passport, and seeing the telegram and a note that Brown had given me, and then discovering I was a doctor, they decided it could be arranged after all. Mary, who was standing in the background, said the change in manner was amazing. They asked us to go and grab a coffee and come back. We felt in need of more than coffee by then, so we had a good meal, and then were back at 3 for the passport: no problems.

I leave here tonight for Holyhead at 10.20. Will probably stay a few days. I don't think there is anything seriously wrong with Mammie but I would like to see her and am dying to get away from Hope. It'll be nice to see good old Dublin, too.

Mike Winstanley went down in his exam again. He was very fed-up because he thought he had got it this time. They have advertised for an Assistant Obst officer, at £350 a year, and I've been told I'll probably get it if I apply. But I don't want another six months here.

HIS DEPARTURE TO Iceland involves her in some strange shenanigans. To stop his parents worrying about the journey, he decides not to tell them he's going. Even when they discover he's due to leave (the flight having been delayed by cock-ups and bad weather), he swears her to secrecy – only *she* must know he's on his way, he'll cable *them* once he's safely there. It's a mark of how things have moved on that she allows herself to be embroiled in his devices. Yet the letters are still comparatively formal. These are only their first exchanges ('of fire', I nearly added, but no fire is visible). Anything could happen. They could lose touch or be killed or forget each other's faces. 'Will you please send me a photo?' he asks. 'Most blokes have their beds surrounded by photos of their wives (funny thing that, by the by – nearly all the men here are married), and I can't be content with nude drawings, etc.' Soon she is making a similar request, for 'that photo of you as a child sitting on the front steps with Mary, the one your Mammie has on the dining room mantelpiece'. He sends love and kisses at the end of each letter – 13 Xs, his lucky number. But he's not sure of her. 'Have you decided to love me yet?' he asks. To which she doesn't respond. She's thinking it over, but no, not yet.

April is a bitter month in Iceland. The RAF station, just outside Reykjavik, is marshy and bleak. The roads are a mass of potholes and laval mud, virtually impossible for the lumbering old Albion ambulances to negotiate. The wind howls and they get all sorts of weather in a day. But he has a bedroom to himself (a perk of being a Medical Officer), they feed exceedingly well (with eggs every morning), there's a bath with hot water in

Station Sick Quarters (SSQ as it's known) and a batman to each hut to make the beds. Beer is 9d, whisky 6d and gin 3d: not bad. Cigarettes are 6d for 20. Reyky itself is modern if crude, with a swimming baths and four cinemas. The blokes in the squadron are a decent crowd. As for the Icelandic girls, he tells her, 'they seem rather similar and pale-faced. Still, they will probably look pretty good when one's been in this place for a year.'

With no patients to see after 11.00 in the morning and little paperwork to do, he throws himself into improving his Nissen hut, which he shares with seven other men. He builds a cupboard, with a shelved door that becomes a writing table. He lines the walls of his bedroom with blankets and plugs the rat-holes. He devises a system for heating water, by hanging a petrol tin on the side of the coke stove. He'd be happier doing a *proper* job, but these ones keep him out of mischief. And it's not as if the pilots are seeing much more action than he is. The role of Coastal Command in Iceland is threefold: reconnaissance (recce-ing from Reyky), convoy work (ensuring a safe passage to and from Britain for American ships and planes), and hunting down German U-boats. 'Aircraft can no more eliminate the U-boat than a crow can fight a mole,' the German naval commander Doenitz claims, and in the early years of the war he seemed to be right. But by April 1943 longer-range Allied aircraft and improved radar devices have turned the tide. Inhospitable Iceland may be but, prangs aside, it isn't especially dangerous. As an RAF doctor, Arthur is aware of the common conditions affecting pilots – anoxia, aero-embolism, fatigue, frostbite and flash burns. He knows about LMF, too – lack of moral fibre – and, on the rare occasions when he comes across it, is understanding: who wouldn't be rigid with fear in a heavy plane on an icy runway? who wouldn't shit his pants with a German aircraft on his tail? But in Iceland the main problem is depression: with the monotonous surroundings and long nights, it is (so the official medical history of the war records) 'a place where boredom, low spirits and loss of enthusiasm for work are quickly felt'. Luckily, once spring arrives at last, and hostilities are stepped up (in May 60 U-boats are sighted and 7 sunk), the depression afflicting aircrews recedes, and Arthur starts to enjoy the perks of the place: hot springs, fresh salmon and pollock, the bar at the Borg hotel. Everyone says he's looking tired, but that's only his 'subocular oedema' (bags under the eyes, in common parlance). He gets ten hours' sleep a night – and dreams of his girlfriend back at Hope.

She, under Reswick, finds herself busier than before. As well as her work on Mider, she has to cope with a spate of emergency admissions – not bombing casualties, but pneumonia cases, so many that every spare bed is taken and adults are sent to the children's ward. 'The sisters are kicking up,' she tells Arthur, 'but Brown says the pneumonias must be put somewhere. I got on to him for admitting an inoperable cancer to my ward but he just said "He'll only last two weeks". Fortunately he only lasted two days. They've had to open another ward, one with 80 beds for chronic females, but it's not relieved the pressure at all.'

The work doesn't get to her; the chaos does. One day she and Reswick have another flare-up, when he snaps at her in theatre for not passing him a scalpel quickly enough (who does he think she is – a nurse? his bloody servant?). Once again she goes straight to Brown, the big chief, and says she wants to leave. Once again he persuades her not to hand her notice in – yet. Her brother Patrick suggests she join the Royal Army Medical Corps: 'He's wanted me to do so since I first qualified,' she tells Arthur. But Patrick's own experience is far from encouraging. A Lieutenant-Colonel with the British army in Sierra Leone, he develops furunculosis – a nasty case of boils. The MO there classifies him as unfit, which opens the door to a cushy number back in Britain. But Patrick, insulted, complains to someone higher up and is posted to India for five years to be in charge of a Field Ambulance. 'Damn silly of him but typical,' she says, and decides that three members of the O'Shea clan are enough of a contribution to the British war effort.

It's not as if she's failing to do her bit. What more important job could there be, when lives are being lost, than delivering new ones?

✵    ✵    ✵

*Mary to Arthur, Doriscourt Nursing Home, 18.4.43*

Probably Gennie has told you a fair amount but I'll start from the beginning.

On Saturday I got up feeling pretty lousy, and lay down in the afternoon, and about 6.30 said to Mummy, jokingly, 'I think I've got labour pains'. Anyway my back ached and the pains kept coming at 10-minute intervals. By 9 I couldn't stand up straight when a pain was on and my desire was to crawl on all fours. Mummy decided to ask Gennie what she thought and she said I'd better get along to hospital.

Matron was busy in theatre and couldn't come out so they put me to bed and left me. I've since discovered the nurse then went to bed herself. About 1 am Matron came in with a hypo, saying it would put me to sleep. Ye gods, sleep! It made matters 20 times worse by giving me a mouth as dry as emery paper and of course did not put me to sleep, so I struggled through the night, talking incessantly. For your medical interest, my waters broke at 3am (bet the censor's eyes will bulge at that). I couldn't tell you when exactly I went to theatre, maybe between 10 and 11 am, but the doctor when he examined me looked very surprised and said the baby was ready to be born. He told me to try hard and I'd have her in 2 or 3 seconds, so I said 'Good God, in the raw?' and turned on my side. To be truthful, I was frightened of seeing her born – I wanted to have her at once, naturally, and I wanted to hear her cry, but I was afraid of seeing her till she'd been attended to. Anyway, I told myself not to be a fool and the next quarter of an hour went by very slowly, with me getting exhausted. Finally he said the baby was distressed and he'd use forceps and send for an anaesthetist, who duly came. They trussed me up like a chicken and gave me ether – you know how I loathe the stuff but of course I'd no alternative. I came round at two and was amazed to hear it was a girl, as everybody had said it would be a boy. I was terribly disappointed I'd not been able to have her by myself, and without an anaesthetic, but that's that.

She's got dark hair which is now going slightly fairer and it grows at either side like Daddy's and her forehead is very Morrison. But from the eyebrows down she is terribly like Michael – everyone sees it at once, which seems absurd when she's so weeny and feminine. Her eyes are dark grey-blue and her colouring is dusky-peachy. Her little hands are lovely. She's a determined morsel, too – sets her little jaw and simply won't do what she doesn't want to. It tickles me to death as I know exactly how she feels.

I hope it feels nice to be a godfather. As you say, it's worth it but I don't understand women who want another immediately. I've had quite a job feeding her, and on Saturday they decided they'd wean her on to a bottle because, they said, I was worrying so much about Michael that it was affecting my milk. Well of course I was heart-broken because I love feeding her and felt I'd let her down, so I pulled myself together and the result is I'm still feeding her and she seems quite satisfied with it. The night nurse says she's sure the difficulty wasn't my present mental state but the shock I had before she was born.

THE SHOCK MARY had before giving birth was a regret-to-inform-you telegram from the Air Ministry. Arthur was still in England when it came. In fact, it was he who collected Mary from Oakington and brought her back to Windyridge. Another five weeks and Michael would have seen his baby. Maybe he still *will* see his baby. All that's known for now is that on the night of 11 March 'the Stirling aircraft in which he was flying as captain set out for action over enemy territory and failed to return.'

Since then, from Windyridge and from her Doriscourt bed, Mary has worked ferociously to discover more, bombarding all and sundry with letters and phone calls. Had Michael had practice at flying Stirlings? Might the plane have been mechanically faulty? Did he take off at short notice? Could he have been flying too low, too high? What procedures were there for bailing out? Had he been wearing his lucky white silk scarf? Why was there no wireless contact when he got into difficulties? Some of these questions are highly pertinent. The unreliability of the Stirling, for instance, is common knowledge within the RAF – with its low speed and slowness to gain altitude when carrying a full load, it's the albatross among bombers, more subject to losses than Halifaxes and Lancasters. But Hamish Mahaddie, the squadron leader (later wing commander) whose crew Michael had just taken over, says nothing about this to Mary. Nor does he mention that bombing missions to the Ruhr – 'Happy Valley' as the pilots call it – were dramatically stepped up on 5 March. Instead, he does his best to reassure her. Michael was an outstanding pilot. Three other members of the crew were also quite capable of flying the aircraft. Stuttgart was an easy target and the perfect opportunity to get Michael together with his 'sprog crew'. Wing-commander Donaldson offers similar blah. Sq/Ldr Thwaites had been flying 'a veteran and dependable aeroplane' (veteran? what comfort in that?). There were two escape hatches in the aircraft, both close to the pilot. The bombing height was about 16,000 feet – no lower than usual. All other aircraft in the squadron returned safely. As to wireless contact, 'a distress message gives away information and might mean action by the enemy to take advantage of a crippled machine. It is therefore wise to keep silent.' The other six crew on board, Donaldson writes, were F/Lt Thompson, P/O Bywater, P/O Luton, F/Sgt Clift, F/Sgt Stewart and F/Sgt Urwin. It's frustrating not to have more information for her, but the father of F/Lt Thompson is personal bodyguard to the Prime Minister, who has been taking a close interest, and they're hopeful of hearing something soon. 'Now please, Mrs Thwaites, don't worry,' Donaldson writes. 'Your anxiety will prove needless when your husband is back with us again. We feel very confident and I want you to feel the same.'

Confident is hardly the word. Mary has heard too many of Michael's stories for that. Her mind is full of the images he planted. His plane racing through a forest of darkness, but a fighter coming from nowhere and latching on to it, like a terrier to the underbelly of a stag, and muscles tearing, and ribs cracking, and blood pouring from gaping holes . . . Hearing nothing, seeing everything, how can Mary feel confident? But at first, as everyone says, she bears up remarkably well. No news is good news, Arthur tells her, and she half-believes it. By the time of the birth, though, a month has passed, and she's sliding into despair. The Doriscourt nurses leave her to herself, bringing baby along only at feed-times. It's standard practice, they say – 'new mothers need rest' – but she wonders if they've diagnosed post-natal depression and think she can't be trusted. As she sees it, feeling low is perfectly reasonable in the circumstances – and holding her baby a cruel reminder that Michael can't. 'Oh Arthur I'm so frightened,' she writes. 'I wonder what the real percentage of saved is – we're losing so many and they can't *all* be alive, can they. Also it was a night-fighter and it seems they shot at Michael before he'd dropped his bombs, so the plane might just have blown up in which case they'll all be dead.' She's right about the many being lost. Since Bomber Command doubled its sorties to the Ruhr, those killed or reported missing have doubled each night, and one man in every twenty fails to return. Churchill and Roosevelt are strongly behind the offensive, and Bomber Harris is pushing it as hard as he can. In May, the Ruhr Dams are bombed, and the campaign is acclaimed a great success. But is Michael one of its victims? One of the eggs broken to make Harris's omelette?

Mary's smaller worry is that she doesn't have a name for baby: 'I've thought of Lindsay, Shirley, Felicity, and can't make my mind up about any of them.' Arthur, replying, tries to help out, and to reassure her about the baby's development: 'I'm sure in my own mind, pet, that the shock you had will not have affected baby as she was eight months then. It is an old-fashioned theory built around one or two children that were abnormal . . . About names. I don't like Felicity – nor Lindsay really. Lindy yes. You should pick a catchy name that still sounds out of the ordinary – something you can shout when a crowd of children are playing, say on a beach, that is quite distinctive, short and sweet.' Helpful advice, Mary tells Kim, but she doesn't follow it. When she next writes to her brother it's to tell him 'I've been into town today to register the snippet whom I can't resist calling Tuppence somehow. However, I named her Anne Lindsay Mikela Thwaites – rather a mouthful, I admit.' Rather a mouthful, because she's hedging her bets. For now, the name she likes best is Mikela. But let Michael decide, if and when he turns up.

As if Michael's disappearance weren't enough, there's soon another blow: the death of Benjamin Blakemore, Arthur and Mary's grandfather, 'called to the Higher Life May 25th 1943: "At home with God, which is far better,/But his love is still with us".' Arthur's wing-commander in Reykjavik gives him compassionate leave for the funeral. Passionate leave is how he describes it to Kim, since his main reason for coming home is to see her. Not that she's forewarned. When Mary invites her to tea at Windyridge after the burial in Birkdale Cemetery, she's expecting to see only elderly Morrison relations — but there he is, in the kitchen, waiting to surprise her. Though it's frustrating for them not to have more time — he has to go off again that same night — at least she can remind herself what he looks like. Her only photo of him is the one she asked for, a little boy sitting on a step, and despite his regular air-mails he had begun to seem like a phantom. His arm around her shoulder in the garden is proof that he exists.

✳   ✳   ✳

TWO CHRISTENINGS AND a funeral, then (and another man missing in action). Two christenings which have as much to with death as birth. Agnes kills herself off to become Gennie, then Kim — a sexless, rootless name that buries the woman she was. And Mary's baby becomes Mikela, after her absent father. It would be good to have a wedding to balance these births and deaths, but there isn't one in prospect. My parents (not yet my parents) have been flirting with the idea of love. But as the novelty of Hope wears off, and summer comes to Iceland, their romance begins to crack.

## CHAPTER THREE

# Iceland/Ireland

*Arthur to Kim, Iceland, 16.6.43*

How are you, pet? I've not forgotten your face when you came into the kitchen a week last Monday to help with the tea – and found me there. I was only sorry we had so little time together, and none of it alone.

The crossing back was very rough. And the moment we landed we were told that the next plane after ours (it was the toss of a coin that I wasn't in it: we'd been split into two groups) had crashed en route and caught fire in no uncertain manner – everybody died. The lads here had heard already and were quite certain they'd be at my funeral. I can only hope and pray – more for the family's sake than for mine – that fate spares me for some years yet. The day after that there was a minor prang on the drome. Then I had a journey of eight miles (first in a lorry, then a jeep) over country that defies description, ending with a climb up a mountain, to identify badly mauled and partially burnt bodies (five – one a pal from the mess) in the wreckage of another aircraft. I was not upset by it but could not help thinking of my own escape and (in a detached sort of way) of where Mike may be. Blast this bloody war.

I haven't mentioned any of this in my letter home, as I thought it might upset them, Mary especially.

Have you decided to love me yet?

*Kim to Arthur, Hope, 17.7.43*

I've told you before how lovely it is to get your letters when I least expect them. Your latest arrived in the afternoon post – I was just coming out of my room when Bill handed me it saying 'A letter from Scotland': he must have misread the stamp. Darling, I'm sorry about my letters. Not that there aren't lots of things to be said but somehow I never say them. I especially wanted to say something in that first letter after you'd gone back. Anyway, you know me well enough by now to know that I'll never say very much.

On Thursday I had a really busy day. Was in theatre from 2–6pm and when I got out found I had nine admissions to see and a blood drip to put up. At 8pm I was on pass ward and had seven admissions. Got to bed at 2am and was called at 3am to admit two kids – then again at 7.30am for an appendix.

Yesterday I went to Matlock with Mary. We had a walk, then a drink when the hotel opened at 12, then a meal. They had good whisky there – it kept me tight till we had to leave at 6. We were going to go for a swim but it was too cold.

Haven't got my passport back from London yet, and am getting worried because I plan to be home in Eire for three weeks from August 5th.

*Arthur to Kim, Iceland, 22.7.43*

I nearly started this last night in a depressed frame of mind, having had so little mail. However, this morning I had your latest, so feel more cheerful. Funny how when I get mail I tear it open and whip through for exciting news – what I expect I don't know, but the result falls somewhat flat. Don't think I'm criticising your letters. I enjoy them a lot, for their news of you and the bird's eye view of home. I also enjoy trying to read between the lines as you never say anything committal – I suppose you do the same with my letters.

I've not worried about Michael much lately. In fact I've hardly thought of it, which I feel rather ashamed of – just push it in the background and interest myself in more immediate matters, mainly booze and idle talk since there's so little work to do. When I do think of it, my feelings are very blunted. I suppose by writing to you about this I must be trying to ease my conscience.

*Kim to Arthur, Hope, 29.7.43*

Don't think I've mentioned Tom, who's a friend from home, since you went away. He's been in Glasgow, and was due to sail overseas, but while he was visiting in Dublin he had some sort of accident and had to go home for a few weeks – and when he got back his ship had gone. So he rang on Saturday, and I said why didn't he come here because there was a sports day on that afternoon, and we stayed till about 6pm (it was the hottest day for years), then went to the flicks in Eccles, then on to a club. But not for that long because he had a train to catch at 11pm – and don't worry, I only had the one drink. He came over on the Sunday too and was staying over in town this time, so we were out till 1am. I've just had a call from him saying he'll probably be back tomorrow since he wants to have a party before he sails from Glasgow on Thursday – I'm not keen but I expect the fishes won't mind. He told me that when he was home everyone he met asked was it true he was engaged to me – even his mother. Don't know how the rumour started, but it's very much in the air. Even Grimmy said a patient had told him Dr O'Shea and her husband were observed at the sports.

Had my photo taken in town the other day and was hoping to send you one but they are all awful – even the good ones are not a bit like me.

You seem to be doing a lot of beering. Don't do so much that you start thinking the Icelandic girls aren't bad.


*Arthur to Kim, Iceland, 11.8.43*

A coincidence you mentioned the local girls in your letter because I took one to a dance the other Thursday. No, this isn't a confession. At a party in the sergeant's mess I met a lady from Brighton who's been here 22 years. 'You're just the right person to know,' I said, and she took the hint and introduced me pronto to this girl, not so good to look at unfortunately, but quite pleasant and I did the noble thing and asked her to come to the dance. We had a good time because I drank a fair amount and there were eight of us at the table – my first social evening in mixed company since I got here. She's now gone on holiday, so last night the W/Cdr and myself picked up a couple more and took them to a dance. I was in a real party mood until mine refused to dance the hands, knees and boomp, after which I got fed

up. Will there be more going out with stulkas, I wonder? Only time
and the urge will tell.

### Kim to Arthur, Eire, 12.8.43

Arrived here a few days ago. Terrible journey over (Irish trains are
as packed as English) and the weather is awful.

Despite that, my younger sister, who still lives at home, has
promised me a real holiday. It seems some of the Irish Army are on
manoeuvres nearby and she has met all the officers. She says they
are nice lads and have shown her a very good time. Like me, they
will be staying on till the end of the month.

Everybody keeps asking if I'm engaged. I suppose they must
have heard the Tom rumours. My policy is to laugh and keep them
guessing.

No other news of interest. Not in good form for letter-writing
today so must finish. How's Iceland?

### Arthur to Kim, Same as usual, 2.9.43

How's Ireland? (Or are you back?) Received your letter dated Aug
12 a bit since. Would have replied sooner but life has been one long
round of drunken parties. Hope you are behaving yourself. Before
your holiday you seemed to be slipping – with your 'husband' at the
sports and about to have a party. I see this Tom is talking about your
engagement already. I wonder what your next letter will have in it.

I went out to a local beauty spot the other day – pretty bloody
day and pretty bloody beauty spot, but I was with one of the lads.

Well, that's all for now.

### Kim to Arthur, Hope, 3.9.43

Should really have written long before now but since I came back
from hols I've been lazy. Arrived here a week ago feeling thoroughly
miserable, having had an immensely enjoyable time in Ireland.
Too much smoking and drinking, maybe, but as people kept on
reminding me I was supposed to be having a holiday. Even had a

hangover on the crossing back to Holyhead, after the previous night in Dublin.

Got here to find a party going on. I was very glad of it. Everyone – about 12 of them – was gloriously tight.

That's all the news of interest.

*Arthur to Kim, Iceland, 12.9.43*

My letter of Sept 2nd will have crossed with yours of the 3rd, but by now you'll have had it.

You are, as I said, slipping. You put 'Eire' on your one tiny letter from home, as if the address was a secret. It hurts my pride but I don't know what to feel or think – whether to be glad or sorry.

Two things are evident. One is that when on holiday you have difficulty writing and don't seem to connect me in any way with the life that is yours. The other is that you bring Tom in again, and everybody says it's time you were engaged.

Well, pet, as I said, I don't know what to feel. Is it that you're worried what to do and afraid of hurting me (incidentally, don't be – I'm too hardened nowadays for anything to upset me)? Or are you realising what an hell of a lot of difficulty it would mean if you did decide to love me? Maybe that's why you say you've more than one reason for wanting to get away from Manchester. Really, I don't know what I want you to do. But surely we could stay friends even if you marry Tom – or if I marry someone. Or could we? I don't know – nor do I know if I want to marry you, or if you want to marry me.

I'm only trying to say what we said that night in the bed and again on the grass at the edge of the wood. We were still happy when we finished talking then, weren't we, and we decided to wait till our next meeting to see what to do.

Reading this through, I'm not sure whether to post it or tear it up. It might make you decide not to stay on after October. But on the other hand I am really just the same as I always was and want you to remain a very sincere friend even if we decide not to be anything more.

Well, that's that. I'm going to get drunk tonight.

WAS THAT IT, then? Had love begun to fade, eleven months on? Would my parents become mere friends and I fail to be born seven years later? I felt like Tristram Shandy, hovering over my own conception, willing myself into existence against the odds. Or like the Michael J. Fox character in *Back to the Future*, rocketed back through time to the agonies of his parents' courtship. I could imagine my father's reassuring voice: 'Just relax, lad. No future in worrying.' It was true. I knew the ending. I kept telling myself: it's OK, things will work out, this is just a counter-plot before the happy denouement. But trapped inside my parents' present tense I began to panic. No future . . . It was dark in there. I couldn't see the light ahead.

My mother was 'slipping' – slipping away from him (and me). She always had that slipperiness. Could change her name, could change her nature. In photographs he keeps the same face, a little more lined as the years pass but forever smiling and unmistakeably him. Whereas she wears a series of masks – Agnes, Kim, Mummy, the Mrs Doctor and countless more, short-haired and long-, wide-hipped and narrow-, gawky, elegant, morose, beatific, shy, introverted, happy-sad, each new mask different from the last. The 'real her' can't be identified and may not exist. No wonder he didn't feel sure of her. What was there to feel sure of? The lack of letters from her that August was symptomatic of a deeper absence. The hole in the middle. The space he couldn't enter. The portal that wouldn't admit him (or me).

As she slipped, so he began slipping too. Took out local girls. Got drunk with the boys. Wondered if it – she – them – the thing they had together – was worth the effort of seriousness. They'd known each other less than a year, most of it spent apart: was marriage a realistic proposition? Perhaps the gulf was too wide. He knew almost nothing about her family, and she'd avoided filling him in – wouldn't give her address or put a name to her younger sister. By definition, being Irish, the O'Sheas must be poor – which didn't bother him but would certainly bother his father. Only the other month, when a pal, Norman Lawtus, married into a well-off medical family, Ernest was urging Arthur to follow suit: 'Never marry for money they say, but believe me it makes one hell of a difference in life. It's all very well fighting your way up, but having connections and knowing you've a little bit behind you does wonders for a career.' The old man had some cranky ideas but this one was hard to refute. Why get involved with Kim and then have to drop her if he met someone more suitable? Better for now to keep a bit of distance. Wasn't that what she was doing – keeping her options open with Tom? 'Surely,' he suggests, 'we could stay friends even if you marry Tom – or if I marry someone.'

How seriously did he mean it? And what was it they'd said 'that night in the bed and again on the grass at the edge of the wood'? Since they'd agreed to wait till their next meeting before deciding what to do, why couldn't they stick to that? I felt frustrated by their vacillations. I'd expected to follow them to the altar, but here they were divorcing. I'd come to find my mother, but here I was losing her all over again.

Some of their problems were due to the vagaries of the post, which gave their conversation an odd staccato rhythm. They kept missing each other. He'd get an affectionate letter from her, feel jaunty, and say something complacent or insensitive in reply. She'd receive this when touchy or depressed, and feel diminished and taken for granted, and come back with something sarcastic. By which time he'd have sent her several more letters, but be suffering from 'flu or feeling browned off, and get angry and go silent on her. Meanwhile she, cheered by his intervening letters, would have written a warm and loving reply, and be baffled by his failure to respond – had she been too amorous? too candid? too pushy? Well, the bastard could stuff it, she'd decide – just at the point of getting his next letter, which, being buoyant and passionate, would soften her, and prompt her to send a loving reply, which would then prompt him (in a glow of pleasure at receiving it) to say something jaunty or complacent and insensitive, making her feel taken for granted . . . And so it would all start again, the endless circling switchback of love.

Not everything was out of sync. Sometimes, checking dates, they'd find they dreamt strange dreams on the same night, or had sore throats or fits of laughter on the same day, or experienced premonitions or 'feelings' which proved correct. Her letters, he told her, were as prophetic as *Old Moore's Almanac*. 'You are already a Mrs Moore,' he wrote, adding, 'I hope it won't be long before the "ore" is altered to "rrison".' I found it funny and heartening to read such stuff. Perhaps this was why my father had kept the letters: because he hoped I (or others) would be touched by them. Even the tiffs and rifts were touchingly comical. Later in life my father liked to tell a joke, about a man whose lawn-mower is broken and who goes to the next-door neighbour in hope of borrowing his. As he waits on the step for the door to open, the man thinks of all the objections the neighbour might raise: that his mower is brand new and can't be risked on anyone else's lawn, that the last time he lent someone something it came back broken, that he now has a rule never to borrow or lend, that there's a perfectly good mower repair shop down the road, etc. When the door finally opens, he's so incensed by these imagined replies he tells the neighbour: 'You can keep your bloody mower, you arsehole.' I thought of this joke while reading my parents' war letters: in many, either he or she will race ahead and become upset that the other (suddenly cruel, cold, selfish, manipulative and untrustworthy) must be feeling this or thinking that. This second-guessing was mostly wrong – and a reminder that we never know what's going on in another person's head. It all struck me as very funny.

Funny in retrospect, that is. In August 1943 my parents were short on jokes and hopes for the future. The war looked set to last, and even when it ended the prospects for them were uncertain. They became, as they admitted, 'brittle and impersonal'. The tone of their correspondence was dutiful. The heart and heat of it began to go out.

✳     ✳     ✳

YET IT LOOKS so promising back in June. Straight after Arthur's flying visit, her sister Eileen (who's heavily pregnant) and brother-in-law Gerry come to stay with her in Salford. Gerry's about to go off to West Africa for an engineering job with the Admiralty, which will be tough, but both of them are in good spirits, and take her to the cinema (*Andy Hardy's Double Life*, starring Mickey Rooney, who everyone says looks just like Arthur), and over a meal afterwards they ask could she get Eileen into Hope when the time comes – and then she, Agnes, deliver the baby. Of course, she says, no problem. The difficulties with Reswick have eased lately, and she has dropped her plans to leave. She feels more at home when she calls at Windyridge, too: Ernest might be intimidating but she's fond of Kathleen, close to Mary and enchanted by baby Kela. As for Arthur, he's hoping to be home for Christmas, and says he wants their relationship to last. His faith in it has strengthened hers. She is not an expansive correspondent but her letters are less wary than before. Buoyed up, secure enough to tease him, she sends him an old magazine article about Iceland, with photos of local women mixing with GIs: 'Unusual ratio of two Icelandic girls to one American serviceman was effected by this soldier at Red Cross canteen', 'Icelandic girls thawed appreciably over Christmas – here a Navy man executes an encircling manoeuvre', etc. The article also includes a poem, which she hopes is *a propos*:

> Somewhere up in Iceland where the rain is like a curse
> And every day is followed by another, only worse,
> Where the north wind's nightly howling robs a man of
>     blessed sleep,
> Where there isn't any whisky and the beer is never cheap,
> Somewhere up in Iceland where the mail is always late,
> And a Christmas card in April is considered up to date,
> Somewhere up in Iceland sits a man whose tender heart
> Is beating for another a thousand miles apart.

Arthur's heart is indeed beating for her, though by now conditions in Iceland are less bleak than those described in the poem. When he first arrived it was so cold he wore three pairs of woollen socks even indoors. But by June it's mild and rainy, and life on camp is almost relaxed. 'I spent a whole day shopgazing,' he tells her, 'and saw the following perfumes: Elizabeth

Arden, Max Factor, Yardley, Icilma, Coty, Ponds, Cyclax, Evening in Paris and La Nouvelle Poudre Simon. Let me know if it's worth sending you any in a duty-free parcel.' He wants to pamper her, and she teases him in return: 'You are having nice weather now, but when it gets cold again don't rub too many Icelandic noses.' Joking and flirting are their own way of rubbing noses while apart. It wouldn't do to admit it, but yes she's decided to love him a little. An incident at Hope brings it home. It happens after a party — doesn't it always? — when two nurses the worse for wear come back to her room to drink black coffee. One of them, Jeannie, has already crashed out for the night when the other, Doreen, catches sight of a photo of Arthur on the mantelpiece (a grown-up shot now, not the little-boy one she had before). 'What's Arthur Morrison doing in the room?' she asks, before passing out on the bed, clutching the photo to her bosom and murmuring 'My old flame'. Well! It wouldn't be right to take offence given how drunk Doreen is, yet she can't help but feel jealous and proprietorial. Slipping the photo from Doreen's clutches, she returns it to the mantelpiece. Arthur's *hers* now. They couldn't be closer, no matter how far apart.

Late June and early July are a high point: white nights and blue air-mails. But then the letters become staccato again and the passion drifts away. He talks of taking out 'stulkas' – local talent. She mentions 'Tom', the boy she knows from Kerry – knows so well that some think they must be engaged. Stung, he is ungracious when she tells him how well she's doing at Hope – 'Ye Gods, I wish I had been born Irish and female' – implying that if better qualified people were around, meaning English male doctors such as himself, she'd not have it so easy. She lets that one pass but then tells him that, 'as he knows', she is keen on leaving Hope, 'for more reasons than one' – which is the first he's heard of it and adds to his feelings of rejection. If she moves away from Manchester, how's he going to see her when he gets home?

What wounds him most is her writing only once – briefly – during the month she spends in Ireland. His letters are petulant about this; jealous, too, at any mention of Tom. What she says about Tom hardly justifies his tone or the notion of marrying others and 'staying friends'. Perhaps it's a ruse to throw her in a panic, so that she'll tell him how much he means to her. What an arch manipulator! I wouldn't blame her if she dumped him. Yet in one respect, he has my sympathy. Whereas he has made her welcome in his family, she excludes him from hers. All that spring and early summer, she calls at Windyridge at least once a week. 'Your wench, Agnes, was here the night before last and is coming again this weekend,' father writes to son, 'wench' denoting sardonic acceptance. Then in August she goes to Ireland, and, back among her own, she clams up. 'You don't seem to connect me in any way with the life that is yours,' he says. It's true. She doesn't. Six months later he's still asking her where she comes from and which college she qualified at. It's inconceivable she hasn't told him. The fault is partly his for failing to hear. But something in her telling encourages forgetfulness. (Years later I too would fail to remember the name of her home town.) Her Ireland isn't for sharing. She won't let him colonise it. She's like the Fenian on the quiz show ('Which two Republicans seized the General Post Office during the Easter Rising of 1916?' 'Who wants to know?') – determined to give nothing away.

Does she foresee, back in 1943, what a life with my father will cost? Is this why she falls silent back in Killorglin, in order to protect the self invested there? Is the disjunction between him and his and her and hers simply too much to deal with, now she's been made to confront it? That August Kerry is almost as hard to get to as Iceland. There's a horrible train ride from Manchester to Holyhead (with a chain-smoking RAMC officer in the compartment who tries to chat her up), a row with obstructive passport and customs staff, a gale-force crossing to Dun Laoghaire, and an equally horrible train ride from Dublin to Killarney (starved of resources, Ireland's transport system is close to collapse). Home at last, exhausted, after a year away, she sees Killorglin through alien eyes – as Arthur might, or as visitors down the ages have. 'For dirt and dreariness, Killorglin may vie with any inhabited place in the universe,' said one in 1822. And so it has continued, down the decades. 'An unprosperous, sequestered and almost squalid seat of population' (1846), 'poverty, decay and dilapidation' (1848), 'a cluster of the most primitive hovels used as human habitation that could be found in the three kingdoms' (1869). After the Great Famine, so she's been told, the turf-diggers of Kerry were so poor that they wore only one shoe – on the foot which worked the spade. There are still barefoot children around. No wonder people move away, in search of better lives. On a single day in February 1921, when she was three, upwards of 20 young men and women left town for the USA. The O'Sheas are part of the diaspora. To 'belong' in Ireland is to leave. Who *wouldn't* leave, given the chance? Tossing in bed, she wonders why she bothered to come back.

But sleep's a marvellous thing. Next morning she perks up. Puck Fair's on, and thousands have come from miles around in order to gawp at the billy-goat (crowned King Puck, and presented with a stash of cabbages, the goat's kept on a fifty-foot-high platform for three days). It's a rowdy occasion, full of beer and tinkers, and in the old days the O'Sheas, summering in Ross Beigh, would keep their distance. But this year they're staying put in Killorglin. Joe and Kitty still live at home, and Sheila's back from teaching in London. The pubs, open all hours, are full of stamping feet and scratchy fiddles.

> Here's to the man who kisses his wife,
> And kisses his wife alone;
> For there's many a man kissed another man's wife
> When he thought he kissed his own.
>
> Here's to the man who rocks his child,
> And rocks his child alone;
> For there's many a man rocked another man's child
> When he thought he rocked his own.

The young O'Sheas trek from pub to ceilidh, from song to song. There are army officers around, and parties to go to, and dancing: not so dreary, after all. If it weren't home, and therefore boring, Agnes could get fond of the place. Dammit, she *is* fond of the place. When Ernest asked after her 'roots', she should have told him the O'Sheas were among the kings of Corcu Duibne, the first Celtic tribe to settle the area. She should have told him that owning the wool business makes her father a man of substance in Killorglin. OK, it's only a one-horse town, but it's her Daddie who has the horse. More accurately, it's a one-car town, and he who owns the car, a Studebaker. Owns but doesn't drive, except at weekends. He has a man to do the driving for him, while he sits in the back doing his sums. Why feel ashamed? By any standards, the O'Sheas are prosperous, entrepreneurial, middle-class, comfortably settled. Shop at the butcher's or baker's or draper's and, being relations, they put it on the tab. Re-rooted, far from bombs, Agnes again rather than Kim or Gennie, she savours the good life, sleeping till lunch, drinking in pubs, cycling to the links at Dooks, watching fishermen hoik salmon from the Laune, burning off her Salford pallor.

One day she, Joe, Sheila and a cousin go for a long drive round the Ring of Kerry. The landscape rushes by like a Thirties documentary on Irish rural life. Peat-stacks by every house and potatoes ripening in furrows. Red-haired children with dusty freckles playing Knucklestones. Rowboats with creaky rowlocks bobbing out towards lobster pots. The silver of lake-water and the gold of scented whins. And horses, always horses, wherever

she looks. Why feel embarrassed to call this home? Any stranger – even Arthur – would think it idyllic.

'And is there someone you're seeing?' Kitty asks, on one of their strolls. 'Nobody serious,' she says. A shifty answer and yet a true one. Arthur's too much of a card to be serious. The relationship's inexplicable even to her. From where she is to where he is it's a thousand miles due north. What hope of bridging all that divides them – not just the war but the differences between their families? And what will Arthur be like when he comes back, after nine months of beer and pent-up celibacy? Almost next door to the house in Langford Street is The Oisin, Killorglin's new cinema. That August it's showing *Star Spangled Rhythm*, which has a scene with a navy vessel disembarking and two eager blondes on shore discussing their chances. One says how glad the sailors must feel to be home in the US again, 'especially those ones – they've just come from Iceland'. 'Oh, *Iceland*,' says the other, and runs straight off in their direction. In the stalls with Kitty, she laughs at this. In bed, alone, it seems less funny. When Arthur's back, he'll be rampant – any woman will do, and the more the merrier. Perhaps he's rampant in Reyky now.

Her stay in Kerry stretches to the end of August. One Saturday, just before leaving, she joins her Daddie while he drives to the other side of Dingle to see a man about a flock. Despite the heat, he's fully kitted out as though for market: double-breasted tweed suit, watch chain, carnation in lapel. At seventy-five, he's getting too old for running the business, and is slowly letting Joe take charge. But at weekends he likes to motor out and keep his hand in. Considers himself young at heart. Self-made. Forward-looking, too, not some mountainy peasant. A patriot yes, but not so much as to fall out with English mill-owners, on whom his trade depends. He isn't the fearsome patriarch sort but demands respect. Would endure no son or daughter of his swaggering back from over the water to pour contempt on the ways of home. But understands his children's ambition to get out. Encourages it. Has educated them into it at no small expense. Depriving the Irish of a proper schooling was how the English used to keep them in place. Education's the answer – not only has he pushed his own children (girls as well as boys) to go to university, he acts as a trustee for Killorglin's secondary school. Beat the English at their own game (not least the game of golf): that's his motto. Of course, there are some who love their chains, whom you can never liberate or raise up – but if people won't be helped there's nothing you can do. Politicians he regards with distrust, as snakes and wolves. Nationalists are the worst of all. Never get involved, he has told his children. He remembers the Easter Rising (not a drop of Guinness to be had in town) and Civil War. The Troubles of 1920 were bad enough – local girls punished for mixing with Black and Tans by having their hair cut off; the burning down of Foley's garage and the Sinn Fein hall; murders and reprisals. But 1922 was worse. Captain Lehane, the Free State commanding officer, was shot right outside the pub, opposite the wool-yard. You can still see the blood-stained gable wall. Agnes would have been five then. Violence like that can mark a child. But she has done well for herself. She's a good girl, they're a good brood.

The route which father and daughter take means them passing the homes of friends and second cousins. With all the stop-offs for refreshment, it's nearly three before they reach the farm. The shearing of blackface sheep, to whose wool he owes his living, usually happens in May and September. This farmer's started early. Led by the mewing of mustered sheep, they find him in a shed out back. His farm's electrified, which means the shearing is done with buzzing blades, a quicker method than cutting by hand and a kinder one than pulling. There are three men working in the shed: one to draw out the victim, one to shear, and one to pile up the fleeces. Each sheep, obese with wool, is fed between the arch of the shearer's legs, gripped, upended, hoisted, dangled, parted from its greasy wrapping then patted on the rump and sent clear. Paddy didn't come for this. It's more a social call than business. All his deals are made at weekly markets (Kenmare on Wednesdays, Kilgarvan on Thursdays, etc). But to Agnes the shearing is absorbing – the silly panic of the ewes in their pen, the heavy rugs peeled off their backs, their milk-white skins with little red nicks as they skip to freedom. How small and light and naked they look, once shorn. Inside every sheep there is a lamb. Standing in the shadows like a trespasser, embarrassed by the farmhands' gaze, she too feels young again. When was the last time she saw sheep sheared? At five? ten? The wool in the yard in Langford Street is lumpen and dead, a commodity for grading and packing. This is different – raw, redemptive and as thrilling as surgery.

In the farmhouse kitchen, where they sit drinking tea and whiskey, the talk is of the slump in wool prices since the onset of war. Loss of exports, broggers bidding low, farms forced out of business, no more golden Irish fleece – the talk is gloomy and tiresome. Every so often, the farmer – fortyish, blood-faced, wheat-haired – casts an awkward glance her way. Doubtless he's unmarried and on the lookout, like most of them: no shortage of bachelors in Kerry. Only the eldest sons can hope to inherit. The rest are tied to their mothers. God save her from one of those. Goats and donkeys are all they own – and all they are. Oh, and their gawkiness at ceilidhs, their rotten teeth and mutton-chops and red faces. Straight to the bar after mass, for where else is a man to go on his day off? No wonder Kerry's women are drifting away, up to Dublin or over the water. Without women, the rural economy can't survive. But who or what will stop them leaving? Those that stay are mired in melancholy. To find a husband with a house or job is thought an untold blessing, but who'd be a farmer's wife, chained to byre and cradle? Her own mother has more spirit, though she too serves a Lord and Master, in church. No, it's no kind of life.

'Sure a pretty girl like you must have a boyfriend over the water by now,' says her father, on the way home. She blushes and denies it. It's not even a lie exactly, since things with Arthur look so hopeless. She knows what she feels about him. Or did know, till she came here. They were on the eve of something. But was it war, not love, drawing them together? Unions rushed into and swiftly repented are a standing joke at Hope, on the maternity ward. It has never *felt* as though she and Arthur were clinging to each other for solace. But what if he hadn't been going away?

And how well does she really know him? To this woman in Ireland the man in Iceland seems suddenly cold and remote. Rolling the window down, she lets her arm trawl the summer wind and changes the subject.

Iceland, Ireland. Just a single letter separating them. But that August it becomes a massive gulf. The difference of a consonant. Yet all the difference in the world.

✳    ✳    ✳

I CONFESS TO A little embroidery there. The trip home, Puck Fair, *Star Spangled Rhythm*, the work and attitudes of Patrick O'Shea, the shooting of Captain Lehane in Langford Street, what Agnes felt about Arthur: all are documented in some way. But her letters from 'Eire' say little, and I've filled in some of the gaps. It's not my usual method, to fictionalise. And even here what I've set down scarcely qualifies as fiction. With fiction you can let go, constrained only by the logic of your inventions. With my mother, who isn't an invention (it was she who created me, not vice versa), there's a demand for honest reporting. I can feel her over my shoulder, scanning the page for stuff and nonsense. Though certain to fail, I want to fail with honour. Which means honouring the truth of who she was.

With family history, facts can be elusive, however. The stories passed down as gospel truth can be more inventive than any an author could dream up. I've been told on good authority that my grandfather was the first man in Killorglin to own a car. But in *Cast a Laune Shadow*, a memoir of growing up in the town, local historian Patrick Houlihan suggests a solicitor called W. Girwan had prior claim. (The chauffeur-driven Studebaker was surely ample compensation.) I've also been told that my grandfather started out as a teacher but was plucked from obscurity by an English aristocrat, for whom he acted as a guide one summer holiday: the aristocrat took a fancy to Paddy, saw opportunities for him in the wool trade and arranged for him to be trained in Bradford, from where he returned in triumph to set up his business in Langford Street (only then winning the hand of

Margaret Lyons, whose father had previously dismissed him as a poor schoolmaster unworthy of notice). Nice story. But the truth, as far as I can tell, is more humdrum. Paddy's father, John O'Shea, had links with the skin trade, too, being a buyer of chickens and turkeys. It was he who bought the house in Langford Street. And there can't have been much resistance to Paddy from the Lyons family, since Margaret married him when she was just nineteen.

I'll do my best not to be fictional, Mum. I've your letters to ground me in fact. But I can't promise to tell the truth in every instance. We should have talked more. There will be things, because we didn't, that elude me. People, too – not least yourself.

✻     ✻     ✻

*Ron to Arthur, 107 Hulton Lane, Bolton, Lancs, 27.8.43*

I hope you got my cable giving the good but hellish overdue news. When I look back I wonder how we made it. Left Africa 15 June and landed in UK 21 August. Better I draw a discreet veil of censorship over the trip but believe me it was bloody – the only redeeming feature was the bar. We were met at [CENSORED, port of disembarkation] by a wizard WAAF MT driver. Boy, was it good to know such creatures still existed after all the rank-conscious, hard-bitten nursing sisters or the tough old Coasters' wives.

I've already been down to Windyridge. Arthur, you certainly have a brave sister. Mary is one of the pluckiest people I've ever met. I was rather worried whether my presence would upset her but I think I managed to cheer her up by shooting a line about the Coast, showing photographs, etc. Her kiddy is really sweet and already seems to have fallen for me.

THERE'S ANOTHER HOMECOMING in August. Ronnie Astle is back from West Africa, as Agnes – or Kim, as I'll now call her – discovers when she next sees Mary. Lean, pencil-moustached and famously moody, Ronnie is an old friend of Arthur. They went to

Bolton School together. They'd have gone to Med School together too, had Ronnie's parents been able to pay the fees, instead of which he settled for dentistry. Browned off, he ran away to join the Tank Corps and had to be bought out. Later he joined the RAF, and learned to pilot Hurricanes and Masters. But it was as a dental officer he enlisted, and lately there've been few chances to fly. His frustration and chippiness make him a natural ally of Arthur, who's a bit of a wingless wonder too. In their letters they ham it up: Ronnie and Arthur, the comic duo, two duffers forced to treat colds or fill cavities while their colleagues are killing Krauts. From his training base in Morecambe, Ron entertains Arthur – or Aha, Abe, Aby, Sod and Herpes-Face as he calls him – with hapless tales and ruminations: the detumescent impact of cold baths, the futility of exams in wartime ('I suppose they will make a bit more fuss over the shell-shattered fragments of a *qualified* bloke'), the difficulty of finding a suitable dame. When he moves on to Hastings, in West Africa, drilling and yanking teeth in an outpost of Empire, the comic litany of troubles continues: it's too hot, he's had to build his surgery himself from Nissen hut-ends, the wogs are dumb, red tape and bull and finger trouble and duff gen are brassing him off, there's absolutely bugger-all to do ('I just sit in a chair in the corner drinking gin and squash, when we have any gin or squash, or rye and dry if we haven't gin or squash, or brandy and soda when we haven't any gin or squash or rye or dry, or sometimes when we haven't any gin or squash or rye or dry or brandy or soda, I just sit and think, or sometimes I just sit'). Back in England, he was seeing a girl called Elise. Since going to Africa, all he can do is read of Arthur's exploits: 'Your sex life leaves me like a baffled chameleon, red and green in the face at the same time. How is that sister at Hope going on? Spare a thought for me (when you are on the job). I've almost forgotten what a pair of white legs looks like. After 12 months here, I'm like that old woman in the joke (remember), watching her grandchild being bathed and asking what its sex is – "It's not my eyes, but my memory that's so bad".'

Ronnie's fifteen months in Africa aren't as uneventful as he pretends: on one occasion he led a search party through a mangrove swamp to retrieve bodies from a crashed plane. But by

August 1943, his first tour over, he's back home in Bolton, unscathed but for a touch of malaria. Within three days he's round at Windyridge, looking up the Morrisons again. And within a fortnight he runs into Kim, who has been summoned to look at Kela's skin. The three of them – mother, doctor and dentist – stand together in the nursery, examining the flaky whorls and pimpled outcrops of baby flesh. Eczema: it's been so bad that Mary once put Kela's arms in splints in an attempt to stop her scratching. More usefully, she took her to see a specialist, a Dr Marianne Peach in John Street, who suggested Mary use olive oil instead of soap and water, and insisted she dress Kela in silk or cotton, not wool. Her skin's improved a bit, though Mary still finds her 'an absolute little vixen'. Kim's good with babies, though as to the skin – at which they stare forlornly, as if a solution will write itself in raised welts – she has no useful advice. Ronnie's stumped too: he's a teeth man, and Kela's all gums. But the women are glad of his company: it changes the chemistry to have a man about. Back in July, Mary was talking miserably of having to 'pick up the reins again and *do* something with my life': were it not for Kela tying her down, she'd join the Ferry Service or Ambulance Corps, 'anything to be in the thick of things'. It's agony to have no news of Michael. But Ronnie has cheered her up.

'She really is bearing up marvellously,' he tells Arthur, not laddish now but pious. 'I just can't express in words my admiration and pity for her.' Admiration and pity? Kim, watching them together, suspects stronger feelings. So do Ernest and Kathleen, who're fond of Ronnie but become anxious as his visits increase. He has always had a soft spot for Mary. What if he falls in love – a cruel fate, since Mary could never reciprocate? Is it irresponsible letting him come as often as he does? In his letters home, Arthur reassures them as best he can, but he too wonders where it will end. Leave a man and a woman alone together long enough and – even with a baby there – something's bound to happen. It's tricky enough with Mary still married, at least in name. But if word should come through, against the odds, that Michael is alive, in a POW camp . . .

Kim, caught up in this, is tempted say something, but Mary beats her to it. It's a Saturday afternoon in late September, and they're trying on winter suits in the women's-wear department of Kendal's, Kim half-heartedly since she is short of coupons and would rather wait to buy one next time she's in Dublin. In the changing room, Mary seems tetchy. Six months on and her figure hasn't come back. Rationing means there isn't much choice: each suit is found lacking, or rather she is. 'How's this?' she asks, in the mirror, then adds, out of nowhere, that she hopes Kim realises her going about with Ronnie is perfectly innocent: she's still Michael's wife, there's nothing more to it than pub lunches and motorbike rides. 'Of course,' Kim nods to Mary's reflection. What's it like to have your man go missing overseas, she wonders? In a way, it's happened to her, with Arthur having become a friend not the Mr Right she thought he might be. But at least he's still alive, whereas with Michael who can say? She catches Mary's face in the mirror.

'It suits you,' she says.

'A bit matronly,' says Mary, running her hands down her sides. 'Just as well I'm not in the market for marriage.'

'Just as well I'm not, either,' says Kim, slipping off a skirt like an old skin.

'Have you ever dreamt of Michael?' Mary asks. 'I know you didn't meet him, but you've seen his photo. It's a silly question but . . .'

It's a silly question, but Mary has been dreaming of Michael, for the first time since he went missing. She'd think nothing of it, but her mother and her mother's friend Edie have also had dreams about him reappearing. Her Auntie Nan, too, has these 'feelings' he's alive; she had them in the last war with her brother who was missing, presumed dead, before turning up safely six weeks later. Michael's brother Gray (Graham) says the same — that he senses he's safe somewhere. The dreams, and lack of news, give Mary hope: surely they'd have heard by now from the Air Ministry if Michael's body had been found and buried some-where. Her own dream always happens in the same way: he comes back, and she walks into his arms and then wakes up.

She's been having headaches, and is thinking of getting her sight tested, and worries that her nerves are driving her crazy. Which is why she asks Kim the question. And why she asks Arthur, too, in a letter: 'Do you ever dream of him? I've never attached importance to dreams before but now I wonder. It's 29 weeks today since I last saw him and feels like 29 years.'

How my parents replied to Mary I don't know – no doubt in as kindly a manner as their scepticism allowed. But half a century on, her premonitions send a shiver through me. For in one respect, she was right: Michael hadn't been buried, and that September he did 'reappear'. The full details emerged only in 1945, after the occupying German forces retreated from northern France. Round 10.30pm on 11 March 1943 his Stirling, on its way out to Stuttgart with a full bomb-load, was attacked by German fighters and became detached from the rest of the squadron. Catching fire, it plummeted towards Minaucourt, a village some 40 kilometres from Chalon-sur-Marne. The local curé was just going to bed when he heard a large explosion and his window-panes shattered. Others saw a plane in flames passing low over the village and crashing near the National Military Cemetery, where 20,000 men lay buried from the Great War. On landing, the plane exploded and broke in two. The rear fuselage fetched up near a German radar station. The front landed in a copse, 200 yards off, brushwood and saplings deadening its fall. In the middle of this copse was a marsh or crater, and the plane sank beneath the surface, bog-water swallowing the crew. Next day, the villagers, using shepherds' crooks, recovered four bodies, including the rear gunner's; the remains of two more bodies were found later. The Germans took possession of all personal belongings and, with the help of the curé, buried the six airmen, with military honours, in the civil cemetery. Ordinary villagers were banned from the ceremony but watched it from behind a hedge and later laid fresh flowers on the communal grave.

What the villagers didn't know was that there'd been another man on board (crews of seven were standard with RAF bombers). Not until six months later, on 21 September, was his body found floating on the surface of the crater. It consisted of head and trunk only; embedded in the chest was a wallet and silver cigarette case belonging to Sq/Ldr Michael Thwaites DFC no. 79550. In the wallet, inside a cellophane envelope, were three photos (one of Mary, one of Michael's mother, one of his brother Graham). The cellophane envelope also contained a letter, a rose and a strand of hair. As the pilot, up front, Michael would have hit the water first and sunk deepest. It had taken six months for him to climb out. The women dreaming at home had all seen the same thing – Michael, unburied, reappearing. And so, after a fashion, he did.

In 1943 Mary knows none of this, and until she learns the truth she refuses to give up hope. But within a month of disclosing her dreams, she receives a letter from the Air Ministry about her 'widow's pension', followed by a run of forms to fill in – each one a reopening of old wounds. Then, hardest of all, a trunk containing his 'personal effects' arrives from the RAF Central Depository in Slough: '4 prs trousers, 2 jackets, 1 greatcoat, 1 raincoat, 1 pr flannel trousers, 3 towels, 5 shirts, 10 prs socks, 13 collars, 17 handkerchiefs, 4 black ties, 4 civilian ties, 2 prs pants, 2 vests, 2 pullovers, 1 brass brush, 5 prs shoes.' The empty shoes upset her most. Afterwards, she writes to Arthur in a rage: 'The Air Ministry say they have no further news but that for official purposes he must be presumed dead – meaning that I am expected to pay death duty. It's a bloody fine world, isn't it? Why not put someone against a wall and shoot him and then tell his relatives they must pay for having him shot. I think I shall be granted relief inasmuch as I have no income of my own and a baby to support. But it's the principle of the thing – and my God how bitter it makes me. Sandy – the little navigator Michael wanted – is now missing and his wife is expecting a baby. And so it goes on and on and still people don't seem to realise there is a war.'

✻   ✻   ✻

*Kim to Arthur, Hope Hospital, Salford, 1.8.43*

As you know, I've been wanting to leave Manchester, for more reasons than one. But it looks as if I'll be staying. The whole thing will

probably shake you. It's certainly got me worried. The fact is that
Grimmy wants to go to Edinburgh for three months (Oct-Jan) to do
his FRCS and he's asked me to take over as RSO. Of course I tried
to talk myself out of it but Grimmy talked me in. I said I couldn't
possibly do it but he said he wouldn't have asked me if he didn't think
I could. I don't mind the wards and clinics, because I've done them
every day since I came here, but the theatre part of it worries me.
However, Grimmy says I'll have very little to do except appendices,
hernias, etc. And since this happened I've spent most of my time in
theatre getting practice. Trouble is, when I get back from holiday I'll
only have a month before Grimmy goes, and I've still a lot to learn.

SHE DOESN'T EXPECT to find surgery so easy. But it's only
cutting and sewing, which she's done since being a child. Not
that her mother sewed – with all those babies, she had no time
– but from maids and older sisters she learned the knack. At
school she was taught embroidery along with the other domestic arts. But it wasn't pushed. There was a notion among her
teachers that the girls in their keeping deserved better. By all
means learn cookery and dressmaking, but let not all your arts be
wifely. There were careers for women now. And even for women
who opted to stay home and raise a family, there was more to life
than plying needles. Latin, French, poetry, music: better for a girl
to be fluent in those. Patrick O'Shea agreed. He'd seen too many
girls become burdens to their parents through lack of education.
No daughter of his would become a spinsterly wraith pining at
home. They'd have careers and qualifications. When Agnes talked
of becoming a nurse he told her to aim higher. And so she did.
But never reckoned on becoming a surgeon.

Back at Medical School in Dublin there'd been a postgrad
on the Ear, Nose and Throat side who, when she asked him
about tonsillectomies, said: 'Why bother your pretty head with
those?' That was the attitude then. War has shaken things
up. Women doctors are no longer wondrous as dancing dogs. Of
the medical students who qualified with her at UCD, a quarter
were female. (I have the list: Mary Frances Andrews, Julia Mary

Dympna Corrigan, Alice Mary Creamer, Ursula Mary Crowley, Rose Mary Domican, Mary Gannon, Bridget Margaret Mary Kelly, Eileen Mary Theresa MacHale, Josephine Mary Needham, and a few more who aren't called Mary – 16 women out of 63 bachelors of medicine.) But there are still the men, young as well as old, who treat a woman doctor as they would a nurse. And who if you dare to answer back, think you're a ballbreaker. Bollocks to that. She's not in competition. Those first women doctors sixty years back, the Elizabeth Garrett Andersons and Sophie Jex-Blakes, might have been tearing down walls, but what she wants is *not to be noticed*. She doesn't care for dirty jokes, but when her colleagues are relaxed enough to tell one in front of her she feels accepted – like one of the boys. Will taking over from Grimmy imperil her status as an honorary chap? Cause jealousy among her peers? Make the nurses (who're soft as putty with male doctors) turn sharp and edgy? If that's what's coming, never mind. Dr O'Shea can take it. If Grimmy thinks she's up to the job, then so does she.

At twenty-six, she looks several years younger. A child wielding a knife – it's just as well the patients are anaesthetised. As RSO (Resident Surgical Officer), she's responsible for anything and everything, but most cases are straightforward enough – so Grimmy says, though it doesn't seem that way in the first 24 hours, with two strangulated hernias in the morning and at night 'two filthy appendices – one gangrenous and oh so hard to get at, the other perfed and a shocking mess.' As well as her own work, she acts as an assistant to visiting surgeons: 'earned a very easy £1.1.0. this morning, assisting Mr Buckley with a private patient – excision of a cyst on a breast, which takes about 5–10 minutes.' But running the show herself is preferable. Battlefield heroics? Man's work? A dangerous front-line activity, requiring strong arms and a stronger stomach? Not at all. It's about precision. Cleanliness, too: the scrub beforehand under a flowing tap – nails, palms, arms up to the elbow, each finger, minutely, in turn. Small hands are an asset. There are a few old lags, the heirs of barbers, who hack in and yank about. But as Grimmy has taught her, it's a tender science. The weaponry is less like a soldier's than

a carpenter's: knife, bone chisel, metacarpal saw, mallet, clamp, hook, tongs, surgical clip. As for the reek and goo assaulting the senses, they barely impinge. You hold the scalpel like a pen, forefinger along the top, the blade at 90 degrees to the skin. A single clean stroke is best for parting flesh – no bevelling, or the sewing up afterwards will be harder. The intimacy is alarming. There you are inside the body of a stranger who's drugged and unable to move. Which is to make it sound like rape, when it's the opposite: a kindly invasion, ending in cure. Work on the wards is a slow cycle of despair. In theatre, you can be quick and effective. She thinks of it as a kind of nunhood: the bleeding victim; the attendant worshippers with only their eyes showing; the discipline, the concentration, the self-transcendence. You can lose yourself while cutting. In time, as her confidence grows, she finds she has a real knack for it. Keeps her nerve, in a crisis. Has a cool temperament, under the lights. A steady hand, too. Begins to feel this is how she wants to spend her life.

Arthur is meanwhile discovering how he doesn't want to spend his. Being an officer, educated and middle-class, with minimal medical duties, he's asked to do some cutting of a different kind: censorship. It's a matter of reading through chaps' letters home and excising sensitive material with a pen or scissors. By 'sensitive' is meant anything that might help the enemy if intercepted: details of manoeuvres, technical know-how, and any suggestion of poor morale. But the only sensitive material he encounters is men pining for the girlfriend or missus. He expects to feel like a voyeur, but the main sensation is boredom. There are only so many ways a man can tell a woman he loves her, and the lads in Reyky haven't the wit to get beyond 'I'm lonely' or 'I miss you'. His own letters are censored too, by senior officers in the next camp. With luck they're too lazy to read closely. And he reckons he knows what he can get away with. Still, letters should be private, even in wartime, and he doesn't like the idea of someone prying. Most censors are clots, anyway. One of his squadron had a sentence struck out giving the latitude and longitude of Reyky, as if such info was classified rather than available on any map. 'I ask you!'

In fact – so I found reading them fifty years later – very few of his letters home were censored, though my mother once had a bundle of them confiscated while disembarking at Holyhead from Dublin (seized in haste, they were returned at leisure). Had my parents felt intruded on, they might have resorted to code, but aside from Xs and DILYs (Darling, I Love Yous) they didn't. Deciphering the language proved an effort all the same. The wartime slang was easy enough – *gen* (information), *prang* (crash), *snag* (problem) and *bull* (bureaucracy) were familiar from childhood – but I didn't know about people getting *whistled* (mildly drunk) or *screechers* (completely pissed). And though Germans were *Jerries*, I'd not heard of the Portugese being *Pork 'n' Beans*. Similarly with abbreviations: TTFN for goodbye (ta-ta for now) and BF for bloody fool were common usage, while SSQ (Station Sick Quarters) and OMO (Overnight Medical Officer) would have been plain to any medic. But was HYDTLMY (Have You Decided To Love Me Yet) his own invention? Was BIB (breakfast

in bed) hers? There are no four-letter words in their letters, nor even many *bloody*s: *ruddy* and *blasted* serve for disapproval, while expressions of happiness come in several forms: *wizzard* (and *wizzo*), *top notch*, *A1*, *bang on*, *full of beans*, *box o' birds* and *happy as a sandboy*. A fed-up person is *browned off* but a *brown job* is someone in the army (unlike those non-combatants who idle on *Civvy Street*). Braggarts *shoot a line*, cowards are *windy*, slackers refuse to *pull their finger out*, and someone who's exhausted is *shot at*. The dead, meanwhile, have simply *bought it*. RIP.

My father, I now see, took pleasure in self-expression, whereas my mother, who had several different selves to express, found it painful ('you know me well enough by now to know I'll never say much'). He should have been a writer, she once told him. But he wasn't enough of one to think words (or the editing of them) a proper vocation. Medicine was what he knew best, and it maddened him to be stuck in Iceland, treating colds, censoring letters or joyriding in jeeps, while she was advancing at Hope. When she informed him of her promotion he congratulated her, but the tone was peevish and condescending. 'So you are to be acting RSO?' he writes in early September. 'Ye Gods, what opportunities this war has presented. You must jump at it, you lucky little devil. I shall be embarrassed to talk any sort of medicine with you when I come back – I know so little nowadays. That's if we see each other.' The churlish sod. Her promotion might make him jealous, but it was unkind to attribute her rise to luck (and gender and Irishness) rather than skill. And then to throw in that last sentence: 'That's if we see each other.' Didn't he want to see her? Or did he think, because she'd written only the once in August, she didn't want to see him? He expands on it ten days later, in his intemperate letter of 12 September, the one that talks of them marrying others and becoming friends – which says, in effect, let's call the whole thing off. How steady was her hand in surgery that night? His letter must have been very upsetting.

Or would have been, had she read it. But in the event he denied her the opportunity, as he explains when he next writes, on the 16th:

Dear Gennie,

Well, pet, here we go again. Was very disgruntled by the 'note' you scribbled to me from Eire, and wrote a long rude letter in reply. I'm glad I didn't post it but I will keep it to show you when I come home on leave – Nov or Dec probably. I still think there must be something on your mind. Come on, what is it? I hope you're not worrying about the RSO job. I imagine it is more than that.

I had my birthday two days ago – did you remember? I've forgotten what date yours was pet. I've an idea March or May, but I may be miles out.

I've written to Ron suggesting he times his leave to coincide with mine. I also wrote to him about my carryings-on – I hope you don't mind. I'm sure you've talked to Eileen or Mary G. I understand your hesitation about still being at Hope when I return. It's difficult, isn't it – and it's our question by the way, not just something for me to decide. I suppose your holiday, and the presence of Tom, brought it home to you. I have thought about it a lot and can still only see it the way I said. I don't think I'm being selfish. Blast the world! But you know what I mean when I say 'Have you decided to love me yet?'

Had he sent his letter of the 12th, that would have been the end of them. But it went unposted, and four days later he's petting and HYDTLMY-ing her as though nothing had happened. 'Here we go again': well, almost. Whereas before he'd hoped to sweep her off her feet, now he's more tentative, keen to impress on her his understanding of the difficulty they face ('I have thought about it a lot'). What this difficulty is he doesn't explain. But clearly both agree there is one. So despite his endearments and her pleasure in hearing from him ('Had two lovely surprises today – first some roses a patient had sent up, then a letter from you in the afternoon post'), there's no easy resumption. They've avoided a final break. But the letters that autumn come more slowly than in the spring.

'Sorry, pet,' runs one of his in November, 'I haven't written for 24 days and the last was, as you say, only a note. I've tried to settle down on several evenings but have got as far as writing the address and then said "hell!" and gone to the flicks or into the club with the lads. Still, it makes us quits.' Ten days later, she replies sarcastically: 'Strange thing happened this morning. I had a letter from you, the first in about 30 days. Thought you had got frost-bitten or something. I've not written myself for three weeks, purely out of pique. No mention of coming home from Christmas, either.' The tone isn't romantic agony, only mild scolding. Nor does she bother to say much more, only that 'I'm really enjoying the surgery now I'm not scared of it any more . . . Just off to do two appendices so I'll finish this.' Not a letter that can have delighted him since she so casually curtails it, as though he came a poor second to her work. Miffed, he doesn't write to her again. Instead he writes to Terry, his old girlfriend, suggesting that when he's next back they spend a weekend together in London.

The relationship seemed to have run out of steam. For six weeks they sent no letters. Despite the evidence (in envelopes yet to be opened) of more to come, I feared the worst. But then in January they broke their silence. And everything changed for good.

# CHAPTER FOUR

# In Love With Love

*Kim to Arthur, Hope, 5.1.44*

Hello darling,

How's Davidstow? . . .

*Arthur to Kim, Davidstow Moor, Camelford, North Cornwall, 5.1.44*

Hello darling,

HYDTLMY? It was nice to hear from you tonight – what bit I could hear. I went into the film afterwards, then came across here to write to all my girlfriends: one letter in all.

I've got a wizzo billet – fire and wash basin in room – private bath with constant hot water and WC – a light over the bed, too. Did sick parade at 8.45 this morning and have been busy cruising around finding out what's what from the SMO, who's going on leave tomorrow night for three weeks.

Oh yes, one more thing – strictly between you and I. I don't think I shall be here for much more than a month after the SMO gets back – nowhere local but very pleasant although distant. Wish I could take you with me.

*Kim to Arthur, Hope, 8.1.44*

Your letter arrived this morning and a good thing too – I'd have had a miserable weekend if it hadn't. Did not like the last part – any idea where you are going? All sounds very vague.

I don't think it would be a good idea for me to come to Davidstow before the 25th. Remember, you have got to live there. I have written to my sister-in-law Ruth in Sussex to expect me about the 20th and I'll probably stay there a week or more, then I'd like a few days in London.

Hope you ring tonight. Hope I have a letter on Monday. Hope lots of other things – like you still love me.

### *Arthur to Kim, Davidstow, 9.1.44*

Hell am I busy. That is – I consider myself very busy having led a nice easy-going sort of life for nearly two years. Honestly my ears are sore as hell from using a stethoscope – I'm going to lubricate the ear-pieces tomorrow.

Got your letter of the 5th and noted the conicidence in the way we had both started. Mental telepathy or something.

I spoke to the SMO about having his house while he's on leave but he didn't bite saying 'Well, there are lots of places nearer – try the Vicarage or Old Major – 's last billet'. Well, pet, I'll investigate. I think it may be a good thing if you come down before he comes back because you'd be able to sit in SSQ with me – you see it's outside the camp limits and then we could have nearly all day together. I can be on call at the local too (if there's a phone there and there's no flying on), so will be able to get about quite well. What do you think?

By the way, I have breakfast in bed every morning. It's perfect. HYDTLMY?

### *Kim to Arthur, Hope, 12.1.44*

I wrote to Ruth last night and asked her if she'd mind my coming down on Wednesday and then going off for the weekend. I will let you know. By the way, do I tell Mary about coming to Davidstow?

Was in theatre from 8.30 till 2 today. Grimmy is due back on Saturday. Big party that night, with me leaving and him returning.

It'll be nice not working for a while again. I hope my trunk has arrived.

### *Arthur to Kim, Davidstow, 18.1.44*

I'm itching for you to get here and I hope you are too. No reason to hide from Mary that you're coming. She knows all about us, so why the secrecy?

*Kim to Arthur, 48 Belsize Ave, Hampstead, 10.2.44*

Sorry about my temper before you left – so unnecessary but I expect it was just because I was so very very miserable. Everything was fine after all – except that you had to get that 1.25am train.

I have mislaid McKay's testimonial, which I need for the interviews. Could you see if I left it at Auntie's?

Did I remember to tell you that I love you very much?


*Arthur to Kim, Davidstow, 10.2.44*

I felt very lonely when I left you last night. It took four hours to Exeter then 3½ hours on the next train and I arrived here at 10am. It's absolutely glorious here today – cloudless and very little wind.

I cycled down to Auntie's at lunchtime – she seemed very glad to see me and has apparently turned several people away saying that she hoped you were coming down again – so there we are! I couldn't find any trace of McKay's testimonial and she hadn't even emptied the waste paper basket, so – though I'll look through my papers – it doesn't look hopeful. I also mentioned, as agreed, that we hoped she didn't think there was any question of – well, anything. She said 'Very nice of you to tell me but I never had any doubts – she's a nice girl'.


*Kim to Arthur, Yapton, Nr Arundel, Sussex, 14.2.44*

Feel so restless (it's a month since I left Hope) that I decided I simply must get a job right away. It's not stubbornness – it's just I'm more happy when I'm working, that is when I can't be with you. I'm having too much time for thinking at the moment. I wept myself sick last night and as a result woke with a rotten headache today. I can't sleep either – there is a chiming clock here at Ruth's which I curse every half hour. The only thing I'm sure about at the moment darling is that I love you.

By the way I'm in bed now and feel a bit better. There's no place I'd rather be than Auntie's but please don't ask me to come down again just yet. I'm at the panicky stage again and must try to relax here for a while.

When I'm with you I never seem able to tell you how much I love you. But you know, don't you?

*Arthur to Kim, Davidstow, 22.2.44*

Paddy, the girl on the phone and at least two other people have asked me whether I got married whilst on leave. Well!!!

It doesn't look as if I'll get any more leave now before I go as the rest of the boys won't and it would be unfair. But we'll see.

TTFN. DILY. DDYLM.

PS When I was censoring their mail in Iceland, I used to cuss blokes who wrote to their wives or girls every day. The letters always seemed so poor – just said 'darling, I love you' over and over again, with perhaps one or two sensible remarks only. I hope mine don't read like that, darling.

*Kim to Arthur, General Hospital, Northampton, 24.2.44*

You know, darling, we are falling in love with each other more and more every day. All the time I think about you. And occasionally I have a quiet weep. How long can we go on like this – you feeling more sure things will work out, me feeling less sure? I know that I love you more than anything in the world and that I could be perfectly happy with you – if things were different.

*Arthur to Kim, Davidstow, 25.2.44*

Helly-ohy My darling,

It's 1.30am and I'm pretty whistled and I've just spoken to you on the phone (it cost me 4/- and then I reversed the charges). I wish not just that you were here but that we were in our own house and this blasted war was over. When we spoke earlier this evening it was as though I'd just rung you at our own home and told you I'd be late as I was going out with the boys so you'd have to bath baby your-self. And when we spoke just now, after I'd got back from Tintagel (20 of us, including three Waafs, but I didn't say a word to them all evening), and after (as the crowd started to dwindle) I asked various different blokes to change all the silver I had in my pocket, and they all said 'You're not going to ring up the girl now, surely', and then left me alone, and I had my three minutes, and nearly all your three minutes, a trio of them came howling into the room saying 'There's Ol' Doc on the phone – Cummon!', so I said 'Well, darling, there's someone coming, so I'll probably have to ring off', and you said 'same here', and then as they didn't open the door to the booth I wanted to carry on, but you seemed to get all self-conscious about being heard saying 'darling' and started talking as though to a distant relative, and then rang off. Anyway, I'm sorry, I know I'm a bit whistled (not drunk) and must have sounded it, and I hate speaking to people a bit whistled myself – they never seem able to stick to the point – but I love you a terrible lot, and always shall, even if I throw this away in the morning.

Following day.

Well, I'm sorry for how I was last night. At least the above (which I'll post, not burn) explains it. It's because you have not yet promised to marry me and any sign that you don't want everybody to know how much we love each other shakes my faith in you. Damn stupid – forgive me?

Phone calls are bloody unsatisfactory, aren't they. But I did feel a bit better after ringing and dreamt you let your hair down again, among other things.

H OW DID I feel reading their letters? How would you have felt? I felt excited, guilty, lucky, furtive, amazed. What did I think? I thought it was miraculous to encounter my parents like this – when they *weren't* my parents, before they married or even knew they'd be together. 'Never put it in writing,' my father liked to say, and yet he had, they both had. Such was the detail – the things they did on particular days, the ideas they had, the emotions they felt – I was more in touch with their past than my own. Whenever I'd thought about them before, even at forty, it was as a child in relation to his elders. But the selves they'd now disclosed were twenty-something, younger than me. I felt protective, avuncular, *parental*. Unlike them, in their perpetual present, I knew what the future looked like — when the war would end, and where and how they'd spend the rest of their lives. This hindsight gave me an advantage, but also created a sense of responsibility. It was like being in charge of children. I wanted the best for them, and shared their pain when things went wrong.

At times I felt voyeuristic. Coming across the print of her lips — like a red seal — at the end of one letter, I quickly passed on: here was an intimacy too many. I was equally discomfited finding notes of his on the back of an envelope containing a letter of hers — headlines to himself of various worries which he must address ('miserable beggar', 'all my fault', 'will say no more until I hear from you', 'can't think of breaking it off now'). But it was he who had kept the letters and made me witness to histories I'd otherwise not have known. The still, small voice of conscience told me: 'This is none of your business.' But it was my business. Family business. The legacy I'd come into. The love to which I owed my life.

'Too many darlings?' Arthur worries. Too many XXXs and DILYs? Perhaps. But to see my parents cooing and billing like this was strangely comforting. Call me greedy or just pathetic, but I needed the proof that they'd once been in love with each other. As a child I'd never been sure. They shared a house, a medical practice, two children, but they didn't share hugs or kisses. My bedroom lay just down the hall from theirs. I once walked in on them having a cuddle, but was never woken by the sound of lovemaking. Most teenagers, squeamish at the notion of oldster sex, would have been relieved. But I felt worried. My mother, always the gynaecologist, liked to talk about sex, and certain wry remarks implied the marriage had become celibate. Was this because of Auntie Beaty? Did he desire only his mistress? Or did my mother feel too affronted to have him? Which-ever, that side of things appeared to have gone. They were affectionate — he called her pet, and sometimes pecked her on the cheek — but not passionate. Passion lay elsewhere: in films, on television, beyond the door.

Yet the notion of romantic love was impressed on me from

an early age. I remember falling in love in Majorca, at the age of ten, on our first holiday abroad (a svelte eleven-year-old from Croydon with whom I didn't stand a chance). And I remember falling in love with love the year before. A holiday again (did love only happen away from home?). A rented cottage in Rhosneigr, on Anglesey. A family friend, Roger, was staying with us – the teenage son of my godparents. Each day we went to the riding school, where the instructor was Karen, a girl of Roger's age: slim, fresh-cheeked, curls spilling from her riding hat. The two of them trotted ahead. I saw it happen. The blushes, the teasing, the first careless brush of hands. Perhaps I recognised the signs because the same thing was happening at home between my father and Beaty. Whatever, I *knew*. On the last day, when we came over the dunes onto the tide-hard sand, Roger and Karen kicked their heels. I hadn't meant to gallop after them, didn't know *how* to gallop, but there was no stopping my pony. The hooves, the blowing mane, the sea-tang in my nostrils, the ecstasy and terror were all part of love. The out-of-control-ness, too, as we hurtled towards black rocks at the end of the beach. My pony pulled up sharp just before the rocks, no thanks to me. Roger and Karen, laughing to find me right behind them, leaned out from their saddles and kissed each other. The ride left me trembling. Or was it the kiss that did? Here was love, no less of a thrill for happening to someone else.

Reading the letters my parents wrote at the beginning of 1944, I fell in love with love again. ('Falling in love with love': a song by Lorenz Hart and Richard Rodgers, written in 1938 and later recorded by Frank Sinatra.) This was my parents as I'd never known them, younger than I was, fresh-faced as Roger and Karen. To pore over old letters might seem a morbid occupation. But it was my parents' youth I loved – their passion for life and for each other. I had nothing to do with this passion. It predated me. By the time I existed it did not, or at any rate had hidden all the evidence. I hadn't known they ever felt like this. I had for-gotten I could feel like this. Racing heart, dry mouth, butterflies in the stomach, trembling hands: weren't these the symptoms? Oh, and those tidal aches and razors of longing, that make you think you'll surely die. I had known such feelings before. Years of marriage and children had subdued them. Now my parents appeared like genies from their urns to bring them back.

The passion they felt was innocent. A simple thing: two people falling in love, and wanting to marry and have children and be together all their lives. Love isn't so simple now. You can't be sure (as they were) there'll only ever be the one person. Even if you are sure, you mightn't choose marriage or see the point of kids. People may be naive still, lovers especially, but the old innocence has gone. It went for my parents, over the years. But at the start it was shining and intact. I ran their love through my fingers. It was no more than faded ink on dry paper. But it felt fresh, incurable, alive.

A new year and a new beginning. Those Hello Darlings chiming together on 5 January. They were back in each other's orbits again, reaffirmed and newly enchanted. Before, they'd only been playing at love, not sure if it was worth the effort. Now they began in earnest – let love seize and abduct them. As before, there are gaps between their letters. But the gaps don't mean what they used to mean. It's something I took a while to grasp: that when the letters between them stop, it's because my parents are together. The old lacunae came from boredom, doubt, estrangement, a sense of futility, things going wrong. That phase is over now. Silence hereafter means they're in each other's arms – that things are going right.

The gaps are protective, a kind of privacy. They prevent intrusion – stop me listening in. I can imagine what it was like when they met at Hope just before Christmas, he (having downed a couple of whiskies with the old man) seeking her out on the ward, she (in the operating theatre) given a message that someone important is asking to see her, he flirting at the nurses' station while he waits, she arriving tetchy and flustered because she thinks it's the registrar or some heart specialist, he wishing she were dressed in something other (or less) than a medical gown, she noticing the bags under his eyes (as heavy as ever), the two of them sharing cigarettes in the corridor, too nervous to touch each other yet immensely happy. But in truth I don't know how it happened. The letters only tell so much, only go so far. I find this frustrating. In love with my parents' love, I want to be there all the time, egging them on. But the letters won't allow it. I can be with them only when they write, and when they write they're not together. There they sit, at a table, on a bed, in a Nissen hut, on the bench of a railway platform, anywhere will do, a notepad balanced on a knee, ink flowing through the nib from the hearts they need to empty, intense and intimate – but always separate. It's the essence of letters. Correspondence: a bringing together. But correspondents are absent to each other. When they write, they're in different places. That's the point of them writing: because they're apart.

There's only one exception. On the back of a sheet of paper dated 23 January 1944, my father has scribbled four questions, and my mother three replies:

1  DYSLM? Yes.
2  HYDTMMY? No.
3  Isn't it nice in bed? Yes.
4  What time are you getting up?

No answer to the last, which is odd, since it's the easiest, or least compromising, question. Perhaps her answer lay in action rather than words: she got up there and then, to prove she wasn't lazy, or because the sun was pouring in, or they'd a walk planned, whatever. Or perhaps some action of his, amatory or otherwise, prevented her from using the pen. No knowing. Still, it's clear they were together during this writing exercise, and that marriage had become a subject for discussion, if only in a jokey abbreviation (HYDTMMY). The dates put the exchange in Cornwall, at 'Auntie's', the house my father rented so my mother could spend time with him at Davidstow. He was between RAF postings, she between hospitals. For a fortnight they were alone together, free of family and friends. ('Alone together': the oxymoronic condition which lovers crave.) The experience transformed their lives.

'Isn't it nice in bed?' Does that mean . . . ? Let me leave that one with you. It's a place no child of theirs should go. I can't pretend that I don't care, since my existence hangs on it, but I'm happy to be spared the details. We can take Auntie's word for it that my mother wasn't that kind of girl. Or accept that two people might share a bed but refrain from having sex, a not unknown phenomenon even now and a common one in wartime (when air-raid shelters and overcrowded lodgings created some strange bedfellows). Or decide that despite what Auntie thought probably, yes, they had become lovers: there was a war on, they were young and euphoric, the forties (like the sixties) loosened many inhibitions about premarital sex, there was no one to stop them, most of us would do the same, it's perfectly natural and they were in love, even if they'd not been in love it would have been natural, let's not be prissy for God's sake, whyever not? The sooner the better, I say. Just don't expect me to be there watching. Their letters keep the bedroom door shut, and I'm not going to spy through the cracks.

For it's their falling in love that interests me, not their love-making. Their falling in love with each other, and in love with love. In my teens, the LPs turning on our record-player were ones that I'd bought – the Kinks, the Who, the Beatles. But sometimes my mum would sneak Sinatra on, with his plaints of foolish love and broken hearts. Sadness struck a chord with her, in middle age. She felt nostalgic for Cornwall, spring of '44. For a fortnight, the moon shone between clouds, and love was honey and fire. Never such closeness. Never such innocence again.

*　　*　　*

*Arthur to Kim, Davidstow, 18.1.44*

The rooms I've got are in a sort of farmhouse. Mother is seventy-odd and the daughter is out working during the day. Sitting room downstairs – quite comfortable the glimpse I saw – and upstairs bedroom (over the kitchen they live in) with, ahem, a nice double bed but nil else at present. She wants you to do your own shopping – OK? – and she will do the cooking. She says coal is very difficult to get at present but

I think that is soon fixed. I said about a fortnight starting Saturday. How much? 'Well,' she said, 'the Polish officer used to pay me £1 a week.' I tried not to show my amazement and said that was OK.


DAVIDSTOW LIES close to Bodmin Moor. A few miles away, on the coast, is Tintagel. It's Arthur's kingdom, and to judge by his new-year letters Arthur feels like a king, an adult with his Guinevere (one of the few new names he doesn't try on her, though Gennie could be Guinevere abbreviated). Do they journey down the coast, past Newquay and Perranporth to St Agnes? Probably not: without a car or motorbike, it's a bit too far. More convenient and no less dramatic is to walk to Boscastle and Beeny Cliff. Thomas Hardy country. Where young Tom wooed his Emma in 1870. And where King Arthur, some say, built his Camelot. Either way, a kingdom of romance.

In the balmy south-west, flowers come out early: snowdrops, crocuses, primroses, bluebells, daffodils. I can't remember my father ever buying my mother flowers, but in her lodgings at Auntie's they keep a plain glass vase on the mantelpiece, and brighten it with what early blossoms they can find. There are walks to buy eggs in the skirmishing fine rain. One day a sheep-dog follows them, as though lost, and keeps nuzzling at their knees and groins. Should ever they marry, they agree, they'll have a gundog, not some little yappy terrier or poncy poodle, but a spaniel, say, or labrador. And a car. And a house in the country. And two sets of golf clubs, right- and left-handed. And three children – a boy for her, a girl for him, a third to stop the other two fighting. Luckily, they agree about most things: what to eat, and who their favourite film stars are, and how long the war's likely to last, and why it's rude not to make an effort with strangers. Only with music is there discord: they both prefer popular to classical, but she goes for slow, sad numbers, whereas his accentuate the positive. Even their disagreements are a pleasure to them. Once, after a row with a nursing sister at SSQ, Arthur mutters about 'Bloody women', and Agnes, in solidarity with her sex, takes umbrage.

'I wasn't getting at you,' he says.

'Aren't I a woman then?'

'Not in that way.'

And she isn't. There's something boyish and Billie-Bobbyish about her, which he finds less threatening than voluptuousness and which she (no earth-mother) likes the shape of too. But just at that moment she bloody well feels like a woman, and wants to punish him for demeaning her sex. They've been having tea by the fire. She turns her back on him and sulks. To stop her nonsense, he pushes her back against the sofa arm, nuzzles her neck, kisses her mouth, tells her he loves her. It's almost worth provoking rows in order to have the making up afterwards.

One day they borrow two push-bikes from Arthur's camp, and plot a route through local lanes: nothing too steep or strenuous. Round lunchtime they stop off at a pub overlooking the sea. (Do I know this because they told me? From reading between the lines? Or has it come down through the genes? What makes me so sure I'm not making it up? I can't tell you. But I can see them sitting there, clear as last week.) After beer and ham rolls, they share a Senior Service. Outside the Atlantic bashes on the shore. There are seals along this coast. They haven't spotted any yet, but he recalls seeing one near Plymouth.

'While out walking with Terry, I suppose,' she says. He doesn't answer. She exhales and peers through the window. In the wintry gloom, the sea's the colour of jealousy, with love the dark shadow beneath.

'I wonder what will happen to us,' she says.

'Whatever happens, we mustn't let it end badly,' he says.

'Is there a way of ending well?'

Afterwards, they cycle some more, then hide their bikes behind a wall and walk along the cliffs. Herring gulls, Atlantic rollers, little pink flowers they can't put a name to. Beyond Penhallic Point they descend to the strand. She feels at home here, as though it were Ross Beigh. There's a tea-place open, and they venture in for scones with jam and clotted cream – the only customers, tea for two in a lovers' oasis, nobody near them to see them or hear them. A perfect day.

Like Ireland, though, Cornwall is damp. After three days she develops a cough, nothing serious, but as a precaution he fetches a stethoscope from SSQ. She catches her breath at the touch of the membrane (cold as a brass penny) against her flesh. He frowns at what he hears. 'A bit sticky,' he says, and asks is there a family history of chest problems? No reply to this, nor to his suggestion that she have an X-ray, once settled in her next job. She should cut down on her smoking, he says — it's unfeminine to smoke except after a meal, and it's doing her lungs no good. 'But who was it taught me the habit?' she asks. And it's true he likes sharing cigarettes with her. The pair of them smoke like Sheffield chimneys. There's a constant drizzle off Davidstow Moor, and sometimes they can see smoke coiled within it, which could be mist or a garden bonfire or just their own cigarettes. The days pass in a pewter haze. Nothing ever really dries: not her underthings on the clothes line, not the leaves and bristles of garden plants, not her cough. But the drizzle is silvery and benign. It's like a blessing laid on them, the press of lips on flesh. They're lucky to have this, when so many in the war have been denied it — the luxury of being alive together. Whole days they barely stir from the sofa. Whole hours they scarcely bother looking out. But what does it matter? If they stare in each other's eyes they can find the window like a cine screen and inside its panes, in miniature, the play of clouds above the moor.

During the day Auntie says they're free to use the sitting-room, which means use of the wireless, too. Mostly it's light music they play — slow-sad for her, fast-happy for him — and sometimes they sing along. 'It had to be you,' they agree. She wandered around . . . and he's finally found the somebody who . . . When the melodies are lost to crackle they turn the dial to the World Service: 'London Calling, London Calling.' The six o'clock news is an evening ritual: they catch it before Auntie comes in and disturbs their peace. Great events are happening — steady advances by the Allies, rumours of plots against Hitler — and they want to keep in touch. And yet history seems another world now. So what if Churchill's closing on the grail of victory? Auntie's four walls are the centre of their universe.

After the news, they wander the empty lanes towards the pub. Tonight it's clear for once. She walks ahead, humming a song. He's content just to look and listen. Moonlight becomes her: it goes with her hair. He catches up and pulls her to him. There's no one around, but the eerie brightness makes them feel exposed, as though the lane were a floodlit stage and they two characters from some historical romance – Arthur and Agnes, English hero and Irish maid. They stop and listen. The only sound is that of sheep chewing tussocks. They resume their kiss. She has never felt so close to someone. And never will again.

✵    ✵    ✵

*General Hospital, Northampton, 24.2.44*

. . . Can't tell you how pleased I was to hear your voice last night. Such a clear line, too. The only snag was that I had to take the call in the dining room and there were three nurses there. I'm sorry if I was bad-tempered but it's so unsatisfactory talking when someone is there. We started off so well and then ended so badly. Hope you are not feeling rotten about it. Expect you are on your way back to the mess cussing women for their cussedness.

*Davidstow, 24.2.44*

. . . Tried to ring you at 8.40. No reply, but no delay either, so came back at 9.00. Of course by then an officer was in the box and a WAAF officer waiting outside. She said she would book my call for me so I started a game of snooker and was just winning well when she called 'Doc' at 9.20, so I dashed out and held on. It's a public call box in the mess, with a penny in the slot and no button B. At 9.23 a male voice came on and said '1/8' in the box so I said 'Is this the call to Northampton?' and he said, all narky like, 'That's what you asked for isn't it?' at which I remained calm and said 'It wasn't me actually but here you are' and put 1/8 in the box, and was greeted with absolute dead silence, and started seeing red, hell I've not been so livid for years, and hung on till 9.28 getting whiter and whiter, then recalled the local (civilian) exchange and she said I had not been cut off from trunks (proving the type was being awkward), so she hung on for 5 minutes shouting 'trunks' and getting mad too and tried another line, which took another five minutes, and then I tried to explain to the bloke (I think it was the same bloke) what had happened and he said 'Oh, just a minute', and I hung on for 1-2-3-4-5-6-7-8-9-10 blasted minutes until suddenly another male voice said 'Trunk Enquiries', and I explained again and he said 'I'll ring you back in a minute', and I hung on for another 15, tried trunk enquiries again and had just got through after 5 minutes when a female interrupted and said 'Here is your call to Northampton', so I then pointed out it was no use unless you were there, so they got you, and I had a personal call and five minutes all for 1/8d, and it was wonderful talking to you at last (did I tell you how much I love you by the way?), but I thought after I would like to fix the man who had messed us about for over an hour so reported the thing to the Divisional Supervisor – not that it will do any good but I feel better.


WHEN MY NINE-year-old son saw his grandparents' war letters heaped up in the basement, he was puzzled. So many words on paper! Why couldn't they have called each other or used e-mail?

I explained that the Internet hadn't been invented then, or text-messaging, and that because they'd been in different countries they couldn't phone.

'But people can phone each other from different countries,' he protested.

'Not then they couldn't – your grandpa was in Iceland, and there weren't any lines to England.'

'Didn't he ever come home?' he asked. 'Couldn't he have phoned granny then?'

'Yes,' I said, 'and he did. But he liked to write letters to her as well.'

He wandered off, bemused: why would anyone write when they could speak? And where did they find the energy – look at all that paper – to write *so much*?

It puzzled me at first, too. Davidstow wasn't Iceland. For as long as he was in England, they could talk on the phone. But the system in 1944 hadn't the beep-beep rapidity of today. Lines were faint, crackly, temperamental and insufficient to cope with the demand. The charges were prohibitive, too: on their meagre earnings, the cost of a long-distance call (five shillings for four minutes) wasn't easily affordable ('And if you have the first quarter minute after the three pips,' Arthur complained, 'they charge you for the full minute, ie 1s 3d extra'). Then there was the lack of privacy. The use of workplace phones for personal calls was forbidden, and with public call boxes there'd always be someone waiting outside, nose pressed to the glass. Worse still were the public phones in corridors, in earshot of irreverent colleagues. Even when the two of them were safely alone, operators had a habit of listening in. One went so far as to imitate them 'kissing' each other. 'Did you hear him?' Arthur asked Kim in a letter. 'I suppose it's silly of me to get so mad at it, but I always feel that our goodnights – in fact our whole conversations – are between you and me, and ought not to be ridiculed by others.' Later in the relationship he would phone her at home in Ireland, which proved more difficult still. He became convinced that the Killorglin exchange had a grudge against him because he was English. Undaunted, he kept at it, till all the operators got to know him and teased him for calling so often ('This Dr O'Shea must be very nice.' 'Indeed she is'). When the Liverpool operator put him through, the response in Dublin was 'Oh, not that man again'. 'So you see,' he told her, 'all England and Ireland know we're in love.'

The expense, the difficulties of getting through, the embarrassments of being overheard, a feeling that there was always something more to say – is it any surprise that they'd begin a letter no sooner than they'd hung up? But in the spring of 1944, there was another reason for writing. The love they felt, so new and hard to credit, was more believable set down on paper. Say something down the line and the words would be gone into the ether, with no record but your own imperfect memory; write them and they were palpable. You could keep them too, and re-read them at leisure. It was so much more *committing* than a phone call – a way of articulating what you felt, and of discovering what your lover felt about you.

The thin blue sheafs of paper, the crumbling envelopes (hers with 1½d postage stamps, his branded 'RAF CENSOR'), the sloping handwriting in faded ink – they look like something from a museum. In the age of e-mails, air-mails are as quaint as trilby hats or one-pound notes. And yet the impulse to set down words is familiar enough. Which is preferable? Hearing 'I love you' over the phone? Or seeing it written in black and white? Surely the latter. My parents didn't live to see it but would have found e-mail wonderful. The instaspontaneity of it was exactly what they were after. Their worst depressions between 1943 and 1945 came not from war setbacks or friends dying, but from delays in the post.

It was good to hear each other's voices. But they preferred the written to the spoken. Ink and paper let them talk heart language. Only in letters could they get through.

✠   ✠   ✠

*Kim to Arthur, 12.1.44*

Don't you think the London weekend idea is a good one? Mary is very keen.

Could you write to her suggesting it? She'd feel awkward about mentioning it to Ron otherwise.

*Mary to Arthur, 20.1.44*

This London weekend would be grand if I dared suggest it to Mummy and Daddy. Will you write to them and say how about it and it would do me good to get away, etc? That wouldn't be a 'line' as I'm dying for a change – baby's skin is much worse and worrying me to death at present.

*Post Office Telegram, 16.2.44*

TO: DR OSHEA YAPTON ARUNDEL HOPING ARRIVE WATERLOO 1800 HOURS OR 2230 HOURS FRIDAY STOP WILL CONTACT BELSIZE PLEASE BOOK ROOMS DILY ARTHUR MORRISON

A WEEKEND IN London for the four of them, Kim, Arthur, Mary and Ron. The arrangements are tricky, to say the least — not the hotel so much (easy enough to book two double bedrooms, and leave the question of who shares with whom till they get there), but the task of prising Mary from home. She might be nearly twenty-four, a wife (or widow) and mother, but at Windyridge she's treated as a child. So much so that she daren't broach the London plan herself but asks Arthur to seed the idea. Though she's duly given leave, it's not before Ernest, who thinks London a hell-hole at the best of times, has made her feel selfish and wanton.

Then there's the Ronnie problem. Is a weekend with the four of them fair on him? The relationship was harmless — friendly, casual, platonic — when he first began calling. In those days he still had the tie with Elise, the girl he met in the Lakes; there was even talk of an engagement. But that's all finished now. A visit to Elise in Uxbridge decides it. As he puts it to Arthur, 'I've had it, or perhaps she has had me. Which of us has changed I don't know, but God, I shudder to think what I'd be feeling now if I'd married the woman. If I ever so much as mention the idea of marriage to her again, please put me in a mental home, chum.' With Elise out of the way, Ron can devote his energies to Mary. But is that a good idea? She has begun to accept that Michael must be dead, but that doesn't mean she's ready for Ronnie. Will a weekend in London only confuse matters?

Given the complications of the heart and the public transport system, it's remarkable the four of them made it. But the lure of the capital was strong — London calling, London calling — and they converged on it with bags and cameras like peacetime tourists. There's a wonderful photo of them together, which dates

from that weekend or soon after. They are crowded on a sofa, all smiling, three of them towards the camera, Ron, obliquely, at Mary. She is wearing a white blouse, and the shadow of a window frame has fallen across her, so that the right half of her face, the half hidden from Ron, is striped with darkness (her right eye is wider open, because it doesn't have to glare into the light, and seems to shine with more intensity than her left eye, as though she was more alive in shadow). Kim and Arthur's cheeks are close together, almost touching. Ron and Mary's, despite the closeness of their bodies, are a foot apart. It's a photo of two couples, one intimate and relatively secure, the other still tentative. It's also a photo of a woman divided, uncertain whether to choose past or present, death or life.

London in wartime isn't the safest of places. When Arthur worked as a houseman in Charing Cross Hospital, at the backend of 1940, the Luftwaffe came over on 76 consecutive nights. He knows the special silence of a falling bomb – like a lift hissing down a lift-shaft – and the earth-shudder when it hits. But they're lucky that weekend: no alerts or sirens. The evidence of war is everywhere they walk: piazzas of rubble, sudden craters of light where buildings stood, chinks of glass on the pavement like spilled trays of ice. But the West End shows go on. The waitresses in Lyons Corner House – 'nippies' as they call them – serve cheap food. The pubs are unrationed in raucous laughter. To eke out the little money they have, the four of them go everywhere on foot. Their only luxury is seeing a film in Leicester Square – *Thousands Cheer*, an MGM musical set on an army base, starring Gene Kelly, Judy Garland, Mickey Rooney and Kathryn Grayson. After a round of whiskies in Victoria just before closing time, they walk to Big Ben, cross the river to Waterloo Station, then come back over Hungerford Bridge, their talk drowned by a train rumbling out from Charing Cross. Below them the Thames is the colour of gunmetal. To their right, downriver, lies St Paul's, the moon polishing its dome, the docks in the east braced for conflagration. To their left stand the Houses of Parliament, unbudging while nations crumble like biscuits. A gust skips across the river like a stone and the air is thick with dust – the drifting pollen of bombed-out houses. Feeling exposed up there on the bridge, an open target, Kim grips Arthur's arm. The few people they pass seem to be silvered in dust, like survivors from the rubble. And the silence, the *siren-lessness*, is eerie. In Villiers Street she pulls her collar tight and shudders, relieved to be away from the river. There are more people here, and an illusion of safety and warmth. They head for Soho, in search of somewhere open after midnight.

For Kim especially, the weekend's over far too soon. By three on Sunday, Mary and Ronnie are already on the train back north, and she and Arthur checking out of the hotel. She'd not noticed the yellowing wallpaper and cheap furniture in the bedroom before, nor the view of slates and drainpipes outside the window. In Davidstow they left flowers behind for Auntie. Here they leave a shilling for a chambermaid they've never seen. The anonymity makes her feel grubby. Wrapped in silence, she wanders with him through Covent Garden and down to the grey, indifferent Thames. Later they order beer and sandwiches, and catch a bus to Hampstead, where she's staying with friends called Maurice and Peg. She feels as leaden as the sky looks. What's the point of love if it makes you feel this desolate? She'd thought it would strengthen her, make her secure. But all it's brought is this infinity of grey.

'It's been such a wonderful weekend,' he says.

'It has,' she says.

'Then what's wrong?'

'It's been such a wonderful weekend, that's what.'

✻   ✻   ✻

*Arthur to Kim, Davidstow, 21.2.44*

Well here I am – back again. Walked to the top of the road after leaving you and it was quarter to when I got to the bus stop. No sign, so I thought of walking, but it would have taken half an hour and as I was dithering a trolley bus came along. I gathered that Paddington station had been hit – also that an ammunition dump in Hyde Park had gone up. (How true were these rumours?) Got to Waterloo about midnight, collected my baggage and joined a terrific queue for the 1.25.

Arrived here in an ambulance, for breakfast (bacon and fried potaoes), sick parade and ward round. And now here's tea – a pancake, Shrove Tuesday. To think that five years ago at this time I was roaring drunk somewhere in the Manchester Rag. Disgusting.

Tomorrow I'm going to cycle down to Auntie's and say that since I don't know how, when and if you'll come before I leave, she should carry on and make other arrangements. But I'll be very surprised if she does take anyone else. So . . .

I still love you, you know darling, and you are very precious to me.

*Kim to Arthur, Northampton, 22.2.44*

I miss you so very much tonight and wish we were still together. I don't want this letter to sound depressing but it's natural I'm going to be lonely. When you went to Iceland I wasn't as much in love with you as I am now, or if I was I didn't realise it. And since Christmas, when we've said goodbye so many times, I've always known I'll see you again soon. But now – not knowing how long you'll be away . . . When I'm with you I never seem able to tell you how much I love you, but you know, don't you?

I went to the flicks this evening. Had thought it was 'Jane Eyre', but that's on next week – it was called 'He's My Guy', which he is. I could go on forever about how much I love him but the censors wouldn't approve.

Tore down to the switchboard just now, because after coming back from the labour wards (to give an anaesthetic for a breech) I thought I heard my phone ring off. But they said they hadn't rung me. I still keep hoping you'll call.

You know, the happiest times in my life I've had since I met you. Don't think I could be so completely happy with anyone else.


THEIR LETTERS ARE more intense after London. 'I love you – couldn't stop now if I tried,' she tells him, while he declares himself in a drunken letter which contrasts how he felt in Iceland – 'not sure of how much I loved you, and determined to try to not see too much of you, so that I could compare you to Terry and any other girl that turned up' – with how he feels now: 'I'm *completely* in love with you and always shall be.' It's true that once sober he turns to worldlier matters, regaling her with a long story about a bloke who won't pay up when he twice beats him at snooker (everyone heard them make the bet) and how even after the third game – when Arthur, twenty or so points behind, gets in such a rage he plays like a man possessed and pots the lot – he coughs up only a measly shilling ('it isn't the money, it's the principle'). But even this digression brings an apology: it's boring of him to go on about a snooker game, but 'there's little else except to keep reminding you how much I love you and how miserable we'll be if we don't get married soon.' He worries that his letters are dull. *Her* worry is that she's becoming an emotional mess. The very thought of him and she loses her powers of concentration: 'I keep thinking about you and wondering where you are and my mind is only half on what I'm doing.' In love, and in love with love, both of them. But how long before they meet again? Will his second tour last one year or two? And who knows if they'll survive till then, given the casualty rates in the RAF and the likelihood the Germans will resume their bombing of British cities, in one of which she's certain to be working? 'Stay as sweet as you are,' he asks her, a line he pinched from somewhere (unless someone – Sinatra, Bing Crosby, Johnny Mathis, Nat King Cole – pinched it from him). Or if not sweet, at least alive.

The imminence of parting is not the only cause of bittersweetness. 'How long can we go on like this,' she asks him, 'you feeling more sure things will work out, me feeling less sure?' He, too, talks of 'the trouble we have', and of the 'terrible overpowering hold it seems to get on people'. It? What's *it*? The same 'difficulty' he speaks of after the London weekend? The same 'question' he'd alluded to the previous September ('it's *our* question by the way, not just something for me to decide')? It seems they've made some kind of pact: 'Remember our agreement darling not to tell anyone what we decided to do?' she writes. 'I've not mentioned it to Ruth, because you know she would completely disagree.' Disagree with *what*? She doesn't say, but he pities her for what she's going through – 'a very lonely little girl . . . a poor little girl' required to 'break the bounds of what she has always been taught'. *It* seems to be more than sex: he would hardly be demanding she surrender her virginity now, when they've just spent a fortnight together and he is shortly to leave the country. Something to do with home, perhaps – though not her Irishness as such, for if that were a sensitive issue he'd not complain with such careless bigotry about Irish overstaffing in English hospitals ('three out of nine at your hospital, and three in GP locally here, and a similar state of affairs all over England'). Not sex, not Irishness, yet touching on both of these. She would like to find a solution. But *it* feels too overwhelming, and can't be conquered without his help.

She also faces a more practical problem: that of finding a worthwhile job. There's one in Surrey, but it's Mider again and when she's pressed to take it she decides against. Applications to Bury St Edmunds and the Middlesex don't work out. A post at the Royal Free sounds more promising, but when she arrives for the interview she finds there are ten other applicants, three of them in-house ('and they usually appoint their own'). Luckily, on her way out, she hears of a locum post at Northampton General, beginning at once. 'So here I am,' she tells Arthur. 'It seems quite a nice place. The medical super is a decent type, though I was rather amazed at the familiarity at dinner tonight – he calls everyone by their first name. My room is good, too – warm, at least. The bed isn't as comfortable as the one I had at the weekend, and something was missing, but I slept just the same.' A happy outcome, it seems. Yet within a fortnight she moves on, to another post, at St Helier's, down in Carshalton, Surrey. Why she takes it isn't clear, even to her, since it's Mider again, and Carshalton is closer to London than Northampton is – close enough to start Arthur fretting about air-raids: 'Don't forget to get a tin hat (I'll bet you look wizzo under a tin hat) and a properly fitting gas mask.' As it happens, he's right to be worried: St Helier's will soon be badly hit. But by then she'll already have gone, to another post, her third in six weeks. Everything she does that spring suggests huge restlessness. Love has made her a new person. But she feels panicked by it, and keeps switching jobs as though to regain control. To him this itchiness is baffling. Troubling, too. Why can't she just stay put? Why doesn't his love make her feel *rooted*? If she sticks at love as poorly as she sticks at jobs, it doesn't augur well for marriage.

They've not been expecting to meet again: London was their swan-song. But she finds herself with two days free between jobs. Though Cornwall's absurdly far, when she hears him on the phone sounding so sorry for himself – he's in bed with a temperature of 103 – she hops on the first train. Auntie, delighted, offers accommodation (five shillings for two nights) and Arthur, granted sick leave, is billeted out to join her. They walk in the rain, lie on the sofa, and wreathe themselves in the comfort of cigarette smoke – just like before. Perfect, they agree, but horribly brief, and to her it makes separation all the harder. 'I think I was on the train for two hours before it sunk in that we'd said good-bye for a long time,' she tells him, and wishes she 'could have stayed until tomorrow – one whole precious day wasted.'

On 7 March he sets sail to a new destination. They consider themselves engaged now, unofficially, and over the next twelve months there will be four times as many letters between them as for the previous twelve. Beginning as he means to go on, he dashes out a few lines before departure and gives the letter to a colleague to post. Where her last letter to him is full of woe, his to her is buoyant – and very bossy.

Remember to have an X-ray on that chest.

Remember I'll always be thinking of you.

Remember you are a little girl very much in love and to stay as sweet as you are.

Remember the glorious reunion we'll have.

Remember to read my old letters about once a month.

Remember to enjoy yourself at parties – but no more than 3 small drinks at any time.

Remember to stop smoking.

Remember to get physically fit and have plenty of sleep.

Remember to make your next job NW of London and to keep in touch with my home.

Here's to that 1945 wedding.

# CHAPTER FIVE

# Medical Records

*Arthur to Kim, 7.3.44*

Remember to have an X-ray on that chest . . . Remember to stop smoking.

*Kim to Arthur, 19.3.44*

Afraid I haven't stopped smoking yet but this really is my lucky week. First my trunk arrived at last. Then today two letters from you came – exactly as I'd dreamt last night. And now my X-ray is negative – the radiologist said I'm A1 in fact and my cough is much better.

A T FIRST I didn't understand: why all the fuss? Her cough in Davidstow hadn't been that bad. But the demand she have a chest X-ray topped his list of parting instructions. In his next letter he was on about it again, urging her to be 'honest with yourself and me if there is "anything".You must be, darling – the whole of our future depends on it.' There was nothing unusual about him giving advice: he was a doctor, after all, the kind who knows best (is there any other kind?), and my mother was his favourite patient. But his language here is untypically dramatic: why so do-or-die? Later in life any suggestions he made about her health would be ignored, and I assumed nothing would come of this one.Yet within a fortnight, meek as a lamb, she had done as told and was able to send him the good news: 'This really is a gala day.' Her cough was history.They could move on.

In health matters, my mother was a sceptic, reluctant to raise her own or others' hopes: drugs could only do so much, most problems were inherited, some conditions were no more than marginally improvable, etc. But the tone with this X-ray was different. She referred to the matter again in relation to a colleague who'd been due to return to the wards but now couldn't: 'she has a spot on her lung, and the specialist has advised a year's light work in a sanatorium. (Tough luck on her; I was luckier with my cough and X-ray.)' It isn't like my mother to count her blessings like this. It's as if she has just stepped out of the shadow of death.

Perhaps she has. The word tuberculosis doesn't appear in the letters. But TB is what they feared the X-ray would uncover. The O'Sheas had a history of TB, her brother Dan having died of it a decade before. Did she tell Arthur about Dan? She wouldn't have needed to. To many people, not least the Morrisons, Irishness was synonymous with TB – and Ireland 'one great reservoir of consumption'. This wasn't casual anti-Irish prejudice. Figures from the 1920s show that deaths from TB were still rising in Ireland when in England they had fallen sharply. And a survey for the years 1941–3, carried out at the Brompton Hospital in London, found that Irish nurses employed there were *nine times more likely* to contract the disease than their English counterparts. During the war a mass radiography programme was launched in the UK, and three quarters of a million people had X-rays. My mother was only a statistic. Yet it's impossible to overstate the importance of her all-clear. Destigmatised and passed for duty, she became a suitable candidate for marriage – a healthy professional woman to whom an Englishman could safely become engaged.

Might she have been dishonest about her X-ray – concealed the true results or never had it in the first place? It seems unlikely. She was capable of fibs but to lie so spectacularly, feigning ecstasy at a fictional outcome, would have been out of character. Yet TB did come back to haunt her fifty years later – as I discovered from her medical card after she died. The relevant entry was dated September 1995: 'Admitted with purpuric rash and nausea. X-ray. Tuberculosis.' My mother had kept me up to date with most of her ailments. But she never mentioned TB.

'No,' said Dr Evans, her GP, when I showed her the entry, 'she'd have been too ashamed. In fact, I know she was ashamed because she asked me to keep quiet about it. There was a stigma about TB, for people of her generation.'

'Would she have contracted it as a child, then?'

'Maybe. It can lie dormant for years. She might have had it and not known it, until her immune system was depressed and it reactivated. Or she could have got it recently.'

'How?'

'I hate to say it, but from hospital.'

'As a doctor?'

'More recent than that. As a patient.'

'But I thought TB had more or less died out.'

'Worldwide, it's on the increase. There's usually at least one case in this practice at any one time. Among the poorer families, especially those who've come here from other parts of the world, it's always a risk.'

My mother was a doctor, middle-class, professional, well-read. She'd have known that tuberculosis wasn't, as many in the nineteenth century thought it, a disease of the passions, signifying moral decay. So the associations she didn't like must have been the social ones: though consumption can afflict the wealthy and well-fed, it flourished (and still does) among the poor – unsanitary conditions, an unhealthy diet, heavy drinking and long working hours are contributory factors. Did my mother think that to own up to TB would suggest she'd come from this kind of world? Poverty was so remote from my childhood that I thought it a city like Portsmouth or Coventry, clearly a big city since ten per cent of the British population was said to live there. My mother's childhood in Kerry hadn't been poor, either: her parents kept a maid and sent their children to boarding school, and though that didn't mean there and then what it would mean in England now, they were securely middle-class. But perhaps she felt that would all take too long to explain, make her defensive, force her to dwell on the conditions of an upbringing she preferred, for other reasons, to forget. And perhaps she'd seen enough of other childhoods in Killorglin, or heard of the harder life the O'Sheas had a generation or two before (the Great Hunger was more terrible in Kerry than in most counties), to fear that poverty and disease were always lying in wait – a calamity visited on Celts, regardless of the kind of life they led.

There was another factor, her instinct for martyrdom. At school, she'd been exposed to the cult of Thérèse Martin of Lisieux, the patron saint of anorexia and TB, whose diary, published posthumously as *The Story of a Soul*, became a worldwide bestseller. Thérèse had borne her sickness bravely, shunning all material comforts. 'My little life is to suffer,' she wrote. 'I'm becoming a skeleton already, and that pleases me.' Hers was a story of phthisis as grace – of the joys of wasting away. Millions were touched by it, and my mother took it to her bosom. TB itself held no charms for her: it had deprived her of her eldest brother. But Thérèse – like Joan of Arc, or the early-Christian monks living on the rocks of Skellig – offered a shining example of asceticism. Suffering must be endured in silence: that was the line. It wasn't what my mother told her patients, when they came with aches and pains. But she expected it of herself.

Had she contracted TB at the age of fourteen, in 1931, when her brother Dan died of it? Did she pick it up as a doctor in middle age? Or was the infection a recent thing, a final blow – leaving cavities for the aspergillus to fill up? Whatever the case, whatever the source, she regarded TB as shameful and couldn't admit to having it – which was to me, too late to offer comfort, the greatest shame of all.

\*     \*     \*

*Kim to Arthur, 1.5.44*

Went back to Hope at the weekend. Everybody says I've gone very thin and am looking rotten. You're not to worry, darling. You'll understand it's just because of the hectic time I've had. And from feeling so miserable. Nothing I can help.

I'D GONE TO consult my mother's medical card in hopes of knowing more about the aspergillus, or fungal infection, that had killed her. Dr Evans met me, one of her successors, the *new* lady doctor (my mother had been much more of a novelty back in 1946). She wore a dark woollen dress and a silver brooch with two fishes swimming into each other. It was nearly Christmas, and my mother had been dead for five months. Earnest, Dr Evans asked how I was doing, as though concerned I might crack up and become a case for treatment. I reassured her I wasn't mad with grief, but she said she had to warn me there was stuff in the file that might distress me. Did I want her to take me through it? No, I'd be all right on my own. Fine, then: she would sit close by in case I had questions. She handed me the 'card' – not the perfunctory two-page sliver I could remember my father's medical record being but a large fat wallet. Dr Evans sat working with her back to me. It was a basement room, chilly like my study at home. I broke the ice occasionally by asking about abbreviations I didn't understand – SOB, for instance, 'short of breath'. Most of what was there was familiar: I'd not been around for my mother's appendectomy in 1946, but the problems of her later years – the sciatica, the fractures, the macular degeneration, the retinal haemmorhage, the severe headaches, the mild cardiac failure, the visits to the pain-management consultant – were nothing new.

The TB, though, came as a shock, and so did the repeated mentions of depression, which she was having treatment for long before my father's death. The depression was no secret. But I'd not anticipated how many such entries there'd be or how low she could go. 1.6.95: 'v. depressed.' 23.6.95: 'sees the future as entirely bleak and wishes she was dead.' 30.8.95: 'v. tired, very very low.' 13.5.96: 'down again. Start Prozac.' 24.6.96: 'Agitated. Worse on Prozac.' Had she told me about the Prozac? I couldn't remember her doing. And then '23.12.96. Desperate.' But that was just before I'd gone to pick her up to spend a week with us over Christmas. And hadn't she seemed, at the time, more or less OK? She was ill, of course. She'd begun to question whether it was worth struggling on. Since my father's death, she had been quietly burning on her pyre of grief, staying alive for the sake of her children and grandchildren. Exhausted, she must at times have wished the trial was over, that the fire from within would go out. I knew that. Even so, the word 'black' again and again in her record. This ledger of pain. These depths she'd plumbed. I felt guilty that I'd not done more to ease the pain, and jealous she'd shared her depressions only with Dr Evans.

Later, reading the letters and ransacking my memories of childhood, I realised her depression had a longer history. There were even hints that it ran in the family – allusions to strange, reclusive aunts or solitary-drinking uncles. My father would have recognised this: his first cousins, Helen and Jean, were (so we children were told, not knowing what it meant) 'tragic cases'. My mother wasn't tragic. But she was often sad, lonely and empty, and my sister and I had grown up learning to allow for her glooms: they were 'how Mum is', 'Mum being Mum', and for a while we got on without her, knowing they would pass. Was depression the price she paid for reinventing herself? Did denial – of who she was and what she felt – add to her melancholy? Too long a sacrifice can make a stone of the heart, Yeats said. My mother wasn't stony-hearted. But her spirits were often heavy as lead.

In 1944 my father was pushing her to reinvent herself and learning that it wouldn't be easy. Her mind was her own: though in love with him, she couldn't be cured of all her worries and glooms. Her body looked more suitable for treatment. He felt certain they could tackle it together, that she, at his bidding, could remedy its flaws. That was the deal they'd made, or he believed they'd made. In his absence she would get herself fixed.

✴   ✴   ✴

*Arthur to Kim, 16.6.44*

How are your headaches? I'll break your neck if you've not seen a specialist.

*Kim to Arthur, 6.7.44*

They did a lipoidal X-ray of my sinuses, but found nothing. Have felt rotten since. Still a terrible pain in my eye. Veganin helps a little but not much. Dosed up, I'm busy working again, though everyone says I should be in bed.

*Arthur to Kim, 21.7.44*

What the hell is the matter with you, darling? They tell you to go to bed for investigation – you refuse! They find a leucopenia, possibly due to Veganin – and you take more Veganin! You're like a big soft kid to whom medicine is some kind of black magic to be distrusted. Or like an adult who thinks the world will stop running if she takes a day off work. Are you a grown woman trying to get fit again for your marriage, or a silly little girl afraid of the big bad ward sister with her stick? If there's one thing that annoys me it's patients who won't tell you honestly what the matter is or who think they know better than the doctor. To read of you behaving like this when I'm out here makes me go wild.

*Kim to Arthur, 27.7.44*

Hell, did you tear a strip off me in your last letter. Well, two can play at that. You call me a 'silly little girl' but if I'd gone to sick bay they'd have kept me in for a week doing all kinds of investigations, whereas I had the blood-count, X-ray and examination done in 24 hours, and the tooth out in another 24 hours, which saved a lot of time. The patient who won't be honest about his ailments annoys me too, but the patient who always complains is worse.

By the way, the world doesn't run, it turns – like the worm.

ONE FRIDAY evening, on the Gyny ward, the pain becomes too much. Collecting her nightdress and toothbrush, she admits herself as a patient in Ear, Nose and Throat (it's her weekend off). X-rays of her sinuses show nothing. The problem must be her teeth, the specialist, Mr Reading, decides, and keeps her in a second night. Stuck in bed and 'rotten with boredom', she leaves her meals untouched or persuades visitors to eat them for her. Mr Reading, after further tests, pulls one of her teeth and advises that two extractions be done under anaesthetic next day – her (L) eye tooth and the (L) lateral one with the crown – followed by a week's rest and a fuller investigation. But by now it's Sunday evening, with work next day, and she says she'll come back another time. Discharging herself next morning, she goes straight to Gyny, dosed up with Veganin. 'You look ill,' her boss says. Well yes, but she'd rather be on her feet than lie in bed.

Arthur, thousands of miles away, is livid. His letters pound her with medical knowhow, as though to prove he has not forgotten all his training: 'Have you had your blood pressure and urine tested? Your ears checked? Have you seen an ophthalmic specialist? Couldn't it be some apical abscess or something irritating the maxillary or mandibular divisions and being referred through the ophthalmic or ciliary branches? Do you really think it is right for anyone to just "carry on" if they're ill?' It's plain to him she isn't looking after herself and without his intervention never will. Soon, predictably, the pain is worse, and she returns to Mr Reading for the two extractions. 'Worried I'd jabber about us under the gas,' she writes, 'but I don't think I did – oh I do love having gas, such a delicious sensation.'

The episode neatly catches my mother's approach to health. My father's too. He was always bullying her to work less. Or rather to work at playing more. She should go for walks, take up golf, explore the countryside: only 'fresh air and exercise' would cure her. As a teenager, I too was subjected to this philosophy of vigour. I didn't know, back then, that 'fresh air and exercise' had been the slogan of the sanatorium movement, the popular remedy for TB. Even if I had known, I'd have resented him using the phrase on me: I might be pustular but I wasn't tubercular – what was the relevance? But I can see why my mother exasperated him. She was long-suffering, and he hated to see her suffer.

The triple tooth extraction didn't cure the headaches but it did leave her with a large gap, for which she needed a plate.

She hated the prospect — false teeth when she was only in her twenties! — but there was one small consolation. Arthur had been complaining lately about her gold inlay and the cracked smile visible in photos: 'I'm not going to have you showing a toothy grin,' he announced. Rude bugger. Who did he think he was? Henry Higgins? Never mind. The toothy grin would soon be gone. Her new look would shut him up.

*    *    *

IT DID SHUT him up. There are no more deprecating references to her appearance after that summer, nor can I remember any from childhood. And yet my mother went on feeling uncomfortable about her appearance. Teeth weren't her only falsies. She also wore padded bras, something I discovered by chance during a pubescent sortie into her bedroom. The guilty garment stared up from the floor: two cups with sewn-in cotton implants. Women didn't have boob-jobs then. But my mum felt small — inadequate — all the more so after the onset of Beaty, whose bosom was classically ample, along the lines of Jayne Mansfield or Marilyn Monroe. It was an age when women were meant to be pliable — and mammaries and malleability went together. In good moods, my mum made light of her unvoluptuousness. Nor was my dad noticeably fixated on breasts. If anything, he was less so than most of his peers. Had any *Playboy* or *Penthouse* been secreted at home, I'd surely have found it in the flush of adolescence. It wasn't that he put pressure on her to expand. But if a wad of cotton could make her breasts look bigger — well, why not?

That padded bra upset me. My mum was beautiful and didn't need it. She had a body image problem before body image problems had a name. Few of us are happy with who we are, but she was unhappier than most. Shyness was part of it. When he asked, from his new posting, for details of her vital statistics, she pretended not to hear. He was offering to have a bra and panties made up from some 'nicely transparent' black chiffon he'd found. But to her this meant revealing more than she cared to. Stringing him along, she teased him for forgetting what she looked like – or for lacking the nous to guess her measurements for himself. At last, reluctantly, she gave him the answer: 'brassiere 35 (smallest you can get), waist 25 and hips (ahem, much too big) 38.' Though she knew how much he desired her, it didn't stop her feeling awkward about her body. She'd have been happier keeping it under wraps.

Christian name, identity, beliefs, physique – my mother falsified them all, not with brio but from feelings of inadequacy. The war and being in England began the process. Then my father pushed it along, bullying her to 'get fit for married life'. Marriage would only be possible if her chest was clear, her teeth repaired, her bosom padded, her Irishness neutralised. No, that's unfair. My father loved my mother and would probably have married her regardless; what his letters reveal is not an unhealthy obsession with her appearance but a passionate concern for her health. Nonetheless, he did make her feel anxious and self-conscious. He was an idealist. And, in her own humble opinion, she fell far short of his ideals.

# CHAPTER SIX

# War Babies

*Kim to Arthur, St Helier County Hospital, Carshalton, 9.3.44*

It is now seven days since I saw you and it seems like years. Funny thing, I can't get used to not expecting letters every day – I still look hopefully at every mail that arrives.

A fairly quiet morning yesterday (ward 9–11, clinic 11–1), apart from having to deliver twins – one hydrocephalic – at 8.30am. Met Sheila at Oxford Circus at 3pm and went shopping but didn't buy anything. Not wanting to be caught in a blitz, we went our separate ways at 8pm. The weather has been lovely, and the moon was full, so all was quiet. Everywhere I go reminds me of you – like Lyons Corner House this evening, and the times we were there together. I keep thinking back to what we were doing at a particular time – and how even Auntie had tears in her eyes when we said goodbye.

Had a fright this evening when one of the wards sent for me to say a girl was dying. She was not my case, though she might have been: I'd been due to give her a blood transfusion on Tuesday, but she refused. Miss Daley took over and eventually persuaded her to have it and she put up a drip this morning. This evening when the drip was finished she suddenly screamed and died – bad thing when she had not wanted the transfusion in the first place. She was only 17. They've not had a post mortem yet.

A letter I had from Mary asks me to come and stay again. You have probably heard the news about Eire – those awful people! – and how all travel to and from there has been stopped, so I will tell her we can have our summer holidays together somewhere. She says at the end: 'Wish you were my sister-in-law.' I wish I were, too – but I wonder. Darling, all the time at Auntie's we never mentioned anything but you seemed to take it all so much for granted that it would be all right. Wish I could feel so certain. 'Don't fail me,' you said, and

I will feel I have if I don't marry you. It makes me wonder if we shouldn't have called it all off long ago when we weren't so much in love.

There was an alert tonight but the all-clear went within half an hour.

*Arthur to Kim, Station Sick Quarters, Azores Force, 10.3.44*

Just a short note to let you know I've arrived. No blackout here – everywhere looks marvellously white and clean from a distance. The women, too – but we can't get near them, apparently, owing to local customs.

When I came ashore I piled into the back of a lorry and came over the mountains for about 15 miles through the clouds. Once here I went straight into the mess for a meal (pretty good). My boss is W/Cdr Carslake (Irish) – several other MOs here are Irish too. By the way, darling, which college did you qualify at and what did you say the name of your home town was? I feel so damn stupid when they ask and I can't answer – makes it look as though I'm engaged to somebody I don't really know.

I landed lucky and am sharing a tent with Steve (who I got to know at Davidstow). We like tent life and intend to stay here rather than move to a Nissen. The weather is quite normal English summer weather (warm but cloudy). Angra and Praia de Victoria are the two big towns in this island. Steve and I went down to Praia last evening to see what the shopping was like – there are watches available at ordinary peace-time English prices, and phials of scent at 1/-. I'm having some house slippers made in raw pigskin and could get you made-to-measure shoes in any colour for £2 – let me know what you'd like. I will get fruit – eg, pineapple – home to you when I can. Isn't it wonderful being in love like this? I am always thinking of you when I'm out shopping now, and it makes it much more interesting.

Ate out in Praia and had a pork chop, 2 eggs, chips and a glass of sparkling muscatel – total cost 3/-. Marvellous.

Darling, I miss Kim a terrible lot but I'm not miserable, probably because I'm in new and strange surroundings. I feel mean not having told the family I was leaving. I should have rung them up to tell them – or at least written before I left. And of course it would have to be the anniversary of poor old Mike's 'Missing' notification. Still can't bring myself to write. Do keep in touch with them for me.

*Kim to Arthur, Carshalton, 21.3.44*

I qualified at the National University, Dublin [UCD], and come from Co Kerry – remember me?
Friday was St Patrick's Day, but not for us: too busy working.

*Arthur to Kim, Azores, 24.3.44*

You've never seen such a downpour as we've had the past 12 hours. Outside everything is a swamp of yellow mud and you just slosh around in rubber boots and oil skins. The damp penetrates everything. When Steve pulled out his spectacle case from a canvas bag, it was covered inside and out with white mould. Even my damn envelopes have sealed themselves in their packet.

Still no letters from you. No medical dramas either, just colds and sore throats, and gastro-enteritis from gorging on pineapples and bananas. But had a real problem case yesterday – possibly some subphrenic lesion – that made me wish I could be getting as much experience as you. Pity you won't be able to wrap it in a parcel and give it to me when I'm back and we get married.

25.3 Still no letters. Rainy and windy. The flysheet vibrating and hitting the roof of the tent sounds like a cross between thunder and machine-gun fire.

26.3 Still no letters. Rain. Very depressed.

27.3 Still none. Rain. Nervous breakdown looming.

28.3 Ditto. Suicidal.

29.3 It's still raining like hell, but I'm feeling like a big soft kid, because I've just had four of your letters. Had a 'feeling' at lunchtime, even though we had no gen about mail coming in. Then some did come, and I pleasantly tortured myself sorting out other people's before reading yours. I kept saying 'This is marvellous' to myself out loud – couldn't help it. Steve had (jokingly) been very rude earlier about my 'feeling', asking what gave me the idea I was psychic. He's been calling me Old Moore ever since.

I keep getting my leg pulled about my resemblance to Micky Rooney. Most unfortunate – and you don't even like him. Have you noticed how my pen keeps running out in the middle of my letters? What a damn silly thing to start writing about, but I just write everything that comes into my head.

TTFN. Please stay away from London and the East coast.

*Kim to Arthur, Carshalton, 30.3.44*

We've had lots of raids lately. The one last night went on for over an hour: not much fun. Our planes have been going over here for the past half hour – they had a bad do last night, didn't they? I'll soon be far away from them, at any rate. Frankly I'll be glad – though if anyone in Birmingham says 'You look too young to be a doctor' (as they all keep saying here), I'll scream.

I hear Mike Winstanley (who's still not passed his exam) is doing a line with Sister Naphthole – he's been engaged for years, too.

Wonder what the censors think of our letters, but expect they are used to 'love' and 'darlings' like ours.

'WHAT DID YOU do in the war, Daddy?' I asked, as boys back then were supposed to. 'How many Germans did you kill? Were you ever wounded?' His answers were all negative: 'Not much. None. No.' It was disappointing. Other kids had dads who'd been war heroes – bombardiers, tank commanders in the desert, Spitfire pilots. Who'd killed tens of dozens of Nazis. Who could show you their shrapnel scars or the dented silver cigarette case which had saved them from an enemy bullet. Or so they said – to be honest, I never met these kids (or these kids' dads), only heard about them: were they for real? At least I couldn't accuse my father of bullshitting. He didn't pretend to be a hero or to have had 'a good war'. The Nazis had to be stopped, which was why he'd joined the forces, but thank God he didn't have to fight. All this was carefully explained to me as a child. But reading his letters fifty years later was still an education. I hadn't realised the infinite varieties of boredom. His chief hardship was lack of mail. And having bugger-all to do.

'What did *you* do in the war, Mummy?' wasn't a question children asked. These were the 1950s and 60s, when mummies, by definition, did nothing of interest. Ever since Eve, it seemed, they'd stayed home painting their nails and cooking for their family. My mother was a bit different: she worked as a doctor. But it was work I didn't see. And what she'd done from 1939 to 1945 never came up in conversation. I vaguely assumed she'd been in Ireland completing her medical training and taking it easy. It took the letters to disabuse me. While my father zizzed on campbeds, she worked in half a dozen English hospitals, rarely staying in one place for more than six months. In Salford, she tried her hand at surgery. In Carshalton, she worked in Mider. Later she moved on to Children. The jobs were temporary, but gave her all she wanted: a salary, a bed, three meals a day. It was all useful experience, for what she wasn't sure. There was a war on, and she kept her options open.

Her war wasn't only busier than his, it was more dangerous. She could have stayed in neutral Ireland, safe from doodlebugs and V-2s. She could have joined a general practice in the English shires and never faced the music of the Luftwaffe. But she chose to work in cities, where bombs were falling. In 1944 St Helier's, in Carshalton, was hit several times. In the last raid many lives were lost, the registrar was blinded, and all surviving staff and patients were evacuated to Guildford. 'Thought you'd like to know,' she tells Arthur. 'It might have been me.' Her restlessness saved her: by then she had moved on to Birmingham. But it was close.

It's not that my mother was attracted to danger. Nor would she have claimed to be courageous, any more than my father did. But being in England was a test of who she might be and how far she could go. That's why she came. That's what she was here for. That's what she did in the war.

* * *

*Arthur to Kim, Azores, 18.3.44*

Daily routine is up at 7.00 (usually 7.15), breakfast at 7.30 (usually 7.45), sick parade 7.45 (usually 8.00). Finish 9.30. Do a few treatments. Coffee at 10. Ward round and odd jobs till 12. Lunch – then across to the tent to write to you and sunbathe (as I'm doing now, on a camp-bed outside). At 1.30 all sorts of odd jobs, including blasted censoring (I had enough in Iceland) till 4.00 or 4.30. Tea. Jobs around the tent (we're still getting ourselves organised, and all the wangling takes time). Dinner between 8 and 8.30 – a chat and a couple of drinks. Bed any time between 9.30 and 11 (not been so early for years but it should be good for me).

I find you enter into all sorts of little things I do and think here – not in a lovelorn stupid sort of way, just as part of me and my life. I wish you could be here to see it all. We might sail here for a week when we're married – when we've saved up enough for a world cruise, or I might try to get a job as ship's MO – sort of pay as you go.

I've been worrying how you've been going on among the blitzes. Have you found a job up North yet? Please get moving. Oh I do wish you were looking after our home and forgetting medicine – and surgery.

*Azores, 1.4.44*

I've decided not to write to you any more. I'm 27 years of age and I want to get married. I've waited for over a year for you to make up your mind, and obviously you don't love me enough, and never will, if you're still undecided. I think I've only been anxious to marry you as a matter of personal pride. Now I'm reverting to my old life – getting drunk and sleeping with lots of women. And I've written to Terry (who I've secretly been writing to all along) to ask her if she'll marry me when I come home.

Well, darling, did you fall for that or did you spot the date at the top at once?

Mary writes to say it's now confirmed. Isn't it a terrible trajedy? Poor little Mikela will never see her father and even if Mary marries she will never be the same. I hope it's Ron, if anyone, but I know she will lead him an hell of a life. Horrible to think of the plane bursting into flames when it hit the ground, especially now I've seen a few results of prangs.

Wonder how you feel in a new hospital with strangers all around. It's no life for a girl to be away from home and not even living with some sort of relative. The sooner you let me put an end to that, the better. Oh darling how I'm looking forward to our wedding day with this blasted silly war over and a home of our own. What rows we'll have, and what happiness.

Well, must go and examine a fellow so he is 'FIT' to undergo court-martial – they have at least one a day here to fill in the time.


*Azores, 3.5.44*

I'm stripped to the waist writing this outside the tent. (I began it lying in the nude – very private here and I'd like to get a burnt backside.) Would be too hot if it weren't for the breeze. I can see clouds of dust blowing up from the runway. Have been told that I look 75 per cent fitter since I am here – pity you can't see me as you would fall in love with me all over again.

✻   ✻   ✻

LANDING LUCKY in the Azores, Flight-Lieutenant 118415 feels like a pig in clover. Beautiful sea, volcanic sand, sub-tropical temperatures, all duties over by midday: who can beat it? His purpose there is hazy. Officially, his Coastal Command unit is engaged in 'closing the Atlantic gap', as it was in Iceland, which means weather and shipping reconnaissance, air-sea rescue and watching out for German U-boats. In reality, the battle of the Atlantic has already been won, and Lagens, where he's based, is eerily quiet: no bombs or raids. Every so often pilots return from sorties boasting of a kill – of U-boats left bobbing helplessly like half-filled bottles. But any action happens hundreds of miles off, out at sea. Four thousand British personnel are stationed in the Azores, most of them, like him, on Terceira, whose chief town, Angra do Heroismo (just a few miles from Lagens), has a population of 10,000. According to the official medical history of the war, 'the inhabitants are a peace-loving peasant people living in primitive simplicity, the men being engaged in cattle breeding, dairy farming and agriculture, while the women occupy themselves working at home for the embroidery industry.' The lads in the mess put it differently: the men are lazy buggers and the women whores.

As a medical officer, Arthur joins a staff of 25, working out of a 50-bed Mobile Field Hospital. Bubonic plague is endemic, and vaccine's flown out from Britain to inoculate the troops. Typhoid's prevalent, too, and all water has to be sterilised. In June the construction of a permanent 150-bed hospital begins. But the occasional minor prang aside, the doctors have little to do. They're not a bad crowd, either: Carslake, Russell ('Mac' as they call him – a touchy bugger), Musgrave (who's prone to black moods), Coffin (the dentist), Grant, Campbell and Throne (a damn nice bloke who never seems to notice when you pull his leg – 'most Irishmen are a bit slow on the uptake but Basil takes the cake'). To make life easier, they've been given a Portuguese batman, who wears an overcoat, carries an umbrella and can't speak a word of English: they christen him Charlie Chaplin.

Underworked and overseas, Arthur's not complaining. The booze is cheap (beer one and six a pint, a double whisky for ninepence), the Atlantic warm enough to swim in, and on 1 May he changes from winter woollies into tropical kit (shirt and shorts). The tent he shares with Steve is on a hillside over-looking a valley, with the treatment block, hospital and Nissens below. When he walks with his wing-commander, Carslake, along the clifftops, he's reminded of Boscastle. The worst nuisance is the lava dust, which gets everywhere – obscuring the runway ('When aircraft come in you can't see them when they land and can't tell if they've pranged'), silting the skin ('if you travel in the back of a lorry or jeep, you get back looking like colliers'), and grating across his notepaper when he writes. Back home he didn't care for camping. But here, under canvas, he discovers the Great Outdoors. Fresh air and exercise have long been his slogan. Now they're his mode of living, too. Animals and insects scurrying by, the wind tensing the guy-rope, the tilley-lamp's moving shadow, the stars like scattered seed-pearls as you step out for a piss last thing at night: who wouldn't choose a tent rather than a Nissen? For the rest of his life, he'll try to recapture the sensation. Other men, similarly, 'never get over' their war. But my father's nostalgia isn't for fighting Germans or hunkering down in bomb-shelters. It's for sleeping bags and a camp-bed under the stars. Any half-warm night and he'll be out there on the lawn. As a teenager, I thought it was to do with sex, or lack of sex, the waning of my parents' conjugal relations. Reading his account of the Azores, I see it was to do with war.

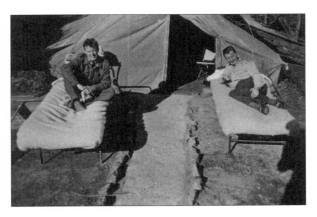

When he isn't sleeping or writing letters Arthur wants action, can't bear to sit. The tent becomes his Windyridge, home from home, a place to do odd jobs around. There are cupboards to make, rockeries to dig, bushes to plant, a palisade and wind-break to build, and extra ropes needed to strengthen the flysheet. When the gate clicks on the palisade he feels houseproud. When shoots come through three weeks after he has planted grass seeds, he's as full of wonder as a schoolkid growing mustard and cress. When a hurricane strikes in October, with gusts up to 100 mph bringing down every tent but his and Steve's, he feels vindicated ('couldn't help bursting out laughing when I woke at 7 and looked outside – everyone was in vest and underpants sitting on top of their tents in the pouring rain'). He paints a barley sugar tin for use as a flower vase. He plants carnations, nasturtiums, sweat peas and cacti. He makes a surfboard from plywood. He's Robinson Crusoe, colonising and civilising the island. His energy is frightening.

Steve, in reaction, takes to his camp-bed and won't budge. When Arthur tries to enthuse him with talk of plants, Steve ignores him or grunts. Long sighs and reproachful stares don't seem to work, either. Finally, Arthur can't resist suggesting that it's time Steve pulled his finger out: it's *their* home and *their* garden, why should *he* do all the work? To which Steve's response is 'It's *your* garden – I admire it, and that's all.' What about the rat-traps, Arthur asks, isn't he grateful for those? (The rats pitter-patter across the canvas at night, leaving ripples as they go along, but he has found a way to snare them, using aniseed and caramel toffee.) Of course he's grateful for the traps, says Steve: as well as pinching soap, chocolate, paper, socks and even matches, the rats carry bubonic fleas. But all this Englishman's-home-is-his bollocks, all this his 'n' hers sharing of tasks – no thanks, mate. If Arthur chooses to spend his time on home improvements, good luck to him. He, Steve, has better things to do – reading novels, writing for the local forces' newspaper, sleeping in after night duty. No offence, but as far as he's concerned, they're cell-mates in a fucking great prison, and the sooner they're out of there the better.

Though steaming with rage, Arthur says no more about it. 'Scotch folk are well known for being touchy,' he tells Kim, and though he can't think of anything he has done to annoy Steve there's obviously been a rift: Christ, Steve even marks his clothes hangers so they don't get muddled with Arthur's and, when the grass grows, mows *his* side of the lawn. Moving tents would be one solution. But in spite of the tensions neither wants to share with anyone else. Arthur sees himself as the practical half of the partnership, though he's not as practical as he likes to pretend. Typical is his sending a dozen eggs home to Kim. Eggs through the post! Though he wraps them as best he can, it's a miracle any are still intact by the time they reach her. And then the wireless, the bloody wireless. It's the Tommy Handley show he wants it for, as well as the news. Light music too — jazz and dance-bands and the songs he associates with Kim. They have a wireless in the tent already, but Arthur attempts to build a better one. Within a month of starting, he has to strip it and begin again because the reception's so poor. Then winds bring down the aerial, so that needs fixing too. Still dissatisfied, he tries to convert to short wave. That doesn't work either. Already he's spent 3 pounds 10 shillings on the thing, and now pays another thirty bob for someone to make him a speaker cabinet. As a last resort, a series of technical-minded underlings are invited to his tent to 'take a look', in the hope they'll offer to fix it. They don't. Six months on, the wireless is still no nearer completion.

While Arthur faffs about, he likes to whistle — music while he works, or idles, songs like 'Tiko Tiko', with their relentless cheer. This too irks Steve. Here they are, stuck in the middle of nowhere with fuck-all to do — has the man no sense of darkness or the absurd? What's there to be so bloody cheerful about? In truth, Arthur's star hasn't been lucky of late. Since the war began, his uncle Ben, aunt Connie, cousin Dan, both his grandfathers, several friends and (it seems) Michael have all died. Quite a share of 'trajedy', as he puts it to Kim. Yet he can't absorb it. He can't even spell it. 'Tragedy' in his letters is always spelt 'trajedy', that 'j' jauntifying and jollifying the despair. The word doesn't exist in his vocabulary. You smile, you whistle, you make the best of it. All of which gets on Steve's nerves.

I identify with Steve. Years later, I too would sit with my nose in a book while my father bustled round and made me feel bad about 'not helping'. I too would grunt when he spoke to me. I too would suffer his belief in 'practicality', while secretly noting how unpractical he could be (like the time we set off camping without tent poles). 'Any man who can't change a wheel annoys me intensely,' he writes in one letter. 'In fact a *woman* who drives and can't change a wheel annoys me too.' But I remember the time he changed a tyre on my mother's car, forgot to tighten the wheel nuts, and after she'd gone, realising his error, tore off in pursuit, expecting to find a wreck in the hedge, a plume of steam rising, bodies over the road. It was all right: she reached the surgery without mishap. But what his carelessness might have made happen went on troubling him, and many hours were spent inducting his son in the art of wheel-changing. No, my father wasn't practical by nature. But the war instilled in him (as in so many of his generation) notions of getting by and making do. He became good at wangling. At manipulating too: men as well as materials were there to be exploited.

What's striking about his letters is their preoccupation with home – not the one he has grown up in but the one he hopes to establish with his wife-to-be. Whereas she will settle wherever she's put, he's a homemaker. 'Went to Angra today', he tells her, 'and bought some lace napkins – will send them to you for our future house.' Then again a couple of months later: 'Went to Angra and bought some hand-decorated linen table mats for our oak table.' The question of marriage is far from settled, but the mats and napkins keep it on the table. The word 'oak' resonates too. In the blowing lava dust of Terceira, oak stands for what he misses about England, being the colour of pub rafters and beer. Later, he would get his oak table. It sat in our dining room until he died. It sits in mine now, a little grebe-shaped hole gouged out of one corner to remind me of childhood (sweet bird of youth!). These days the fashion is for a lighter furniture: Ikea and scrubbed pine. The old oak heirlooms have come to seem oppressive. But to my father in 1944, they embody strength and solidity. While dust blows through his tent-flaps, rats chew his chocolate and clouds flit overhead, he dreams of an Irish girl in England. And of oak.

✢   ✢   ✢

*Kim to Arthur, Dudley Rd Hospital, Birmingham, 4.4.44*

Sorry I didn't write last night. Arrived round 5pm, after a crowded train journey, to find my predecessor was still here. He managed to depress me, and later I discovered why. It seems he didn't intend to leave and they advertised the job over his head. Then he went on two weeks' holiday – and didn't know I was coming till he got back yesterday. Also, he was getting £200 pa and I'm getting £300 – no wonder he was peeved. Anyway he tried to be nice and showed me round. The Maternity block is delightful – very modern, with 120 beds, plus two Gyny wards of about 25 beds each. The chief, Taylor, who lives out, is Irish and has been here for years. The other man, Mitchell, also lives out and is very nice. I'm the only MO who lives in, and (here's the bit you won't like) on call every night, so you can guess I'll have some work to do. I get one half day off a week and one long weekend a month, that's all. I can't kick up about being on call, because the other two are on call, too – if I'm in difficulties they have to come in.

Went to bed pretty miserable hearing all this, and wished you were here or that we were engaged. Got up at 8.30am (there was a forceps at 4am but Mitchell very decently came in to do it and they didn't wake me), and did some rounds with Taylor, then went into theatre with him.

My room is very nice – coal fire if I want it, a couch, two wardrobes, bookcase, shelves and cupboards. Horrible bed, though – like yours in Davidstow. The mess is quite good and the food all right. When I gave my ration book to the elderly woman in charge of the mess she asked me how old I was, because 'If you're under a certain age I must have your date of birth, and you look about 22'. I didn't scream.

No one can talk about anything here except the second front. I was reading an article about the Azores today, which Peg fished out for me – it says the troops there refer to the aircraft that carries the mail as the 'passion wagon' (do they still?), and that there's never a shortage of hands to unload it.

Letter from Mary this morning. Ron is on holiday but she wonders how much she'll see of him. Seems there is a misunderstanding between them. Reading between the lines I gather Ron is falling more and more in love (if possible) and she is in a quandary. She still talks of Michael all the time.

What a life! Why can't it be like it was in Cornwall or London? Will I ever feel so happy again?

*Kim to Arthur, Birmingham, 21.5.44*

How's the digging for victory going, darling? Wish I could be there with you, messing about in my slacks.

Funny thing, but I think I've written 'I love you' more than I've ever said it.

Two clinics today, morning and afternoon. Do I hate pregnant women. You can imagine – after seeing about 80 of them in one day. Was feeling rotten after being called about six times in the night. But went into town to collect my suit – which I like very much – and had a good blow in the breeze and now I'm fine again.

Whit weekend. Much too hot, especially in London, where I stayed with Maurice and Peg. Why is it nothing's quite the same when you aren't there? Caught the 6.10 back and got to Brum at 8.50pm. Louise had supper ready. Had a cold bath and am here in bed but it's still much too hot to sleep. In my white pyjamas, Louise says I look like a corpse. Feel sorry for any woman pregnant in this weather. It's 86 degrees on the labour ward – too sticky to hold forceps.

They've been agitating in the papers for less letter-writing in the forces – to cut it down to a minimum and use thin notepaper. So since there's no news I will do the right thing by my country and stop here.


SHE HAS NEVER been to Birmingham and is surprised by its poverty and gloom. Founded in 1887 as an infirmary to the city's new workhouse, Dudley Road Hospital is still a refuge for the urban poor. The staff-patient ratio is daunting – nine full-time doctors to 873 beds (170 of them in Gyny and Maternity) – and some of the cases she has to deal with are horrendous. But her salary is a decent one for someone so young, and she's safe from the Luftwaffe (who have given up long bombing missions to the Midlands). 'You'll be working long hours,' they warn her, but she's used to long hours: which hospital doctor isn't?

What's novel is working on a labour ward, where the hours are crazier than anywhere else. Take her first weekend, over

Easter, 8 and 9 April: she works in surgery, cutting and stitching, on the Saturday evening; gets to bed after midnight; is called for a breech delivery at 4.30am, a forceps at 7am and the manual removal of a placenta at 8am; at 9am grabs a bath and breakfast, scribbles some words to Arthur; and by 10 on Easter Sunday is 'ready to start the day's work'. On the 12th, while delivering twins – one forceps and one breech – she's called to an emergency involving a collapsed uterus. On the 16th she's present when a woman dies on the operating table during a Caesarian ('a terrible feeling, darling, don't think I'll ever forget it'). On the 22nd, she's forced to do a general anaesthetic for a forceps delivery: 'I had to use dope because the woman was terrified of being touched – wouldn't let anyone near even to palpate her. As sister said, how did she ever get pregnant?' On the 23rd, she sees 13 new admissions, has a crisis with a woman who's been in theatre to have a bit of placenta removed, then deals with a ruptured ectopic. The following week she's called to a case of delayed labour; the baby is dead, it seems, but still has to be delivered: 'Stayed there for a while hoping she'd manage on her own but no. Everyone thought it would be a nice one for a student to do as there would be no hurry but it was not nice and I had to help him out. Later had an eclamptic and had to put forceps on her. She wasn't so good and still isn't – several fits since delivery.'

So it goes on. All the routine stuff – breech deliveries, Caesareans, heads tugged out with forceps. And all the complications – ectopics, prolapses, subphrenic abscesses, retained placentas, eclampsias, puerperal insanities. Here's a not untypical day:

Didn't get to bed till midnight because of a forceps. Ward round from 9–10.30. Clinic from 10.30–1.30. We saw 91 patients – just Mitchell and I. Doesn't sound a lot but it seemed like hundreds, and nearly was. Did two inductions after lunch. Afternoon clinic from 2.30–4 – a bit better, only 38 patients. Tea, and then an anaesthetic for Mitchell, and here I am at 5.30pm, with a forceps due any minute. Contemplated one of those Welfare Clinic jobs once – but not now. I'd be bored stiff in no time.

There's my mother speaking: overworked, stressed out, but certain she'll be bored if she does any less.

In theory, she's employed only in Gyny and Maternity, but her room lies close to Casualty, and sometimes she sees cases that aren't her call (ovarian cysts which turn out to be obstructed hernias, vaginal haemorrhages that prove to be rectal). As for births, Dudley Road averages 3,000 a year – between 8 and 9 a day. On one occasion she does 16 deliveries in 24 hours. 'There are times when I hate women, and tonight will be one of them,' she tells Arthur, with 14 new patients awaiting operations. Sundays are the worst, when she sees her admissions for operation on the Tuesday. 'Only one in four of these really need doing, and only one in a hundred D&Cs.' Where Arthur's letters to her are written at leisure, from a camp-bed, hers to him often break off mid-sentence because of an emergency: 'Sorry darling, there's the phone . . . Midnight: that *was* urgent.'

Despite the workload, she's not unhappy. A couple of other doctors are Irish, and she becomes good friends with a nurse called Louise, who makes a fuss of her – fetches her toast and boiled eggs at teatime, massages her scalp, brushes and washes her hair. Her room's cosy, with a fire. And most days bring a letter from Arthur, on one occasion five in the morning post and two in the evening. He sends her parcels, too: Louise is in her room when one of these arrives, and Kim torments her by ever so slowly undoing the string. They whoop with delight when it's finally open: inside are bananas ('which I haven't seen for years') and a pineapple ('How did you know it was my favourite fruit?'). The pineapple sits ripening by her bed for over a fortnight till on a cold night in early May she and Louise 'make real pigs' of themselves. He has sent an enticing recipe, which involves cutting the ends off, enucleating the fruit from its skin, creating six circular slices, pouring 2oz of port over, reassembling and serving. But they content themselves with scrounging a tin of Nestles from Sister. 'Thank you, Arthur,' says Louise to his photo on the mantelpiece. What can they send him in return, Kim wonders? Themselves as stowaways, says Louise. She likes Louise, who wears glasses and makes funny jokes, not least about her own appearance − 'I'm not fat,' she likes to say, 'I've gone beyond that stage: I'm gross.' She thinks Arthur would like her, too.

About the rest of her colleagues, she's less flattering. There are four senior physicians, three male and one female ('very female too: we all hate her − she is very pally with the chief, so if you want anything out of him you just say it in her presence'). One of the males is German, 'and he's not the worst of the bunch'; her predecessor was a conscientious objector. Then there are the surgeons − nice enough but with a pernicious habit of starting operations about 11pm and going on till 3am. She'd think more highly of her boss, Wentworth Taylor, if he weren't so suspicious of pain-killing drugs and so brutal in his delivery methods: 'he sits on the floor with a forceps and does he pull! He gets the baby out but always with a third-degree tear.' Still, he's not as bad as the grumpy old burns specialist, whose flat is situated below her room: 'The phone doesn't reach my bed, so every night I pull the bed out to the middle of the floor so it will. He rang this morning to complain about all the "furniture-moving". I was furious and let him know it − why couldn't he say it to my face? Anyway, I'm moving rooms tomorrow − a sister's leaving and is letting me have hers, it has a phone by the bed and a gas fire, which is better because they've stopped coal fires here now.'

It's intriguing to see my mother getting 'furious' with someone. I never knew her to raise her voice or lose her temper. But in Birmingham she stuck up for herself. If her hours were over-long, so be it. If the work exhausted her, at least she wasn't bored. But she wouldn't take crap from colleagues. She was just about to have her twenty-seventh birthday. How dare they try to push her around?

✳   ✳   ✳

*Arthur to Kim, Azores, 9.4.44*

Since tea I've been reading for an hour – the unabridged version of Lady Chatterley's Lover by DH Lawrence. Yes, darling, I know it's disgusting but I've heard so much about it that I'm reading it while I've the chance. Don't mind, do you darling? After all, it must broaden the mind, even if purely on one subject – Sex. (Later: Have now finished it, and apart from being rather nauseated by seeing 'that word' and quite a few others in print, found it fairly well written.)

*Azores, 1.5.44*

Was chatting to Musgrave about a week ago. He said:
   'When are you getting married?'
   'Oh, soon after getting home, I think.'
   'I wouldn't if I were you. You can't trust women.'
   'Oh, but I trust this girl.'
   'Don't be a damn fool – you can't trust any of them. They're all alike. This love business is nonsense.'
   Well, darling, I used to think so too. But not now.
   Funny thing, but despite the fact that I'm senior F/Lt by a long way, Musgrave (without saying anything to me) appointed Mac to act as SMO. It's OK by me because it's a moithering job on a bloody station like this. But it's just not done, and Mac takes it all far too seriously, worrying about everything. Last night he saw I was giving a lecture and rang me up: 'Why wasn't I told?' I was madder 'n hell and we had a hell of a row over the phone – verbally shook hands at the end but relations are still strained.

*Azores, 6.5.44*

We're getting a lot of Sulpha-resistant gonorrhoea – probably due to constant medication of the pros. Can't understand the mentality of anyone joining a queue, reading a paper, smoking a cigarette, etc, all while you wait around for the blokes ahead in line to do it first, and then finally getting in and knowing they've been in there just before you and there are half a dozen more right behind. But we are getting cases. Gave a lecture to my crowd on VD the other night, and laid it on pretty thick.

AWAY FROM KIM, Arthur finds his mind turning to sex. He's not a great reader, but every book that comes his way has a sexual content: *Solomon's Vineyard* by Jonathan Latimer, which he can't imagine being much broader ('From the way her buttocks looked under the black silk dress', it begins, 'I knew she'd be good in bed'); *Congo Song*, 'about a woman among seven men who loves them all and also suckles a baby gorilla'; *Dr Haines's Encyclopedia of Sexual Knowledge*, which is 'interesting in parts', though less so than *Lady Chatterley's Lover*, a pirated copy of which is doing the rounds. (My mother would have to wait till 1960 to read it: the post-trial Penguin edition used to sit in her bedside cabinet.) But it's not only books that bring up sex. There's also the behaviour of his fellow servicemen, with their trips to the local brothel. It's the sort of clap that's hard to treat, he tells Kim. She, puzzled, asks why he hasn't been using penicillin – a barbed question, since she too would like to get her hands on the new wonder drug (only in widespread use since the previous year) but has been told it's reserved for the armed forces. So why doesn't he have it? Because it hasn't reached outposts like the Azores, he says. In its absence there's only sulphur – and fire-and-brimstone lectures from the medics.

Arthur's the last person you'd expect to give a lecture. But Musgrave butters him up by alluding to his recent triumph in saving the life of an eleven-year-old Portuguese boy with tetanus. In truth, Arthur's only task was to take some serum

(ATS) to the island of San Jorge, so the boy could be given an injection. At the time what most excited him was being allowed to fly the plane on the way home. But since then there've been reports on Lisbon Radio, the Portuguese Governor is planning a champagne party for the crew, and even Ernest back in Manchester reads about his son's adventure in the morning paper. 'The lads are in awe,' Musgrave tells him. 'You're a hero. I can't think of a better person to talk to them.' Which is bullshit. But enough in a weak moment to win him round.

Come the hour, he regrets succumbing to Musgrave's flattery. The mess hut, with forty or so empty wooden chairs. A handful of boys drifting in with pints after supper. And him sweating like a racehorse. Earlier, on his camp-bed, sand blowing across a mild sun, he jotted down half a dozen headings from *Dr Haines's Encyclopedia of Sexual Knowledge*, trying to remind himself what he was taught at Med School. Treating is one thing, talking another. He suspects the other MOs of setting him up: Christ, they're used to pontificating, do nothing else, so why delegate this to him? Steve, his tent-mate, pops his head round the door, asks when Arthur's starting, and pops back out. Then Musgrave, Donald, Grant, Throne and Coffin enter, the whole of the medical crew. Then Mac, still sulky that no one thought to tell him. Then Carslake – Jesus, the bloody Winco as well – tilting his wrist-watch as he takes a seat to indicate it's gone 8:30. Arthur stands and clears his throat. But then the door bursts open, and thirty pairs of feet clatter in: Steve has brought the whole bloody bar with him. Arthur can feel his legs shaking. Every bugger's there to see him make a fathead of himself. 'Come on doc,' someone calls out, not unfriendly, and the boys start drumming their feet.

'Now lads,' he begins, 'you know what I'm here to talk about: VD. The clap, the pox, syph, dripsy, French gout and all the other things they call it. Common enough back home. But I didn't expect to come across it here, stuck as we are in the middle of nowhere with scarcely a woman in sight. I was wrong. Quite a few of you have already been in for treatment. A damn sight too many, in fact.'

Remarkable: they're listening. Not his doing, but the subject: the endless fascination of sex. He hates sounding like a priest. But that's what Musgrave wants – to hellfire the lads out of the brothel. He tries to think of Florence Desmond in that ENSA show the other night – she was trembling too, but it didn't cramp her performance. Just hide the nerves.

'VD, they call it, but the term covers two or three different diseases. First, the mildest and most common, gonorrhoea. The incubation period is usually short, two to five days. The first thing you notice is a burning sensation when passing water. Next day you find yourself leaking pus from the urethra. Gradually the burning gets worse – having a pee feels like pissing broken glass or having a hot poker inside you. By this point, most of you will have been to see the doctor, thank God. But if you don't, because the inflammation seems to have eased, there's worse in store: a swelling in your scrotum that can get as large and red as a cricket ball. Whichever side it's on, that testicle will stop producing sperm; if it affects both sides, then you'll become sterile. I won't labour the other complications.

'Then there's chancroid, or soft core, very common in the sub-tropics. Again, there's not much chance of missing a chancroid – it's an ulcer on your penis, a bit like a honeycomb. Sounds pretty, doesn't it: a honeycomb. But it doesn't *feel* very pretty, and what with the pain, and the loss of tissue, and the leaking pus, most men won't hang about, they'll be in to see me sharpish. And if they do, no problem. A week's treatment, and both gonorrhoea and chancroid can be cured.

'Now the last and most vicious kind of VD, syphilis, a cunning blighter because if you're not careful you'll think you've beaten it, only to find it coming back. Harmless enough, at first. It can take as long as three months before the sore appears on your penis – that's supposing you're not a pansy, who's more likely to get his on his b-t-m. It'll have a crust, this ulcer, making it round and hard, like the suspender button holding up a woman's stockings (undoing which was probably what got you in trouble in the first place). The ulcer may weep a bit, but it won't feel sore, and any tests in the first few weeks will be negative – which is why, when it disappears, you may think you've got off scot-free. Forget it. You haven't.'

He remembers Brenda, the chorus girl in Plymouth. When she showed him the copper-red rash on her arms, like measles, he, naive, had said, 'Oh, it's nothing.' Next time he saw her, she was close to suicide, diagnosis having revealed it to be syph. She swore she was a virgin – her only 'intimate loving' had been with a medical student. At the time he had believed her: those earnest tears, her hand resting in his. Later, knowing more, he decided she must be lying.

'As well as a skin rash, sore throats, swollen glands and jaundice may be present too. You can go on with minor symptoms for up to five years, and not know what's behind them. The parasite is taking a rest, or offering a temporary truce, but it hasn't been defeated. The latent phase lasts anything from ten to forty years, then it's mayhem. First you find your balance gone and start walking like a sailor just off the boat. Then stabbing pains in the legs, headaches, insomnia, impotence, blindness, paralysis, madness. A living death for years. And then you die. And still the story isn't finished. Any children you have risk being infected. For them blindness, deafness, deformity and premature death are all in store.'

The sudden scrape of a chair. A lad, green-faced, rushing for the door. The other lads parting for him, afraid that he'll throw up. Good, thinks Arthur, I'm getting through.

'And all this because you couldn't stop yourself jumping on a woman you'd not have looked twice at back home. Because that's how you get VD: through intercourse. Toilet seats, dirty towels, baths, swimming pools, donkey bites – come on, lads, don't waste my time. Intercourse is the way, and on this island the only women who'll consort with the likes of you work at the brothel. I've been there – strictly on a recce. I have to tell you, I was not impressed. Hand-picked, those ladies are: fat, greasy, middle-aged, and with faces more pitted than the moon. Serve you right if you come to me with yellow pus oozing from your knob. By then it'll hurt so much you'll be pleading with me to amputate. Perhaps one day I will. If you're such fatheads as to keep running to the whorehouse, you deserve the guillotine. And don't try telling me that what your wives and girlfriends don't know can't hurt them. What you do in the brothel can infect them. Even if it doesn't, you'll have to live with your conscience. And there's no medicine for regret.

'Yes, it's tough living without women. We go a little mad. But there are ways for a man to relieve himself. Self-abuse is a dirty habit, but rather that than dipping your pail in a poisoned well. And poison's the word. It isn't civilised on islands like these. It's *syphilised*.

'To sum up. VD is nasty in all its forms, at best painful, at worse life-threatening. If you think you have symptoms, come see me at SSQ, and I can treat you. But why run the risk at all? Stay away from that brothel and the only time you'll ever see me is in the bar.'

He sits down. Twenty-five minutes, longer than planned. He'd meant there to be time for questions. But the lads look shell-shocked, and their glasses are empty, and no one raises his hand. Carslake steps forward and expresses his 'sincere thanks to F/Lt Morrison for a most sobering talk. I'm sure no one here will have missed the point. But if there are any questions, the MOs will be happy to answer them afterwards.' A shuffle of khaki out the door. 'You might have mentioned condoms,' says Mac, even sulkier than before. The others merely nod on their way out. Stuff them. So what if they don't rate his lecturing skills? At least he got the message over.

Who was the lad who rushed out? he asks, at the bar. Harrison, they say – and isn't it Arthur's turn to get a round in? Harrison, eh. The one who keeps getting his letters by mistake, because of Kim's scrawled, all too doctorly hand. At least he has the decency not to open the envelopes. Not the type to visit brothels, either, by the look of him. Who would be the type, after what they've just heard? Cheers. Your health. It's not often you can change people. But maybe this once, tonight, he has.

✳    ✳    ✳

*Arthur to Kim, Azores, 3.5.44*

Yesterday afternoon went to the beach. Damn good: cloudless blue sky, and so hot you had to keep your sandals on walking across it, loads of chaps bathing. We were all talking about how marvellous it would be with our wives – had to stop in the end because we began to get depressed.

Glad to hear your smoking is down. I hope it's the same with drinking. I'd hate you to get like you did that night the Christmas before last, just after we'd met. Don't like this calling up women into the forces again, either – a bloody racket. I should be terribly jealous if you were, because I know you'd be in great demand. It's certainly an experience and education, but you're doing a much more important job of work there.

Why do I write every day? Because I want to tell you every little thing I do. Nothing yet everything, for pages and pages . . .

WHOOAH, DAD, STOP there, it's not your turn, you're taking over. It's difficult, I know: you'd rather be *doing* something, not bloody writing. But all this leisure time makes your letters longer and more frequent than Mum's. To me, partial as I am, they're interesting letters; it's as if I'm there with you on the beach, in the mess, under the stars. But this book's supposed to be her book, not yours. You're part of it, just as I'm part of it. But if we're not careful, she'll be crowded out. Knowing Mum, she'd welcome the chance to fade into the background. But it's her story we've come to hear. If you want the best for her, and I know you do, let her get a word in. She's reticent at the best of times. And her work doesn't leave much time for self-expression. But she does have things to say. Let's sit patiently and listen while we can.

(And if you could back off in other ways, Dad, that too would be appreciated. Just let her be who she is for once! Don't be so domineering! I find it hard to discuss this with you. I never did discuss it with you. It was a thing that needed saying, not just to you but to other men like you. It was there, at the edge of speech, but if ever I faintly implied it you got the hump. So let it pass. My lips are sealed. This is a silent parenthesis. But the words are here anyway, in loving reproach.)

✻ ✻ ✻

*Kim to Arthur, Birmingham, 19.4.44*

It's pouring rain but I'm in front of the fire feeling very very happy, having had seven letters from you today, five this morning and two this evening. The mail is haywire, but I'm having a gala week, with two letters yesterday as well. It's marvellous. The only problem is getting back between ward rounds and clinic to read them, alone.

A girl here had her papers today. I'll soon be due for mine. So if you want to keep me out of the war I'll have to get married – how about it? I could be so happy, even here, with a ring on that third finger. It would make me feel more confident about going to your home, too. How perfect it would be to be standing on a platform somewhere a year from now waiting for you to arrive.

I remember when Jerry and Eileen used to write to each other every day and I thought they were quite crazy and said 'I'd never do that'. And here I am. Dammit, there's the phone . . .

Later: Sorry about that. A real emergency. She was a ruptured ectopic, who'd been down as a query ectopic pregnancy for a few days and was due for a laparotomy tomorrow – but she decided to rupture tonight. Dr Taylor catheterised her and got pints off. For a horrible moment I thought it was nothing more than an acute retention – I'd have felt such a fool getting Mitchell in if so – but all went well.

The night before was terrible too. Called at 1.30am to do a forceps. Another sticky case after that (large brow, hard pull needed) and didn't get to bed till 4.30am. I never mind getting up to do work like that at night, but it is maddening to be called to admit cases when they're not urgent.

How I'd like to be at Auntie's now. I loved her couch, despite the lumps.

BACK IN BIRMINGHAM, illicit sexual liaisons are also occupying Kim. It's a full-time job trying to keep up. For every baby she delivers, there are several foetuses ripped untimely from the womb.

Her letters speak of D&Cs – dilation and curettage, aka cervical scrapes. 'God it makes me furious the way everyone has a D&C in this place,' she complains, 'including kids of 16 with dysmenorrhoea [painful menstruation] who should have their bottom smacked instead. Sent one home yesterday and told her to have more sense. Mind you I blame Mr Taylor, not the patients. He seems to feel under obligation to every GP in Birmingham.' Though D&Cs are a routine procedure, intended to reduce heavy menstrual flow, many are done in order to remove 'waste products' after home-made abortions. Others, in effect, *are* abortions – in the first fourteen weeks of pregnancy, dilation of the cervix followed by curettage of the internal uterine wall is a safe method for destroying an unwanted foetus. Better that, though, than backstreet abortions, numerous enough in Manchester and even more plentiful in Brum. Blame the war and its brief encounters, to which the rising birth-rate (15.6 per thousand in 1942, 16.2 in 1943, 17.5 in 1944) is testimony. Forty per cent of babies born are illegitimate, and many more are secret cuckoos in the nest. If an unmarried woman falls pregnant, or a wife does while her husband's on a year-long posting, abortion is the obvious answer; otherwise it's marital trouble or – horror – single motherhood. (There's also the fear of birth defects, cases of syphilis having risen sharply.) A hot bath and bottle of gin. Castor oil, mercury salts, mustard, laburnum, pennyroyal, quinine, even a spoonful of gunpowder. A bumpy bike ride or heavy fall downstairs. The insertion of slippery elm bark, which swells as it gets wet. Or if all else fails, crochet hooks, scissors, a pencil, a hat pin, a knitting needle, a bicycle spoke . . . The old-wives' cures are unpleasant but numerous, and every district has its expert to assist – not ogres, but saviours, someone (usually an older woman) who can 'put you right if you get caught'.

In England in 1944 abortion is still illegal and carries stiff penalties. As Kim well knows, Section 58 of the Offences Against the Person Act, 1861 (amended 1891) decrees: 'Whosoever, with intent to procure the miscarriage of any woman, whether she be or be not with child, shall unlawfully adminster to her or cause to be taken by her any poison or other noxious thing, or shall unlawfully use any instrument or other means whatsoever with the like intent, shall be guilty of felony and being convicted shall be liable to be kept in penal servitude for a minimum of three years and a maximum of five . . .' The law applies as much to doctors as everyone else. (It's also part of the Hippocratic Oath not to 'give a woman means to procure an abortion'.) But with all the dangers of backstreet abortion, many hospitals quietly ignore the law. They've been encouraged by a test case from just before the war, when a surgeon at St Mary's in London, Dr Alec Bourne, was acquitted after performing an abortion on a fourteen-year-old rape victim. Since then the notion of 'therapeutic' abortion – performed for the well-being of the mother – has become more widely accepted. Many abortions at Dudley Road are of that kind, officially performed for obstetric reasons but in reality for socio-psychological ones. On her first weekend at the hospital, my mother performs eight in a single night.

Her letters are reticent on the subject. But she can't have felt good about it. Many of the girls are called Docherty and O'Connor, and they come from Ireland, not Brum (for the next fifty years, half the Irish girls visiting England will do so in order to get an abortion). She feels odd about that, and has a further reason for hating the work, as will become clear. But she gets on with it. Done properly, it's as safe as lifting an egg from a hatching-box, and infinitely preferable to cleaning up others' botches – though that too is all in the line of duty. In July there's a particularly horrendous example of a termination gone wrong. A girl with long black hair Kim vaguely recognises from some-where is admitted with rapidly spreading peritonitis: a suspected septic abortion. She and Taylor do a laparotomy, an incision into the abdominal cavity, and put in a drain. But the girl's condition doesn't improve. They'd give her pencillin, but are told, once again, that it isn't available: supplies are being kept for the troops.

They put up drips for her, but in her restlessness she pulls them out, so they tie in a cannula (a hollow tube). Then she begins to vomit, and is put on gastric siphonage. It does no good. Five days after admission she dies. 'Saw the post-mortem on that girl,' Kim writes to Arthur, 'no evidence of criminal abortion, but that's what usually happens. She was toxic all over – liver, kidney, heart, etc. She was known on the stage as Gypsy Nina. I think I saw her once. She played an accordion.'

Cases like that take some getting over. Worse still are the women who die in childbirth, the first within a fortnight of her arriving – a very bad 'APH', losing heavily, and 'almost gone before we started', though knowing that is no consolation: 'terrible . . . somehow a maternal death always seems worse than any other.' One night, she and Taylor do a Caesar on the wrong mother. It's not a disaster – the woman was due to have one anyway, later in the week – but the muddle shows how over-stretched the hospital has become. Four days later there's another death:

Last night was called at 4.50am by Sister on the block. She had a patient over there (having her fifth baby) who was being a bit slow to deliver and she rang me to ask if she could give her some Pituitrim to help her pains. For some unknown reason – just a 'feeling' – I said no: I personally hate giving it but they give it rather freely, expecially in a case like this – head showing and poor pains – and it usually works. So I told Sister not to give it but that I'd do a forceps if necessary. She said she'd probably deliver it herself – she had things boiled up and ready. However, at 5.30 she rang again to say she still hadn't delivered and there was maternal and foetal distress. So I got over quickly but the woman had collapsed in the meantime and was moribund. I gave her oxygen, put up some plasma and rang Mitchell, not wanting a death on my hands, though I guessed she'd die. She did, at 6am – the post mortem is tomorrow. It must have been a ruptured uterus but why I can't think. She didn't have very good pains and there was no obstruction and she'd had four normal deliveries before. But it could only be that or a pulmonary embolus, and she had no symptoms of either – complained of nothing, just suddenly collapsed. It was horrible. I hate maternal death. Thank heaven I didn't give her the Pituitrim or I'd be blaming myself. (Later: the post mortem showed it was a ruptured uterus – though why we can't tell.)

Maternal deaths are rare even in 1944 – two women for every thousand births. But labour complications are common and, with foetal monitoring such a crude technology, the perinatal mortality rate is high: 45 babies per thousand. In other words, nearly one birth in twenty ends in a death. Since Kim's delivering several babies a day, she experiences a death most weeks. In her mother's time, at the turn of the century, it was worse: one in ten. Things are improving, everyone says. But how to quantify improvement? Every statistic is a tragedy.

Despite the traumas, she *likes* working in Gyny. The great thing about crises in the operating theatre is that the patients are unconscious and amenable; whereas unanaesthetised, on the ward, they thrash about and answer back. It's the routine stuff that wears her down. After each ante-natal clinic she swears she'll never examine a pregnant woman again. The great cowlike docility of them, oh and the stupidity – it drives her nuts. She feels a sense of mission, all the same. Here she is, in the middle of 1944, ushering in a postwar generation: babies the colour of clay from whom the future will be moulded; babies who when they grow up will remember nothing of the war. It's not only that she feels lucky to be in on these births. She feels at home, too. Life back in Killorglin was all fecundity and plurality, and it's the same in Dudley Road: you can't stop the babies coming. There's a joke she hears doing the rounds which makes her smile in recognition. It's about an Irishman – called Paddy, of course – whose wife goes into labour one night. Their rural cottage has no electricity, so the midwife asks Paddy to hold up an oil-lamp to help her see what she's doing. There are places he'd rather be, but after an hour his wife gives birth and he breathes a sigh of relief. 'Not so fast, Paddy,' the midwife says. 'Hold that lamp high – I think there's another one.' And so there is. He relaxes –

nothing wrong with twins. But 'Not so fast, Paddy,' the midwife says. 'Hold that lamp high – I think there's another one.' So a third child is born – triplets, and at last he thinks he's free to go. But 'Not so fast, Paddy,' the midwife says. 'Hold that lamp high.' To which he protests: 'Sure, and I won't – it must be the light that's attracting them.' My mother never told jokes but she liked to tell this one. After years on maternity wards, she knew about babies being born in numbers. What I didn't realise till after her death was the other connection: her own mother's score of births.

Her sister Sheila, teaching science and maths in London, says that English children are worse off than those in Kerry. That's how it looks from where she stands at the blackboard. Free milk for every pupil, and free meals for half of them, but still some are half-starved because their parents eat their rations. Oh, and the head-lice and scabies. Kim knows about those, too. The rickety kids coming in to see their new siblings, already scarred by hunger and neglect. It would be hard to be a worse mother than some she's had lately, all joy and tears at first but clueless how to look after a baby. Margaret O'Shea (née Lyons) made a better job of it, despite the largeness of her brood. Never so cared for as in the womb. Never so safe as when wrapped in a layer of cheesy vernix. Kim will make sure it's different with her own children. Not that motherhood or marriage is imminent, with Arthur away and no knowing when he'll return. Even when he's back, supposing he does come back, who knows if it will work out between them. Sheila hasn't met him yet. She likes the sound of him but doubts that their parents will, him being English and all that.

The two sisters meet in Birmingham late that May, during Sheila's half-term break. Two weeks later, on 6 June, the Allies achieve a major breakthrough, with the D-Day landings in Normandy. For the first time since 1939 it's possible to speak of peace and not feel idiotic. In the Azores, after the initial elation, Arthur's main feeling is one of shame and helplessness: 'Won't it be nice for me after the war when people ask "Where were you?" and I say "Oh, sunbathing in a neutral country". It will certainly be good to be alive to tell the tale, but I'd rather have a tale to tell. I'm no hero, and it must be terrible in France, but I wish I was there. Here I am safe and sound, whereas my family and wife-to-be are near the front line and may be right in it any day – hell.' In Birmingham, Kim is more directly affected by D-Day – she hears the planes going over at five in the morning, and has her leave cancelled until further notice: 'They've been keeping the wards empty for some time, and now it's all hands on deck.' But despite the excitement, there's no influx of casualties. On the maternity wards the works goes on. Business – that's to say babies – as usual.

✳   ✳   ✳

*Mary to Arthur, Windyridge, 19.5.44*

It's nice of you to think over my present problems. Honestly, I don't know what to do – I'm so desolate, and the spring and everything makes my heart ache for Michael lying cold and dead somewhere. I think Ronnie is in love with me and I'm afraid of making a mistake. Is he the best second best? He is wonderful with baby, and kind, and more or less understands me, but whether marrying him is right I don't know. In any case, I'm taking a lot for granted – he's never asked.

WHEN ERNEST AND Kathleen write to Arthur, they begin their letters in the same way: 'Everything is going on here just as always.' A soothing message to an absent son: don't worry, you're missing nothing, Windyridge will be the same when you come home. But it isn't quite true. As well as Mary's emotional ups and downs, Kela's skin problem is causing concern: when Mary feeds her custard, her eyes stream and she comes out in a vivid rash. Tests indicate that egg is causing her allergy. Relieved to know the cause, they cut all trace of egg from her diet. But it doesn't stop the irritation.

Irritation is the family tune that spring. They're fed up with each other, and fed up with Arthur for clearing off to the Azores. He had no choice, of course, but might at least have phoned before he left. Instead of which he writes a letter which Kim (under orders) doesn't give them till after she hears he has got there safely. The Icelandic saga all over again. Bloody daft, everyone agrees, including Ron, who's also sworn to secrecy and has to throw a 'dismayed surprise act' on learning of Arthur's departure. What is it with Arthur? Why couldn't he tell them straight? If he'd been killed en route they'd still have felt as bad or worse. As it is, they spend a fortnight worrying that he has been sent to Burma, where young men are dying every day.

It doesn't help that he falls silent just before the anniversary of Michael's disappearance. March the 11th: Mary has been dreading it coming, and on the day, a Saturday, something terrible happens. Lunch in the dining room. Kathleen (despite rationing) has served everyone's favourite, roast beef followed by semolina pudding. They're just finishing off when a plane comes over, very low, just as Mike used to do on practice runs. Their thoughts are already with him, of course. And when the pilot keeps circling back over the house, and divebombing, as though waving to them from the air, it seems a kind of signal. It must be someone who knew Mike and has remembered the day, they decide, but it's a stupid trick. The stunting goes on for half an hour. By the end, poor Mary's calling for Mike – crying out his name and telling him she can't live without him. They're all relieved when the pilot clears off at last. Later, Ernest rings the RAF, in hopes of getting the culprit's name and playing hell. But no one seems to know who it was, least of all Mike's old friends at Upper Heyford. Mary keeps to her room that night. Far into the small hours, they hear her muffled weeping.

Even if it weren't for her grief, Mary would find it hard living with her parents. When Michael went missing Windyridge was a refuge. A year on she feels different. She's twenty-four, for God's sake, with a mind of her own, and unused to spending her days among *old* people, especially old people who presume to order her about. Oh, Mummy's all right, but he, Ernest, Daddy, is a nightmare. He objects to the length of her phone calls. He objects to the 'County' types who sometimes visit (the wives of squadron leaders she got to know at Boulder Dyke and Upper Heyford). He objects to her painting her nails red, toes as well as fingers, which to him 'means only one thing' (well-manicured nails, fine; slightly tinged nails, maybe; but flaming red nails – NO!). Most of all he objects to how she's bringing up baby.

After years without a child in the house, Ernest finds Kela a shock. At first he makes gruff jokes about joining the RAF to get some sleep, or about 'persuading baby to become a herbivore' so as to keep the lawn trim. But soon he's drooling with delight. 'Baby is a perfect rascal,' he tells Arthur, 'misses nothing, can wangle anything out of us, likes reading (though the words may be upside down, and she prefers my colliery *Guardian*, full of adverts, to any of her own books), requires only to be shown a thing once, and is becoming more like Grandpa every day. She is boss of the house already and in another week or two will be riding your motorbike.' Who's boss is more vexed an issue than this suggests. Mary thinks it should be her. She has read the latest manual by Truby King, which says that mothers must crack down. Strict four-hourly feeds, leaving the baby to cry itself to sleep, and no picking up even during tantrums – that's the Truby message (anything less rigorous, and the baby will laugh at your gullibility). Ernest dismisses this as 'tripe' and 'Red Tape Book Rot', preferring a more flexible system: 'I didn't know that newly born babies were expected to be mechanised on behalf of the war effort.' Kathleen, he feels sure, secretly agrees with him, but pretends to side with Mary and tells him to mind his own business, etc, which needless to say he does during the night. Given Kathleen's black looks and Mary's nervy state, he keeps his mouth shut as best he can. Even so, they find him too interfering by half. He may be out at work all day, but his soppiness when he is there – his 'poor wee mite' this, and 'poor little thing' that – drives Mary up the wall and (as she sees it) undoes all her careful discipline.

The rows rumble on for fifteen months. The last of them is sparked by Ernest saying, in reference to Kela being in a playpen (another new-fangled idea), 'You wouldn't bring a dog up like that.' If he thinks so little of her mothering, Mary storms back, then it's time she moved out. Let her try managing without the free childcare she gets at Windyridge, snarls Ernest. Now now, says Kathleen. In fact Mary has been talking about moving for some months – 'Every woman must have a home of her own,' she believes – and the row is the push she needs to start looking. To rent somewhere is the plan. But suitable places are hard to find. Ernest, guilty at pushing her out and unable to resist taking over, comes up with an alternative to renting. On Moorside Road, near the golf links, stands an empty bungalow, a 'lodge', with a large portion of land alongside. It's in rotten condition, but could be made comfortable – and there's room for a pair of semis if they sell off the adjoining land. He reveals his plan to Arthur, stressing the financial benefits to the family as a whole: 'The bungalow will cost £630 including legal fees, and the work on it will cost £250, so you can say it has cost £900 in all. I have no doubt I could sell it for £1,000 or even £1,200 and still retain some of the land, so I am not worried in the least if Mary doesn't want it.'

Stuck in a tent as he is, Arthur feels peculiar about his younger sister having a house. His reply precipitates another row, by referring to Mary as 'spoilt'. The reference is meant for his parents' eyes only, but Mary, sitting next to Kathleen at breakfast, catches sight of her name, reads the offending sentence and hits the roof. Soon letters are winging back to the Azores. Ernest tells Arthur he should have more sense than to refer to female perversity in a letter. Ron tells him that, 'stuck out there', he has forgotten how difficult his father is. Mary simply tells him where to get off: 'You seem to be getting a very low opinion of me since you've been away. First there was your bloody nasty attack when I saw you last and which I've not forgotten. And now you say I don't appreciate what Daddy is doing for me. Well, chum, I've taken quite a lot from you over the years and said nothing, but I don't promise it shall continue.'

The aftershocks reach Kim in Birmingham, as Arthur and Mary vie for her support. She plays the pacifier, as always, the Irish neutral, and in time both of them cool down. But the volatility of the Morrisons never ceases to surprise her – and still surprises me fifty years later. My childhood home was quiet, because everyone gave into my father, but at Windyridge rowing was the house-rule. They even fell out over Noël Coward. 'A clever man and knows it,' sneered Ernest, who had seen him in *Play Parade* in Manchester. A conchie and a nancy boy, growled Arthur, who found nothing funny or ironic in the song 'Don't Let's be Beastly to the Germans' – and if ever he got to meet Coward would be happy to greet him with two lovely black eyes. Whereas Mary leapt to Coward's defence, citing all those concerts he gave for troops and mill-workers: 'No matter what people say about him, his every thought is for Britain and our fighting men.' Coward was hardly the populist Mary suggests, but the case for and against him isn't the point. What's striking is how claustrophobic the Morrisons are: on each other's backs, in each other's pockets, too close by half.

It's something my mother begins to grasp round about now: that if she marries Arthur, she will be marrying the rest of them. Of course they'll forever regard her as an outsider, because she's not blood, but that won't stop them entangling her in their feuds and dramas. The O'Sheas have a different model: strong on kinship but less possessive, the family scattered far from Killorglin. For them, going away is a natural part of growing up. But at Windyridge, the sons and daughters aren't ever allowed to leave. Look at Mary, unable to bring up baby as she'd choose. Look at Arthur, 1300 miles away in the Azores yet fully participant in family rows. Is this what she wants for herself? Is this what she wants for her children? Is this what Arthur thinks a home should be?

✻   ✻   ✻

*Kim to Arthur, Dudley Road, Birmingham, 2.6.44*

Had the strangest feeling last night that you weren't very far away – wouldn't have been surprised if you'd walked straight into the room.

HER PREMONITION ISN'T far wrong. In mid-June, without warning, he comes home – because of a crisis at his base. It begins with an epidemic of gastro-enteritis, attributed to poor water, hot weather, swarms of flies, and the farming methods of local peasants (who use human faeces as manure). Then comes a major panic. Late at night, on the 13th, Mac admits a coryza, a case of catarrhal inflammation, and the poor lad wakes next morning with 'bilateral complete upper limb paralysis: polio'. 'We started oxygen inflation at 3.30,' Arthur tells Kim,

and loaded him aboard a plane at 7.30pm, with Mac having to turn the tap on the oxygen bottles every 20 seconds: goodness knows if he'll make the journey. We've isolated SSQ and hospital, taken over new quarters for other patients and are trying to organise bedding. Every sore throat is damn near getting lumbar punctures. I can think of one bloke who wouldn't mind being in Mac's place and is almost hoping there'll be another case tomorrow. In fact, he's about to do a lumbar puncture on another dubious case (neck rigidity), so perhaps his turn will come.

It did. The official medical history of the Second World War records that, in the absence of an iron lung, 11 cases of acute anterior poliomyelitis, 4 of whom die en route, were evacuated to the UK from Lagens between 14 June and 20 June. (In all there were 20 cases and 9 deaths.) Arthur was the second doctor-escort to fly back, on the morning of Saturday the 17th. On the Sunday, his rescue mission a failure (like Mac's, his patient dies en route), he phones Kim from Newquay. She is given time off, passionate leave, from Monday to Wednesday. They meet midway, at Swindon station, then travel north together to see his parents. He has brought her a watch, but not a ring. Their 'three perfect days' are spoilt only by a mix-up on the Wednesday night, when he phones to say goodbye from Newquay and the staff at Dudley Road fail to locate her, despite her having left careful instructions. Afterwards, he has nightmares about neck rigidity. His worry is that he has contracted polio, or passed on the infection to her: 'I remember an MO going to see his wife in hospital two days after her tonsillectomy – he gave her one kiss and she died of bulbar paralysis 24 hours later. Oh darling I hope you're all right.' She is all right. The only after-effect of their meeting is love, there again in all its pain and excitement.

At Windyridge, Ernest understands for the first time about Arthur and Kim. When she was working nearby at Hope their spending so much time together seemed innocuous. But to bring her up from Birmingham with him when he's home so briefly – things between them must be getting serious. To Ernest this is very worrying. Oh, he likes Kim well enough as a person. But should the question of marriage arise, there's her Irishness to think of as well as her lack of good connections (and money). What's her family like? He hasn't a clue. But at a guess not his kind of people. And then there's the other thing. He isn't sure, but he suspects. Next time they're together he must have it out. And if need be nip the relationship in the bud.

*It.* I've been avoiding broaching the issue. But *it* now threatens to come between them. It's the *difficulty* he glancingly refers to in that unsent letter of September 1943, when he says 'what an hell of a lot of difficulty it would mean if you did decide to love me'. And it's the *things* that make her say, in February 1944, 'I could be perfectly happy with you – if things were different.' In all love stories, there's an impediment. What's the impediment here? Till now, I haven't faced the matter, because they didn't. But hereafter, it's mentioned almost every time they write. Time to address what *it* is.

# CHAPTER SEVEN

# Once a Catholic

*Kim to Arthur, Carshalton, 22.3.44*

Went down to breakfast this morning to find FIVE letters from you. They were marvellous – except for one bit, which made my blood boil. You know the bit. You always imply that RCs are uneducated people (and vice versa). Please remember that I am one.

Anything else in the world I could give up willingly for you. But can't you see how much it means? Can't you just get used to the idea of my being what I am?

*Arthur to Kim, Azores, 29.3.44*

Now let's be quite clear on this. What I said about the natives here was:

1) they get a very strict religious education

2) they get no other education

3) a purely religious education does not enable them to fend for themselves among modern civilised peoples.

To me, being religious means striving to improve the world and the lot of every single individual in it. I'm not asking you to be an atheist. I'm just asking you to accept that certain teachings of the RC church, excellent though they may have been a few hundred years ago, no longer apply among happy healthy humans of today. Oh darling I do love you, you know. I hate having to try to teach you to learn my beliefs. I want you to reason them out for yourself, and to see that what it means to be one of God's servants is very different from what it means to be an RC. It is difficult to explain but please remember I am a truly religious individual too.

Rather strange but about a week ago I got talking to an Irish lad (one of my corporals) who was an RC – he used to be a true one and to practise the safe period, too. But he said the more he saw of the world the more he despised the over-ruling control the church had. He has travelled a lot and has been horrified at the power the church has over the people of these islands – poor uneducated slaves, whose teachers are the wealthy ruling minority who pay 1/- per week per man whilst trading for large sums with other countries.

Please don't think I've been going round talking about this subject to everybody, but it does worry me. God didn't put you on this earth to be miserable. He didn't give you sexual desire to be curbed irrationally. He didn't mean you to bring so many children into the world that you couldn't give them decent protection, food and education (you yourself must have seen the misery in slum districts caused to a large degree by the absence of contraception). He didn't intend you to educate your children in one set of opinions alone (if he had, there wouldn't have been more than one church). It hurts me to keep this sore open but I can't do otherwise, or I may lose you.

A S A CHILD, I didn't know about my mother's religion. The village church was C of E and though my parents, as the local GPs, were expected to attend, neither of them did. It surprised them when, around the age of nine, I asked could I join the village choir – not out of religious zeal, but as a way of getting to see my mates at weekends. They were resistant, my father atheistically (he thought church 'a waste of time', and worried that my going would 'bugger up Sundays'), my mother for more obscure reasons and mainly (I thought) out of solidarity with him. In the end they gave in. I was given a cassock and surplice, and – like some Mellstock rustic – stood in the choir-stalls with my friends. On special occasions my mother turned up to hear me sing. It was more than my father did, but hardly evidence of spiritual longing. Easter, harvest festival, the Christmas carol service – she showed no itch for more, nor any emotion beyond maternal pride. Worship was for kids. She had put it behind her. There were better ways of spending Sunday.

I learned the truth only because of her sister Sheila, who

when she stayed during school holidays caught a bus to Colne, six miles away, every Sunday morning.

'Where's Auntie Sheila going?' I asked.

'To church.'

'Why can't she go to Thornton church?'

'Because the church she belongs to is different.'

'Different how?'

'It's another religion.'

'Which?'

'Roman Catholic.'

But if Sheila was Catholic, I later worked out, then my mother must be too – or must have been once. She didn't deny it when I asked. But she didn't want to talk about it, either. Like her name, like her accent, like her origins, like the number of her siblings, she preferred to let it go.

More than letting it go, she was active in concealing it – as I discovered when I came to write a book about my father. It was a book that described his final illness and also mentioned his relationship with Beaty. Apprehensive about hurting her, I gave my mother the first draft, promising myself that if she didn't like it I would put it away in a drawer. In the event, she objected to very little, but asked me to remove one detail about her: the fact she'd been brought up a Catholic. There were friends and neighbours she hadn't told, she said, and they might be shocked. I doubted this but didn't want to upset her. The reference came out.

\*     \*     \*

*Kim to Arthur, Birmingham, 14.4.44*

I know that one can be good and religious without being an RC. But I just can't understand any RC chucking everything away. If you knew how miserable it makes me to think of it you'd stop asking. I can't imagine life without you, darling, and yet I wonder what's going to happen. I can hear you saying, 'Well, it's up to you.' But I think sometimes, 'No, why can't he give in?' I could be such a different person if I knew for sure I was going to marry you.

*Arthur to Kim, Azores, 24.4.44*

All I can really say is:

1: You won't marry me in a C of E church, and I won't marry you in an RC church. It will have to be a Registry Office. Pity because we both want a church wedding but there it is.

2: Our children can be what they like after the age of 21, but they are at no time to receive any biased religious teaching from either of us – at NO time. We'll give them a general outline but they are not to go to any church until they are at least 12 or 13 – probably older. That's the only way round the trouble.

3: We want two boys and a girl, don't we? We're not going to have any more, though, and we're not going to impose any nervous strain on them by suppressing their natural instincts. We must agree on that.

THOUGH I KNEW about my mother's religion, it wasn't until she died that I saw how deep its influence had been. The morning after her death I ransacked her wardrobe, in search of God knows what. 'She may have put the will there,' I told my sister, and half-believed it. Unlocking it seemed a transgression all the same: the intimacy of scent as I clicked the door open, the bric-a-brac facing me when I swung it wide. To the left hung coats and dresses; on the right were wooden drawers. She'd lost most of her jewellery to burglars years before. There were no valuables left, only these infinitely precious bits and bobs: scarves, tights, kirbygrips, unworn earrings, empty buds on silver rings from which the stones had slipped, a lady's face in an oval brooch. In one of the drawers I found her make-up. There was make-up on the dressing table as well, but the main supplies were here: the lipsticks, facecreams, mascara brushes, powder puffs and false eyelashes she used to make herself beautiful or someone else. Dazed and elegiac, I forgot all pretence of being businesslike, and ran my hands through her hangers and drawers.

I knew that wardrobe. Many times as a child I'd climbed

inside and pulled the door shut, breathing its sweet maternal air. But high up, in a plastic bag, lay something I'd not seen before: a plait of auburn hair, eighteen inches long. At her boarding school in Killarney, so she told my sister, she'd let her hair grow down to her waist. We had no photographs but here was the evidence. Snipping the plait must have been a rite of passage, an entry to adulthood, a literal cutting off. Had she lopped it in her last years at school? Or did the university forbid women medical students from wearing hair that long? It had gone, whichever, but she had hung on to it, like an old self she could inspect in secret. Now I hung on to it too, as if by doing so I might hang on to her, or, better still, be put in touch with the girl she'd been, who spoke in a different accent and went by another name and religion.

On the shelf where I found it lay something else: a package of slippery green paper, neatly tied. There was an address label, half torn off, and a postmark, 21 May 1948. Inside, three items: a brown crocodile purse; a green pamphlet of Rosary Novenas to Our Lady, printed in New York in 1925; and a small, black, leather-bound book with a sixteen-year-old's hand-writing on an inside page, 'Agnes O'Shea, Loreto Convent, Killarney, 2 June 1933'. The book was a prayer-book or rule-book, I wasn't sure which: the Manual of the Children of Mary of Loreto Abbey. As I flicked through, several cards fell out, with prayers to assorted female saints and '300 days' or '100 days' written underneath or on the back – indulgences to win the obedient an extra lease of life. In size and texture, the cards were like the slips we used to get when placing bets at the Gisburn point-to-point races. Two of the cards depicted St Agnes. Another had been made 'in loving memory' of my mother's brother Peter, who had died of peritonitis in 1931.

I put the book down and unzipped the purse, releasing a waft of incense. Inside were a string of rosary beads, a plastic Christ splayed on a wooden cross, two silver medallions with the Virgin enovalled in swirling robes ('O Mary conceived without sin, pray for us who have recourse to thee'), and a fragment of green cloth showing Mary on one side and a heart with a sword

Sancta Agnes, ora pro nobis!

through it on the other. The cloth came with a piece of paper explaining what it was: a Green Scapular. Anyone wearing it who said this prayer – 'Immaculate Heart of Mary, pray for us now and at the hour of our death' – would be miraculously healed. Many a leper, cancer-sufferer, haemorrhaging woman and incurable man had been saved by the Green Scapular. All you had to do was take Mary into your heart.

Had my mother taken Mary into her heart? If so, she never let on. But for a moment I was out the other side of that wardrobe and back inside the childhood of her faith. A row of Loreto girls in navy uniforms and white blouses; nuns giving them lessons in Science and French; the May altar decorated with wild flowers in honour of Our Lady; the soot-black spot dabbed on foreheads each Ash Wednesday; the house in Langford Street open to all comers, taking its turn as one of the Stations of the Cross. An Irish Catholic girlhood, that was all. Ordinary enough, but not to me, who found it both enchanting and faintly repellent. Why hadn't I seen all this before? It was an old story:

someone goes, and too late – much much too late – you discover where they came from. Did my mother have to die before I started getting to know her? I zipped up the purse, folded it with the book and pamphlet in the green paper, returned the package to its shelf, and closed the wardrobe door.

✳   ✳   ✳

*Arthur to Kim, Azores, 25.4.44*

The trouble with RCs is that they place religion and everyday life in two completely separate cubby-holes in their minds. They do this because they're brought up to believe that questioning in any way the teaching of the RC church is sacrilegious.

I know how miserable you must feel, having been married to the RC religion for so long. And you will want to be miserable (having married me) during the first few months of your divorce. But I know you will be perfectly happy after 12 months.

*Kim to Arthur, Birmingham, 2.5.44*

Afraid I can't agree with you that RCs place religion and everyday life in separate compartments. To RCs religion is part of everyday life. When I start on this subject with you, I feel utterly miserable and say to myself 'Oh what's the use?' We'll never agree, will we? What's going to happen, I wonder.


DESPITE THE MARIOLATRY in my mother's wardrobe, it didn't occur to me to hold her funeral in a Catholic church. The local vicar was fond of her: they'd often shared gossip and theology, and he was keen to do the service. In his address he spoke of her 'deep sense of the spiritual', and how for years, to judge from the conversations they'd had, 'her faith had been underplayed'. How apt, he added, that her funeral should fall on the Feast of Mary Magdalen, 'an unusual saint', since my mother had also been unusual, 'an Irish Roman Catholic steeped in the

168

faith of that corner of southern Ireland who encountered events in the course of her work which gave a different shape to the Christianity of her childhood'. He'd guessed, or she'd confessed, or someone had gossiped. It wasn't a secret kept from him. The service was moving, everyone said. Afterwards I had misgivings nonetheless. She'd been seen off on Anglican ground, with no priest at the nursing home to say last rites – had we failed to do right by her? (And the nursing home she'd died in *would* have to be called Cromwell's, after the greatest anti-Catholic of them all.) I rang Beaty, who I remembered was Catholic too. As a child I hadn't realised this, being too conscious of her other denomination in our house – the 'Auntie' who was a mistress. As an adult I'd become aware that there was more to her. She may once have been a rival but my mother came to see her as a trusted friend. Now as an orphan I needed her spiritual guidance.

'Your mum often spoke to me about dying,' she said, trying to reassure. 'I don't think she was worried about last rites. Though I noticed she came back to her religion after your dad died.'

'How do you mean?'

'When she was worried about someone's health, or upset on her own account, she'd phone me and ask would I say my rosary. And if someone died, she'd get me to have a mass said for them, and send money – a fiver or tenner. Sometimes, she'd make me say a Hail Mary with her, too. But if ever I asked her to say a prayer in return, she'd laugh and say: "But why would God listen to me?"'

I was intrigued by their religious intimacy (intrigued too that, despite his prejudices, the two women my father loved had both been Catholic). Saying Hail Marys with her relations would have faced my mother with the origins she'd lapsed from. Beaty was different: easy, understanding, and – like her – a martyr to my father's love.

'When did Mum first tell you she was Catholic?' I asked.

'Oh, I knew more or less from the start. It was after I'd met her one time with her brother Joe or sister Sheila. I asked her straight out. She didn't answer. Just inhaled a cigarette and said: "Do you really believe in all that nonsense?" But she didn't deny it. Takes one to know one, I suppose. She used to tease me: "How can you stand all that twaddle?" But I can, I do, it gives me strength.'

So Catholicism was 'twaddle' and 'nonsense'? There spoke a sceptic rationalist, a mid-twentieth-century doctor, the agnostic created by Arthur. It was the side of her I knew, too: I remember her saying, sardonically, after Auntie Sheila died suddenly in Tralee (where she'd retired after a lifetime teaching in England), that what had caused it was 'over-excitement at the Pope visiting Ireland for the first time'. The secular cynic. But Beaty had come to know another side – Agnes rather than Kim. The name might have been dropped but the identity wasn't so easily broken with. 'Names have more significance for Catholics than they do for other people,' writes Mary McCarthy, in *Memories of a Catholic Girlhood*. 'The saint a child is named for is supposed to serve, literally, as a model or pattern to imitate; your name is your fortune and it tells you what you are or must be.' Agnes told my mother to be lamb-like and pious; Kim let her skip confession and smoke cigarettes. Yet she missed the old patterns and couldn't wholly shed her beliefs. So she'd told Beaty, and now Beaty, over the phone, was telling me: 'I say my rosary every night, the five decades. I'll never lose my faith. I don't think your mum lost hers, either.'

The letters, when I read them, were a shock, nonetheless. Protestant versus Catholic: to me, that versus was the stuff of historical textbooks. Or a versus for cultures other than the one I'd been raised in – for the people of Belfast and the six counties, for Celtic and Rangers supporters, but not for our family, not for my Mum and Dad. I hadn't realised how large religion loomed in her life. Now I'd found her at last. Or had I lost her more irretrievably than before?

*      *      *

*Arthur to Kim, Azores, 25.4.44*

How will it work? I can't honestly say, darling. We really love each other – there is no doubt about that. We'll have lots of rows in any case, even if religion will undoubtedly increase the number. How blind an eye I'll be able to turn to the weekly demonstration of faith I don't know. But you should go to church occasionally if only to give yourself an uplift when you're feeling low. And I think I can safely say I'm a fairly broad-minded individual. Some of my best pals have stolen things. I've slept in the same bed as a person with syphilis, and another friend has gonorrhoea. All had a relapse for a few hours from rational behaviour. It isn't how I live but I've never held it against them.

I feel very sorry I ever made you love me in some ways, that I'm responsible for turning your whole world topsy-turvy. You are such a beautiful, sweet, straightforward little girl and you have had the whole world crumble round you. I wish you had run away with another man or something so that you were happy and that I could take all the worry on my shoulders. I have had so many upsets during the past two years that I feel I can put up with almost anything. I am absolutely certain I can make you the happiest girl in the world but I don't know how to do it. If I could marry you tomorrow and we could go into a place miles away from civilisation – the middle of Africa, or more practicably the Shetlands – then I'm positive you would understand it (and prefer it) my way. If we could at the same time run a country practice and have children, I'm sure we'd be happy. But our happiness has to be found on this earth. We cannot live in an ideal little world of our own – we are very small cogs in a very big wheel but we have got to help that wheel turn in the right direction.

Had a 10-mile walk today along the cliffs with an Irish orderly called Hollywood – quite a gentlemanly type. We tried bathing at a couple of places, but it wasn't possible. He is an RC and, as you might imagine, we got into a discussion of religion. He not merely agreed with my views, but propounded theories similar to my own – without any prompting.

After dinner, at the bar, I got into a very involved discussion with some other chaps on the glycogen breakdown theory related to diabetes – then anaesthetics – then Darwinism and religion – and how wrong the RC religion is in the present world. Again I didn't start or even enter into the religion issue. But you see I'm not a crank. One of the boys tonight said: 'My sister is an RC – brought up in a convent – had it drilled into her – she can't face a reasonable discussion – just carries on in blind faith.' Don't you see, darling, Hitlerism has some fine principles, too. So has the C of E (which is 90 per cent identical to RC). But 'physical manifestions' such as eating bread and drinking wine at communion ruin these principles.

If I could ignore religion, I would turn RC and marry you tomorrow – and be a hypocrite like so many others (not you). All I want you to do is reason out those principles upon which we differ and realise where they are wrong. Then you can do what I do when I write down my religion: I put C of E (you can put RC) because I can't say 'atheist' (I'm not one and anyway it's not allowed) and I can't say 'Modern religion' because no one has yet initiated it even though 99 per cent of people I know practise it.

Don't apologise for your letters being depressing. I want to hear what you are thinking. It stimulates me to try to convince you. If I didn't have such faith in you I'd have given up the struggle long since.

I wish you were here so I could have my arms around you all night and talk to you. I wish I could practise mental telepathy. Please don't get upset by this letter. And promise me now you'll never do anything crazy because if you did I would have to follow suit, even tho we'd both then be stupid cowards. See how worried you've got me. Goodnight.

(Just counted – 25 pages in this letter)

*Kim to Arthur, Birmingham, 10.5.44*

Don't know how I expected you to answer my letters, but not the way you did. Don't think I'm disappointed, darling, they are marvellous letters. But I do think the only way it will work is by my giving up being an RC, and I know I couldn't do that. You say you have faith in me, and I have faith in you, but things just can't work out the way

you think they will, darling. I begin to feel such a fraud. You say you
know I can do this for you when I know I can't. It sounds easy, but
I really think that only RCs realise what being an RC means. If you
wrote to me and said 'All right, if you can't give it up, that's that', I
know how utterly miserable I'd be. You talk so naturally about being
married and what a marvellous future we'll have. Somehow I just
can't convince you can I? But I must go on trying to tell you how I
feel, even if it makes my letters morbid. What's the use of writing
cheerful letters for 12 months and then telling you when you come
home?

Darling, do you honestly think you won't marry me unless I give
up my religion? Please tell me.

Being in love isn't all fun, is it?

*Arthur to Kim, Azores, 15.5.44*

If the thing was not of such importance to me and my children and
millions of other children not yet born I would ignore it and marry
you tomorrow as you are. But the future will have to bring some very
great changes on this earth – that's why I criticise old-fashioned,
bigoted, narrow-minded views.

*Kim to Arthur, Birmingham, 19.5.44*

I should have known you better than to think you would change
your mind about anything. Don't think I can't appreciate your point
of view: if I weren't an RC I'd probably feel the same way. But I can't
honestly say I'm sorry I am one. The only comparison I can think of
with something that means as much to you is your family. If I said
I'd marry you only if you had nothing more to do with your family,
I'm sure you wouldn't do it. Suddenly saw last night that if we
did marry all your friends would have the same views as you and
gradually you'd become very conscious of my religion and would
eventually hate me for it . . .

I think I know deep down that we'll never be married now. But
you mustn't blame yourself. People can't help falling in love, can
they? I often think the best thing to do would be to hop off back to

Ireland and forget about you. But even the first part wouldn't be easy – and the second impossible.

THEIR LETTERS SAY a lot about them. *Le style, c'est l'homme (et la femme)*. He hopes to wear her down, or to a frazzle. Says he has faith in her. Feels sure that by debating with her, he'll persuade her of the flawless logic of his position (*her* position being mere emotion and superstition). Threatens, failing that, to practise mental telepathy, or mind-control, to win her over. Believes in the absolute rightness of what he says. And feels stimulated by trying to bring her round. In other respects his confidence has been dented: friends have died, he feels to be falling behind in his career. But his faith in his faith is unwavering. What is that faith? In one letter he presents himself as a trembling worshipper, a 'truly religious individual', never so earnest as when alone in church ('I know I am far more sincere and deeply engrossed when I go into an empty church where no one can interrupt my thoughts – no talking or singing to prevent me getting near to God'). In truth, he is humanist and secular, and would describe himself as an atheist if he dared. Later, he did dare, but for now he's scared of scaring her off (difficult enough to win her over to his notional, undevotional Protestantism, impossible if he admitted he had no faith in God at all). I'm being unfair. He does believe in God, a Lawrentian God (he has been reading *Lady Chatterley's Lover*) who wants to save the world from repression. He even claims to have a hotline to this God and to know what his wishes are ('God is our friend – and wants us to be happy'). As a true servant, he is obliged to point out Kim's impiety. She is abasing herself before the wrong icons. Her fellow-worshippers are primitive and uneducated. It is time she altered her ways.

Her letters are briefer and more tentative. While he enjoys the argument, she feels battered by it and would like to have done. It's 'hopeless' she says, over and over: no future, no solution, no way out. To her, faith can't be debated or articulated. There are no words to explain why she believes, she just does. Her whole identity is at stake here: RC is me. She explains it to him in the only way he can understand: to surrender her religion would be like him never seeing his family again. Even this doesn't budge him. His intransigence leaves her weeping in pain and frustration. Why should *she* be the one to compromise? His jibes against her faith wound her deeply. He even attacks the Catholic propensity for large families, suggesting that the children of such families are denied proper care and attention. That he can make such a crack suggests she hasn't told him how many children she is one of, which would fit with her general reticence about home. 'Do you realise,' he accuses her, 'I've known you for nearly two years and I've met only one sister of yours and don't even know your home address?' A good thing he doesn't know everything, perhaps. Just as he overplays his religiosity in order to win her, so she underplays the size of her family in order not to lose him.

More than once she weeps with frustration. It makes it worse that Arthur's so ill-informed. What are the Stations to him but places where trains come in? What's Mass but something in physics? The holy trinity, the light of God, the mystery of the Virgin – to him they're airy mysteries, to her a way of life. When she prays to 'our Queen and Mother', she means Mary not Elizabeth, the Madonna not the wife of George VI. Peasant nonsense, says Arthur. But she eats the wafer and sips the wine, and feels better for it: that's no illusion. The hard instruments she uses in her work – the glass tube of mercury pushed under the tongue, the stethoscope's cold membrane laid on the chest, the rubber bulb of a blood pressure gauge – are enough to drive the spiritual out of anyone. But to her religion and medicine are parallel activities. Wasn't she taught in church 'Your priest is the doctor of your soul – show him your wounds so they may be healed'? Didn't the retreat she went on back in 1933 insist on 'Personal Holiness and Active Catholicity'. Once a week she needs a space to recognise the numinous, a rite to prove that life is more than ward-rounds. Arthur's trying to deny her that, to wrench her from her own being. Well, he can't. She isn't having it. Anything else she'll do for him but not that.

It's not as if she's asking him to convert. She only wants him to go through the formalities. Once they're married, she'll not expect him to enter a Catholic church again. If he loves her, why can't he do this for her? What does his love amount to, if he won't grant her this one thing? Their affair almost faltered early on, for lack of passion. Now there's passion in abundance, but also *it*. And *it* can't be defeated without one of them giving in.

Their battle is not fought out alone. Both of them have allies, and look to those allies for support. Handily for Arthur, the Azores seem to be full of lapsed Catholics, mostly Irish, who, unprompted, articulate views exactly like his. Kim, unimpressed, calls on her own battalions – her brother Patrick, brother-in-law Gerry, sister-in-law Ruth, and sisters Eileen and Kitty ('Have been talking to Kitty about it, who before I said anything said "Well, it should be all right if the kids are R.C." I had to explain to her. Naturally she is on my side'). She also cites her boss at Dudley Road, Wentworth Taylor, 'Irish but not RC', who on her first day 'did a hysterectomy on an RC which he thought I would rather not assist at. Very decent of him: can't you see, darling, it is easy to appreciate other people's principles and not let them interfere with you?' She is over-simplifying, of course: soon enough her duties at Dudley Road involve her performing abortions, and these she carries out unprotestingly, knowing it would be awkward to refuse. Even with abortions, she's willing to compromise. So why can't he compromise, in relation to marriage? And why's he so stubborn about their putative children? According to him, any they have will not be permitted to enter a church till 12 or 13. Later he raises the stakes and says he 'won't allow them to go into any RC church until they are 21, and I want a sincere promise from you that you will never try to influence them in any way.' His obstinacy about this, years ahead of them becoming parents, seems remarkable. She must have wondered whether marriage would be worth it, with him on the lookout for secret indoctrination and the children lined up for daily interrogation ('And when did you last see your mother cross herself?').

What makes me wince even more than his obstinacy is his

condescension. He had a habit, later, of presenting her to the world as his vulnerable other half – her body the frailler (though he would die before her), her mind the more subject to worry and distress. This was him being gallant and old-fashioned, solicitous as men of his generation were supposed to be. But in these letters he's simply patronising: she is a 'sweet, straight-forward little girl', a 'very lonely little girl' whose world he has turned topsy-turvy, and other yuk besides. Is she being belittled as a woman or as a Catholic? Perhaps both. His contempt for weak and credulous Catholics is rehearsed at some length: in that vast letter of 25 April, he goes so far as to equate Catholicism with syphilis, presenting them both as diseases consequent upon a lapse from reason. He also implies a loving contempt for the opposite sex, who may try to act tough and rational but whose woozy emotionalism always wins out. It's a view that prevailed in middle-class English homes of the time. Women, it was agreed, were incapable of rational argument. A man's job was to cure them of their affliction. So Arthur set about healing Kim.

'I've done nearly all the reasoning,' he says, 'now it's your turn. Let's have some tabulated facts and deal with them as we would with a patient. Let's do a blood count and find out what the score is. Let's diagnose sensibly and rationally.' Briskly pragmatic, he plans to banish her Catholic illogic. To de-programme her. And to batter her with facts facts facts.

☆　　☆　　☆

*Arthur to Kim, Azores, 23.9.44*

Hitler has supposedly been offered shelter in the Vatican. No comment.

*Kim to Arthur, Birmingham, 24.10.44*

I see Hitler has now turned his attention to the RCs – has killed hundreds of civilians and priests. Probably some people will think it's a good thing. Seemingly this has been going on in Germany for the past two weeks, and the Nazis now blame the RCs for all their misfortune. So I don't believe what you said about Hitler being offered shelter in the Vatican – nonsense.

THE WAR BEING fought at large is drawn into their smaller one. While bombs fall on London and Dresden, while the Allies take the Normandy beaches, while the German army withdraws from Paris and Rome, Arthur and Kim clash swords and icons. The Pope's a Nazi in disguise, says my father, having heard it on good authority over a pint. Rubbish, she replies, the swastika wants to obliterate the cross.

History suggests that neither got it quite right. Before becoming Pope Pius XII in 1939, Eugenio Pacelli had brokered a deal with Hitler, the Reich Concordat, agreeing to surrender the political rights of German Catholics in exchange for strengthening the Catholic church there. To that extent, there was a Nazi–Vatican alliance, and Pacelli effectively silenced Catholic opponents of National Socialism in Germany. Neither the Night of the Long Knives (when prominent Catholics were among the 85 'enemies' whom Hitler massacred) nor the invasion of Poland (a largely Catholic nation) prompted a word of protest from the Holy See. Worse, Pacelli raised no voice against Hitler's persecution of Jews, even when made aware of the Final Solution. For years after the war, historians defended Pacelli: his duty had been to stay neutral, they argued. But new evidence uncovered by John Cornwell in his book *Hitler's Pope* suggests the Vicar of Christ was culpable – and something of an anti-semite himself.

To that extent my father (not yet my father) is right: metaphorically, the Vatican was a shelter to Hitler, and the Pope his pawn and dupe. But my mother (not yet my mother) is right to refute the claim that Hitler, when he began to lose the war, was literally offered refuge by Pacelli. Nor, as she says, was the Führer a friend to Catholics. Though raised in the faith, he once told an SS rally that he would crush the Catholic church under his heel 'like a toad'. He also announced, in 1943: 'We'll clear out that gang of swine. Do you think the Vatican impresses me? I couldn't care less.' The Pope could and should have spoken out against Nazi atrocities. But he wasn't acting in concert with Hitler — as the Allies implicitly recognised by refraining from bombing Rome.

As war correspondents, my parents (not yet my parents) are too remote from the action to report it accurately, and too caught up in their own battles to pretend (as the Pope does) to be neutral. What's at stake is their peacetime future. Catholic *v* Protestant. Catholic *v* Agnostic. Catholic *v* Atheist. However it's framed, the argument spills over into every aspect of their life. They argue about Hitler. They argue about a film, *The Song of Bernadette* — 'well acted,' says Arthur, 'but you know what I think of the subject matter.' (The subject matter is a peasant girl having a vision of the Virgin Mary at Lourdes: 'For those who believe in God, no explanation is necessary,' goes the film's prologue. 'For those who do not believe in God, no explanation is possible.') Most fiercely of all, they argue about a bestselling novel, Howard Spring's *My Son My Son*, first published as *O Absalom!* in 1938. Arthur reads it in his tent. Kim remembers reading it in Ireland and says that she found one part of it offensive. Was the offending passage near the beginning, Arthur asks, when Bill, the Mancunian narrator, and his first wife Nellie (whose background is Nonconformist) visit Dermot and his wife Sheila, who are Catholic and Irish Nationalist? No, she says, that wasn't it, but a passage of a sexual nature 'which seemed to me unnecessary to the story'. He's still baffled. 'I can't think which bit was bad in that respect. When Maeve slept with Oliver or when Bill slept with Livia?' Isn't she being rather narrow-minded, he asks? The suggestion enrages her. 'I've been waiting to write to you all day until I cooled down a little. I read the book when I was about 17 and my morals were probably better then. But I've read other books with that sort of thing and they've never bothered me.' Abashed, Arthur backs down: 'I don't think you are narrow-minded (I can say things to you I'd never dream of saying to anyone), except in one respect and you know what that is.'

He means religion, but sex *is* part of it, too. The description of Bill going to bed with Livia is risqué by the standards of the time ('She thrust my hand under the loose jumper to the warm flesh of her straining breasts. She pressed herself against me, limb to limb, each limb alive and passionate . . .'). Arthur finds it rather sexy. Kim objects because the sex is happening outside marriage – whatever her own conduct ('who am I to criticise others' doings?'), she regards pre- or extra-marital activity as a sin. Sex within marriage divides them, too, because of the issue of birth control. He disparages the safe period; she won't countenance contraceptives. Deeper still is the issue of physical intimacy. He has been thinking of having some matching pyjamas made up for him and his would-be bride, he says, but then 'Throne said I was a fool because when you've been married a fortnight you never wear anything'. An appealing prospect, he says. It 'certainly won't apply to us,' she replies. 'Not a natter, just letting you know. Otherwise it will have to be twin beds. And both being used.' The tone is teasing, but he worries how seriously she means it. Could sexual inhibition be a side-effect of her faith?

War, films, books, bed, birth control – the curse of her Catholicism tainted everything. Even The Curse itself.

✳   ✳   ✳

*Kim to Arthur, Birmingham, 4.4.44*

Before coming, saw Maurice and Peg in Belsize. After lunch and cocktails, Maurice went golfing while Peg and I just sat. That was all I wanted to do as I wasn't feeling my brightest – curse. (It's a month since I was in Cornwall.)

*Arthur to Kim, Azores, 16.4.44*

Wondered how the censor would feel about the 'curse' bit in your letter. 'A month since I was in Cornwall' rather gave the impression that I might be worried. Actually it wasn't censored, but . . . I'm damn glad I'm not a woman.

*Arthur to Kim, Azores, 19.10.44*

Just got your letters. What can I say I haven't said already? I just hope and pray that by repetition I will convince you.

Incidentally, you mention having your curse on the 15th, after you'd written that miserable letter on the 13th: do you realise that all your worse glooms have been closely related to that? It's quite evident in your letters.

*Kim to Arthur, Manchester, 16.11.44*

Have been putting off replying to your last letter. Didn't know what to say at first. Then in view of your remarks about the coincidence of my miserable letters and the curse, I thought I'd wait till that was over – however, it's been awkward too and still hasn't come.

*Arthur to Kim, 2.12.44*

Your letters lately seem very impersonal: don't know why. On the 18th you were rather miserable again – I don't think my theory is anything but proved – and I even add that irritability the preceding day is evident in you, too, darling, although not as marked as with some women.

As DOCTORS, THEY discuss her periods without embarrassment. In August she tells him how she 'found why I'd been so irritable the last couple of days. Fine today, but plans to go swimming with Louise have been cursed.' Another month she complains of heavy loss and that, days in, 'my curse is still going strong'. She has other phrases to describe her periods – 'sudden fit of the blues' or 'not in form, for a very good reason'. In October it's enough for her to say 'discovered why I've been feeling off colour – funny how time flies' for him to know what she's on about. 'Your letters have been much happier lately,' he observes, 'but I suppose by the time you get this you will be cursed again.' In December, he ventures 'You're getting irregular aren't you' (no, she contradicts him, not getting, she always has been), and then he adds, with something between a leer and a marriage proposal, 'I'll do something about that before we are much older.' She ignores this, but tells him about a staff nurse in Outpatients who has been asking her advice: the nurse has just started a period and is terribly worried that – horror of horrors – the next one will coincide with her wedding day in four weeks' time.

To Kim it's natural talking like this. She's in Gyny, pre-occupied with births and blood and monthly cycles, so why not? To him, it's part of the special intimacy they enjoy, and he doubts that other lovers (even other doctors who're lovers) are so candid. 'Isn't it grand to talk to each other so openly, darling?' he writes. 'From letters I've censored, I doubt whether many married couples know each other half so well as you and I do. We talk of curses, houses, nothing yet everything, for pages and pages.' Though unable to reciprocate, he does his best by keeping her in touch with his bowel movements – or by disclosing that he sometimes reads her letters while sitting on the lav. Whether she wants such detail is doubtful, but she's pleased they can confide so freely. Other aspects of her life – and her body – are closed to him. But her periods cause no such inhibition.

Did she relish talking about them because a common objection to women doctors, even after their pioneer, Elizabeth Garrett Anderson, entered the British medical register in 1866, was that menstruation (as well as physical weakness and small brain size) reduced their capacity and usefulness? Was insisting on her difference, her femaleness, a means of fighting such prejudice? Perhaps. But that's to make her sound feminist, which she wasn't. For his part, Arthur's told as much about menstruation as a man could wish to know. Unfortunately, being told only confirms his view that her periods are an unfortunate 'problem', just like her religion. Indeed, he suggests a direct link between the two – that it's when she's pre-menstrual that she feels most hopeless about their situation; that it's PMT inciting her to be more fanatically RC. How does she feel about this? Patronised or understood? Like a case-study for a quirky medical thesis of his? Or the butt of crude male prejudice (the kind he describes to her when his colleague Musgrave says, on receiving a grumpy letter from his fiancée, 'Helen must be in the middle of a curse: I shall have to live away from home one week in four')? She agrees that PMT affects her badly – 'Re the curse and "irritability all the previous day": with me, more like all the previous week' – and after one awkward exchange imagines him 'on your way back to the mess cussing women for their cussedness'. She even delays writing to him on the matter of religion until her period has started. But in this way, she also refutes his thesis. See, she's saying, even when the blood has come, I still feel the same about my religion. *In sanguine veritas.*

Her periods and her religion are a trial to him. He wants to be happy but he won't be happy till her makes her happy too. Happiness, in his eyes, means marriage, pregnancy and an end to the Catholic ritual of blood as wine.

Six years later, he temporarily stopped her monthly bleeding, or I did. The candour disappeared as well. I've no memory from childhood of menstruation being discussed: or of sanitary towels or tampons being left about the house; or of sexual education of any kind. Till they married they were (so I now see) remarkably open. But by the time I arrived, sex and fertility weren't up for discussion. Catholicism and Ireland were also off the map. All were connected in some way. But none was mentioned.

☆　☆　☆

*Arthur to Kim, Azores, 23.8.44*

What do your family know about me – anything? Perhaps you're waiting to get home before you broach the subject – am I right?

*Kim to Arthur, Birmingham, 1.9.44*

My family know nothing about you, darling, except Eileen, Sheila and Kitty – and I suppose Patrick, from Ruth. I mean Mammie and

Daddie know nothing – I told you once they wouldn't approve: I don't mean of you personally but of what you're not.

*Arthur to Kim, Azores, 23.9.44*

What have the family been saying, seeing you writing letters every day? Didn't they ask you about me?

*Kim to Arthur, Birmingham, 30.9.44*

The night before I came back from Ireland Mammie asked about us – she'd noticed your letters coming. (The mail was quite good, see – amazing, from one uncivilised country to another.) Of course the first thing she asked was if you were an RC and when I said 'No' she was worried and didn't approve. I know she would be terribly disappointed if I married you. I had a long talk to Daddie, too, but not about us, because he was ill and I didn't want to upset him. But Mammie will tell him and anyway I know he feels the same. Not that that would stop me marrying you, darling – they wouldn't want to see me any more, but I wouldn't mind that if I had you – so long as we were married in an RC church, because I wouldn't feel married if it was a registry office.

You probably think they're being a bit hard but being brought up in a Catholic country religion is very important to them. You know too that your Dad wouldn't approve and that that would worry you.


IF ONLY SHE can be honest with her parents, Arthur tells her, everything will work out. But he's wrong about that. The O'Sheas are good Catholics – her Mammie especially, who goes to Mass each day and would have liked nothing better than for one of her sons to become a priest (Paul, the youngest, actually trained for the priesthood but then, to her dismay, discovered women and ran off to join the British army). An O'Shea wed a non-Catholic? Perish the thought. None of Agnes's siblings has married out. Indeed her sister-in-law Ruth, in marrying her brother Patrick, became a Catholic convert. Fat chance of Arthur following suit. Which is why when she tells her Mammie that her boyfriend is a Prod she gets the expected response.

She could endure her parents breaking off all relations with her, she says, so long as Arthur agreed to marry on her terms. It's a courageous offer, but I doubt she means it or, if she does, could see it through: the wound – both theirs and hers – would be too deep. Among the photos she has is one showing her parents seated on a bench, deep in conversation. Margaret leans on Patrick's shoulder; he frowns and closes his eyes, as though having just learned something he'd rather not hear. It's a picture of what Patrick's reaction might be on learning the truth about about her boyfriend, and she loves him too much to want to expose him to any such shock. It's bad enough having to tell her mother and seeing her disapproval. Honesty? What's so great about honesty? All it brings is worry and dismay.

The pressure to be honest is a bit rich, coming from Arthur, since the real concealment isn't in Langford Street but at Windyridge. Her parents haven't met Arthur, but when they ask she tells them the truth. His parents have come to know Kim quite well, but they've been kept in the dark about her religion. It's not just that he has made a point of saying nothing about it.

He has asked her to take pains to keep it hidden. This is why when she spent weekends at Windyridge, the previous year, she'd slip out on Sunday morning under the pretext of doing a ward-round at Hope – when in fact she was secretly going to Mass. Mary was aware of the deception. In time, Kathleen was let in on it too. The one person who didn't know was Ernest. And can't be told now. And mustn't ever find out, come hell or high water.

In a letter to Arthur in the summer of 1944, Mary makes clear what they're up against:

I thought I'd better let you know that Daddy will probably write and ask you about Kim's religion, as he seems to be on the warpath about it at present. We all say we don't know and I, for one, am not going to be dragged in by Daddy. You know how stupidly bigoted he is about religion, and you must please yourself, but take my advice and don't let him spoil your life. He's lived his as he wanted to and now it's your turn. Kim is a perfect pet, and so in love with you, and her life will be utterly ruined if she doesn't marry you. Don't be a BF. You're ideally suited. You're young. You've a right to be happy. Take it Arthur – I know what it's like to lose it.

Arthur's grateful for her support, but replies that his religious views are 'very like Daddy's' and that he can't imagine changing them, not even to marry the woman he loves. The obvious solution is to 'let Kim remain RC', says Mary. But that still leaves the problem of Ernest, who 'threatens all kinds of things' should Kim prove Catholic (his great fear being that Arthur would then become a convert). These threats extend even to suicide: he has taken to locking himself in the bathroom and saying he'll use a razor on his wrists. Telling Ernest the truth would be a risk (just as Kim telling her father would be a risk), but Mary thinks it safer for him to know.

At Mary's behest, Ron also offers his tenpenn'orth to Arthur: 'I don't know if you've decided on any line of action, but it is a situation that has to be faced, chum. If your father persists, he is bound to discover the truth. I know it's none of my business but I would tell him straight. It will make a hell of a row but I think it will be better – after all the trouble, wangling and deceit about one thing and another when we were kids, I'm becoming convinced that honesty is the best policy. I know that sounds trite, but . . .' Arthur replies that he'd be willing to tell his father face to face, but not in a letter – which means waiting till he gets home, another six months at least. He hopes Ron and Mary can be discreet in the meanwhile. If the truth should come out . . . well, it doesn't bear thinking of. His father will ban Kim from Windyridge. Or insist on the relationship ending. Or even do himself in.

The virulence of Ernest's anti-Catholicism is hard for someone of my generation to understand. He wasn't a church-goer, or remotely interested in religious affairs – why such venom? Perhaps the point about the truly prejudiced is that they don't know they are prejudiced; instead of holding beliefs, they merely inhabit them, without self-consciousness. Ernest reminds me of Daniel Defoe's description of anti-Catholic bigots in the eighteenth century – 'stout fellows willing to fight against Popery without knowing whether it be a man or horse'. Where did his sectarianism come from? In part, it was the Nonconformist spirit of the north-west of England, the chapel air he breathed without ever going to chapel. And in part it was simply the language of bourgeois Britain. Hatred of Catholics was endemic to its modern mercantile class – hatred of blacks, Jews and homosexuals, too. Ron writing from Africa describes his servant in terms which we'd call racist but which commonplace at the time ('I have my own dhobi boy. I don't know his real name but the first two syllables sound like Mo-Mo, so Momo he is. He is just as dumb as the rest of the wogs but by constant reminding, and occasional boots in the right place, I manage to get him to do my washing, fetch drinking water, bring me bananas and pineapples, etc.'). And here is a doctor friend of Arthur writing in 1941:

Penrith is becoming a real funk-hole. It must be pretty good because the jews have smelled it out, and one sees many a fat jewess waddling through the town. Since there is a shortage of fat, I think these jewesses should volunteer to be boiled and used as grease. I may sound a spot bitter and antisemitic, but one or two of the breed have been in to see me and my God do they get up my shirt. With all these bloody rabbits hiding in Penrith, I am kept pretty busy.

Until pictures of Belsen and Auschwitz made it clear where such prejudice led, many people in Britain talked this way. Writing to Arthur in September 1944, on the Hitler–Vatican issue, Ernest rounds off his deprecation of Catholics by comparing them with Jews:

Well, the war news exceeds all expectations. I don't give the Japs six months once Germany's finished. So all being well things will be very different by next June. The only question is who we are to make peace terms with – certainly not Hitler. I note Rome says he can shelter in the Vatican. I never had any time for that religion and still less for the priests. In fact I hate the sight of all the b—s and I speak from experience. They will shelter anything and anybody for money. They are as bad as the Jews.

As a guest at his lunch table, Kim had often heard Ernest air such opinions. Perhaps he exaggerated his prejudice against Catholics (how primitive they were, how uneducated, how vast their families) in hopes of flushing her out, but if so the strategy failed. Away in Birmingham, no longer a visitor at Windyridge, she was spared the strain of silence and concealment. But even there she felt afraid that religion might be held against held her, and let on only to Taylor, her boss. One day the secret would come out. But for now, to anyone who asked, she wasn't, never had been, and had no intention of becoming RC.

*　　*　　*

As a child, I didn't know my mother was a Catholic. As an adult, I was asked to keep it quiet. As an orphan clutching his cache of letters, I discovered what a huge issue it had been. All those battles. And all the lies she had to tell. I felt torn in half – my father, English humanist, ruling my head, my mother, Irish Catholic, ruling my heart. The letters gave no clue how they'd breach the great divide. I knew they must have found a way, otherwise I wouldn't be here. But in 1944 neither side was in a mood for compromise. As with the war, there could be only one outcome: my father (and England) would win. But peace was a distant prospect. A lot of ground would have to be surrendered. And for now, neither the Germans nor my mother would give in.

# CHAPTER EIGHT

# Oodling

*Arthur to Kim, Azores, 1.8.44*

Oodled around after lunch, then spent the rest of the afternoon on the wireless again. Makes me wonder what I do with my time. First of August! Will soon have finished five months here. When is this blasted war going to finish? Here I am sitting on a canvas chair trying to pretend I'm enjoying myself, when what I really feel is that I'm wasting my life. I know millions of others have said the same since the war started but it still gets me wild. I've never been so moody.

Yesterday caught the 5pm transport to the beach at Praia, threw a medicine ball about for an hour, then did some swimming, paddled about in a canoe Bugs and Smithie made, and finished off with a sprint along the sands. What a war effort, eh?

*Kim to Arthur, Dudley Road, 5.8.44*

Pounds of fruit here lately, which I love – apples and pears and plums. For supper last night had dates (along with lobster salad and hors d'oeuvres). Thought you'd like to know. They're the only kind of dates I'm likely to have here or anywhere for a long time. Oh darling, do you remember the walk to Boscastle and the cycle rides and good old Auntie? Don't you wish we were back in Davidstow?

Yesterday sat out in the sun and got very brown. The weather has been marvellous, very unlike English weather – or Irish. Have been told I'm looking well now – wish you could see. The front of my hair is quite bleached – I might be a blonde yet. One of the boys today said 'You are sun-kissed', but that's not much good – a very poor substitute. Maddening to think of us both burning under the same sun but, oh! so far apart.

M Y COMPACT *OED* gives nothing between 'oocyst' and 'oof'. Other dictionaries have 'oodles', a plural noun meaning lots and lots. But to Arthur in 1944, *oodle* is a verb, an action word for inaction. He is young and alive, with oodles of time on his hands. But there's nothing to do but idle. And, ooh, he finds it hard.

The D-Day landings are the start of it. He hears about them on the wireless and is soon enviously watching the newsreels. Why can't *he* see some action in France? Why can't *he* have the luck of Ron, who's expecting to be posted there any minute? He makes plans to see the Winco, Carslake, and say, 'Look, I've been in Plymouth (after the blitzes), in Iceland, and in the Azores. I've a good record, so what about *letting me get into this war?*' The risk is that they'll post him somewhere like Burma, which he knows would worry his family, who have suffered losses enough. But at least he could prove himself a man. He puts all this to Kim, but she's discouraging: 'Why volunteer, darling? You're doing your part in this war, the part they've made you do, so why worry about it? I hate to think of you in Burma. I hate to think of you in France, I hate to think of you in the Azores, too, but at least I know you're safe there.' Unpersuaded, unpersuadable, Arthur duly speaks to Carslake, but is told he's wasting his time. They don't need RAF doctors in Europe. He must stay where he is and serve out his second tour.

Time weighs heavy. He plays a lot of sport – hockey, rugby, even soccer, which he's useless at – encouraged in this by his father, who tells him it's his job as medical officer to keep the squadron fit: 'You can't have enough games to please the lads.' Some of the activities are sillier – clod-throwing, for instance ('grabbing hard bits of soil – stones banned – and hurling them at each other and running for shelter in the tents'). Some barely rate as activities: he spends a whole afternoon with a friend sitting watching an ants' nest ('That's how it gets you after a while'). He finds a good place to swim, near Praia: a sandy – i.e. lava dust – beach. But then some stupid devils get out of their depth one day and nearly drown in the offshore currents, after which bathing is prohibited. Of his various trips into town – to

eat, to shop, to get whistled, to visit the house of his Portuguese batman, Francisco, to check out (but not make use of) the local brothel – the most bizarre is to attend an aquatic bullfight. In a small cove at the foot of vertical cliffs, hundreds of people gather, some safely ensconced behind a concrete wall, others out in the open to test their machismo. Off shoots a rocket and a bull is released at the end of a long rope. It charges down the road, along the quay, across the beach, scattering spectators. Then it rushes back up the hill it came from, young men running like mad just ahead. Then down to the beach again, where it disappears up to its neck in the waves. After a while the rope is shortened and the bull re-penned. Then the performance is repeated with another bull, and another. No one is injured – not even the bulls. The whole event is an excuse for the local lads to fight and get drunk ('zigzag' in local language). Running with the bulls. Running with the waves. Arthur would like to enter the festive spirit. But he feels out of it, an Englishman among Latinos. The absurdity of him being there in the middle of war strikes him with new vigour. 'What a bloody awful waste of time, and of the best years of my life.'

The bull in the mess oppresses him too. A new rule is passed that members can't take drinks into the lounge, owing to past 'incidents' (though no one knows what these are). Carslake inaugurates a daily 5pm parade – compulsory for all the squadron, including MOs – thereby buggering up afternoons off. There's also a new fortnightly dining-in night for officers: as Arthur describes it to Kim, 'like a lot of schoolboys following teacher, we collect in one room at 7.30 to drink sherry or gin (but no beer and we mustn't smoke and on our way in we must say Good Evening to the President of the Mess Committee). Then silence falls while the Big White Chief comes in and orders his drink; once he's ready to go, he leads the way into the dining room and we all stand to attention behind our chairs till he sits down. Impressive, eh?' Arthur doesn't think so. Nor do Throne and Coffin, who later receive damning reports for their lack of discipline, though they do a grand job. Arthur is scathing about it when he next writes to Kim, perhaps rashly, since censorship of letters is being stepped up. To cover himself, he sometimes writes in the third person, his thoughts and actions attributed to a fictional character called Jack. But it may be no coincidence that shortly afterwards Carslake sends a letter to the Air Ministry drawing attention to the fact that, though officially posted to the Azores on 3 January 1944, 'F/Lt Morrison spent two further months in the UK awaiting instructions' (and had also 'enjoyed a few days off in the UK in June' because of the polio case he flew back with), thereby inviting the Ministry to extend his tour. 'The artful devil,' Arthur complains to Kim. 'The underhand, double-faced rat.' Is there any difference between Nazism and RAF bull, he wonders. If Carslake really wants to impose some discipline, he ought to be tackling 'that there', homosexuality, which is, claims Arthur, 'spreading like wildfire', the latest case involving two officers. 'It's getting as bad as Reykjavik,' he tells Kim, 'where that lad shot himself. Best thing they could all do.' There are even stories of sheepshagging. Balls and bull and bestiality and buggery and bugger-all to do. 'What a war effort, eh?'

Twice he escapes. First there's a trip to Gibraltar, followed by a more exotic outing to a place of 'Arabs and sheikhs and marvellous-looking French girls and sultans throwing parties and bags of opportunity for going astray. I'm not allowed to say where, for obvious reasons, but do you remember that film with Humphrey Bogart we went to see in Manchester?' (She did: *Casablanca*.) Then he fills a notebook describing a trip to Furnas, another island in the Azores, where he stays in a lavish hotel, watches children skinning a calf and plays golf with three pilots, a number four iron and one gashed ball between them. His travel notes run to the length of a novella. 'You should have been a writer,' Kim tells him, when she gets the letter. 'No, I mean it. You give wizard descriptions of places. I started reading it in bed at 1.30am and didn't finish till 3. I'm dying to read it again.'

These escapes (and writing about them) briefly dispel Arthur's gloom. But soon he's back at SSQ, glumly oodling the weeks away. What he's suffering from, he tells Kim, is TXitis: 'TX – pronounced tea-ex – means time expired, i.e. the end of one's tour overseas. TXitis means being restless for this time to be up.' The war will soon be over, everyone says. But after the visit of an Australian padre, Arthur begins to doubt it. The padre talks of his time in New Guinea, and of the 'filthy horrible things' he saw the Japs do there – officers pinned alive to trees and used for bayonet practice, women tied up, raped, hung alive from trees and then their breasts cut off – and of how it will take at least eighteen months to clear those islands. By then who knows what will happen to him or to his family. 'Everything is going on here just as always' the letters from Windyridge begin, but he wonders. His mother wasn't well last time he saw her: might it be cancer coming? And his father was looking overweight, fat thickening his jowls and silting up his veins – at fifty-four a heart attack's not out of the question. If only Kim could keep an eye on them. But with her in Birmingham, and him stuck out here . . .

His 1944 Christmas card to Windyridge is signed 'Arthur – On Inactive Service'. It causes ructions, of course. 'Cut out the hero stuff,' his father tells him. 'Mike might have been here except for heroics. So might Dan. It's too late in the day to look for trouble.' Mary is angry, too, tearing him off a strip and accusing

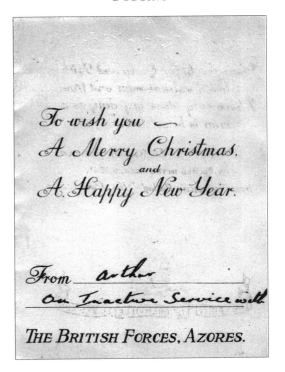

*To wish you —*
*A Merry Christmas.*
*and*
*A Happy New Year.*

*From* arthur
On Inactive Service with

**THE BRITISH FORCES, AZORES.**

him of 'P/o Pruneishness' – there are thousands of people who'd give their right arm for a post like his. But Arthur is unrepentant. Isn't it better to die a hero than live a coward? He's bored with pretending to be useful. 'Can you imagine what it'll be like when I'm home – going round to The Cock, and blokes there looking at me and saying "Hell, he should laugh – Iceland and the Azores, whilst all his pals were getting killed, how dare he even show his face let alone be happy?" I love being alive. But wish to hell I was in the war. So put that in your b- pipe and smoke it.'

   ✻  ✻  ✻

*Kim to Arthur, Dudley Road, 7.10.44*

Was called twice the night before last – at 3.30 then again at 7. Fully intended an early night tonight but just as I was going a case came into casualty, a septic abortion (criminal). She died this morning anyway but there'd have been hell to pay if I hadn't seen her. After that had a retained placenta. Was 1am before I got to bed.

BACK IN DUDLEY ROAD, Kim's frustrated too. The *impasse* with Arthur is part of it. But there's also her work, which has begun to seem repetitive. One night she has a ruptured uterus, the third in six months, all of them different from the pictures in textbooks ('I wonder where they collect those textbook cases from – they never look like the real thing'). Another night she finds herself having to deal with a mad patient, her second within a few weeks. The nurses want to inject the woman with morphine but can't get near, so Kim has to give her a whiff of chloroform first ('Don't ask me how I did it: two sisters and four nurses didn't really do much to help'). She has a hell of a row about it with the powers that be – the woman should have been in a mental hospital: what was she doing on the Maternity Ward? – and has only just cooled down when another sticky case comes her way, a woman whose baby has died *in utero*. Even tragic cases like this are now repeats. The familiarity helps relieve the stress. But doesn't it also mean she must be burning out?

'Those doctors in Brum are exploiting you,' Arthur tells her. 'Have it out with them right away. It's not being bolshy. It's common medical sense – if you don't have plenty sleep and recreation, not only your health suffers but your work does.' Needless to say, she doesn't have it out with them, but Mitchell notices how run-down she's looking, and insists on coming in two nights a week, which means she's on duty only five in seven ('it's really my own fault he hasn't done it before – he did offer'). With one half-day off a week, and a long weekend once a month, she's not complaining. By her standards, it's a life of ease. She starts to socialise a bit, with colleagues. She even has time to get a tan. But her health continues to deteriorate. She's been having headaches and sinus pains again, and everyone says she's looking thin. The Ear, Nose and Throat Man says it's nothing a holiday won't cure. Arthur, too, bullies her to take a break. Work's

only meant to be a hobby, he tells her. And nothing's more important than her health, 'not even me'.

Under duress she spends a long weekend at Lytham St Anne's, down the coast from Blackpool, where Mary has rented a house. They loll in the sandhills, cook fish and chips for supper, and when Kela's asleep discuss their respective difficulties: if only they could share a house and make a life together untroubled by men. The religion problem is worrying her still, but what Mary notices, and reports to Arthur, is that 'Kim's not at all an ardent R.C. I laughed because she was so *mad* (can't you hear her saying it?) at having found an RC chapel here – she had hoped there wouldn't be, but once she found there was she felt she had to go on Sunday morning. It's the only day she does go, though.' As a thank-you for the weekend, Kim buys Mary a book of RAF poetry which she saw her admiring in Boots: ordinary chaps in the forces expressing their feelings about war. It was the first poem in it that Mary seemed to be mooning over:

Give them their wings:
They cannot fly too high or far
To fly above
The dirty-moted, bomb-soured, word-tired world.
And if they die, they'll die . . .

Does reading such stuff help Mary cope with Michael's death, she wonders? Are other war widows helped? It's hard to imagine what helps, but RAF anthologies are selling well, so they must be of use to someone. There was a poet who dedicated a book to her once: Michael McKenna. Nice to have sonnets written for you. Arthur's not the poetry type, but she'll forgive him that. What she can't forgive is his intransigence.

Before she leaves Lytham, there's a comic incident involving Ron, who, in these last weeks before he's sent to France, often comes across from nearby Kirkham on his motorbike and, if it gets late, stays overnight. Unfortunately his comings-and-not-goings are tuttingly observed by the landlady and her sister – the Watch Committee, as Ron later christens them. Not that the landlady says anything at first, but after they run into her one morning and she cuts them dead, Mary has it out with her. A single man spending the night with a married woman – the landlady has made herself quite ill worrying about it. Mary explains about Ron being a friend of the family. That's all very well, says the landlady, but what will the neighbours think? Later she and Kim have a good laugh about the old bitch and her sour, sex-starved imagination. But the incident rankles with Mary, so to emphasise the point about Ron being a family friend, she persuades her grandmother (over for the day from Knott End) to stage the most fulsome of greetings in front of the twitching living-room curtains, till poor, bemused Ron (who has never met the woman before) is quite overcome by her embraces.

Back in Birmingham, Kim scans the *British Medical Journal*. Her six-month contract will expire in October, and though they want her to renew it she's keeping an eye open for other posts. The work meanwhile continues, unrelenting – no let-up in babies just because there's a war on – and soon she's ill and exhausted again, as though she'd never been away. She still has two weeks' holiday owing, and when Mitchell urges her to have a proper break she arranges to spend a fortnight back in Kerry. The temporary travel ban has been lifted, and she takes the ferry from Holyhead. Once home, her troubles recede, as they did the previous summer. She drinks, plays cards, goes dancing, gossips with her parents (who're looking old, suddenly), and sleeps – especially that. One day she cycles to Ross Beigh with friends and on the way back stops off at the nearby golf course, Dooks, where her brother Joe is playing in a tournament – he sinks a long putt on the eighteenth to win, and afterwards treats them to a meal at a nearby hotel (chicken and ham, sherry trifle, coffee and brandy). By the time they set off back for Killorglin it's 11pm, and very dark and they've only one lamp between seven bikes, but in the end they get there, more sober than when they set out. Arthur seems hundreds of miles away – he *is* hundreds of miles away, but now she knows it, and tells him so: 'Dreamt about you a couple of times before I came and you seemed very near. Why is it that since I came home you seem farther away than ever, my darling? I know this place is miles from everywhere but you seem twice as far away as you did – miles and miles and miles away, and not just in physical distance.' The Atlantic Gap is the least of gaps between them. Her old doubts return, plus a few new ones. The prospect of marriage seems remote.

Once back at Dudley Road, she resigns. Taylor tries to dissuade her: it's like losing his right arm, he says. Dr Burns, the big chief at Dudley Road, threatens her with the Central Medical War Committee and warns she'll be called up if she leaves his haven. But she sticks to her guns. Louise, her room-mate, is also leaving and there's nothing to hold her. A few more weeks, then goodbye Brum.

✳   ✳   ✳

*Arthur to Kim, 25.7.44*

What a party we had last night, for the arrival of the new group captain. A couple of Madeiras before dinner, then red wine with dinner, which consisted of grapefruit, soup, omelette, chicken, baked potatoes, peas and beans, trifle, cheese and biscuits, bananas and pineapples, followed by coffee. The speeches were inaudible. At some point a fight started with bread rolls and banana skins, then a game of rugby with a pineapple, and only then did we learn the speeches had finished.

THROWING BREAD ROLLS and banana skins, eh? Even by the standards of a wartime piss-up, it's pathetic stuff. He'd like to be involved in *real* fighting – or at least a little wanton destruction. It's not unknown, when there's a war on. At a party in Ron's mess, for instance, vases fly round and chairs are broken, and at one in Hope Hospital which Kim attends a piano's pushed downstairs and smashed to bits. That's the kind of vandalism war induces, a poor substitute for tearing the enemy limb from limb, but a release of sorts. Whereas the only vandalism in Lagens is ... throwing bread rolls and banana skins. It's frustrating for him; frustrating for anyone reading him, too. There are no epic battles, only boredom relieved by horseplay.

Still, this is what it was like for many people. They mightn't have eaten as well as Kim did in Ireland or Arthur in the Azores (fresh fruit, fresh vegetables, roast chicken, red wine, etc.), but they knew about boredom. A pacific generation like mine imagines war as violent death and destruction. But that's to forget the humdrum in-between bits, the endless hanging around – waiting for transport, waiting for instructions, waiting for the All Clear, waiting for the Germans to surrender, then the Japanese, waiting, waiting, waiting. Better to wait than to come ashore at Omaha Beach, as the US 116th Infantry did on 6 June 1944, only to be slaughtered. (If my father had seen *those* D-Day pictures, of bodies floating in the surf or splayed in the shingle, he'd not have been so itchy for action.) But to feel you were at least doing some good – that would have made the waiting more bearable. Yes, 99 per cent of war is boredom, but what about the other 1 per cent? Kim, back in Birmingham, was doing more for the war effort, and running greater risks.

I'd like to invent a dangerous mission or two for my father. But this isn't a novel and it's important that he survive. Besides, in a workaholic age like ours it's good to be reminded of oodling. Do people oodle any more? Only poets, perhaps. There are some poets I know so indolent they barely move, and yet their poems can be moving – as Edward Thomas's 'Adlestrop' is, though nothing happens in it. Great poetry slows us down. It makes us concentrate on minutiae which prove, on close inspection, less minute. 'What is this life if, full of care,/We have no time to stand and stare?' are the only lines of poetry I can remember my mother quoting. To stand and stare wasn't her style, but she knew that oodling had its place. So did my father, impatient though he was. To observe small commonplace acts in a time of breaking nations; to hear people whisper nothings to each other while dynasties pass; even to see them throwing bread rolls or watching an ants' nest – there's a value in this. We're addicted to adventure and noise. We've seen too many action films. We envy the dead for having lived more dramatically than we do – when all they wanted was a bit of peace.

It's the little things in life that hold the story. The oodling you never know if you're in a hurry. As I was, till my mother, stopping in her tracks, stopped me in mine.

\*     \*     \*

*Arthur, Azores, 26.8.44*

Another Caesar? My little girl is doing too many things that I couldn't even attempt. (Wonder if I'll ever get anywhere in this world.) Of course I approve, but not if it is taking up more than a small percentage of your total ambition. The main part of your life must be me, darling. Work is just a placebo until we marry.

*Kim, Booth Hall, 6.11.44*

Have been reading 'She Would be a Doctor'. Lets us down a bit – the gender not the profession. However, she redeems us in the end – as books will have a happy ending.

*Arthur, Azores, 18.11.44*

'She Would Be a Doctor'? Add 'Until She Was Married' and it will do.

IT'S A THEME of his, that autumn. Her next post, after Birmingham, will be at a children's hospital. He approves of this, in so far as it's 'practice for looking after our own'. But what she should really do is 'Go home and get yourself acclimatised for the life you are going to lead after the war. You know, practise cooking. Yes, I said cooking, a most important factor in a happily married life.' Just in case she's missed the point, he repeats it: 'I don't like you saying you feel lazy for not taking any more exams – and I don't want you to feel lazy when you become a common or garden housewife.' Or again: 'Glad to hear you are getting domesticated, ironing, sewing, etc. Could use you at this moment, with all these holes in my socks and buttons off. When you finish your next post you must go to a Domestic Science college.' It's a wind-up: he knows how much she loves her work. But, like most men of the time, he also believes a woman's place is at home. To the O'Sheas, back in Killorglin, Agnes working as a doctor doesn't seem radical, but the Morrisons take a different line on female emancipation. Ernest, for example, disparages Winston Churchill (in every other respect his hero) over his 'stunt' of equal pay for women in the forces: 'It is wrong to say women are equal to men. In the past a man married and expected to work and earn enough to keep his wife at home to look after the house, his meals, his children and the running of things in general. If pay in all trades is going to be the same for women, then the man is going to stop at home and the wife work.' Which is, to Ernest, unthinkable. To Arthur, too, when his father fires him up. On one occasion he tells Kim: 'I'd absolutely loathe it if you took any job after we are married even if we had no children on the way.'

Mostly, he's less dogmatic than this. But he doesn't like the idea of her working hard. Given her history – the headaches, chest problems and willingness to be exploited and exhausted – she will have to take things easy *après la guerre*. He says this because her loves her and wants her as his (healthy) wife, and because he believes medicine should come second to leisure ('work's only a hobby to help while away our short time on this earth'). But he's also unnerved by how far her career is streaming ahead of his. It's brought home to him when they discuss one of her cases at Dudley Road, a pregnant woman with a query subphrenic abscess – a post-operative infection causing pus to gather between the liver and the diaphragm. Despite the fear she'll go into labour prematurely, Kim and Taylor decide to explore. Surely it's a crying shame to leave the baby inside, Arthur objects. God, what *is* he thinking of, she replies, doesn't he know that abscess cases who miscarry invariably die, because their adhesions break down and they succumb to general peritonitis? It would be like murdering the woman – does he want that?

Exchanges like this make him feel small. In his first three months in the Azores, he had the polio outbreak and the flight to save the boy with tetanus. Occasionally there are minor dramas still: a lorry turns over, trapping one of its passengers; a drunk pilot coming back from Angra is set upon by locals and badly beaten; one chap electrocutes himself and another ('one of those') tries to sever his arteries. Mostly, though, 'flu or bruised fingers are as bad as it gets. Every fortnight, to keep themselves up to scratch, he and the other MOs meet to discuss cases cited in journals. In theory, very useful. Yet lately he's stopped attending. He finds he hasn't the time to read up, or would rather spend it working on his wireless. What's the point of sitting there in silence, rudely reminded how much he has forgotten from Med School or how little he knew in the first place? He hates the big-mouthed show-offs, the Musgraves and Carslakes; it's not as if they're any good *clinically* just because they talk a lot. More to the point, he resents the doctors back home – all those conchies, Krauts, Yids and *Irish* busily passing exams and staying out of the forces. He'd like to send them back to their own countries – or to the East, to fight the Japs. They're stealing a march on him. If he's not careful, they'll steal his future: the job, the wife, the peace.

Kim too is a rival and usurper: 'My little girl is doing too many things that I couldn't even attempt.' It gives him an inferiority complex, the kind afflicting a more recent generation of men, made to feel useless by the rise of women in the workplace. But he won't succumb to envy and torpor. On his campbed in the Azores, as the nights close in, he begins drawing up post-war plans. What kind of doctor will he be? He could go back to Hope, he's sure they'd take him, but he sees no future in hospitals unless he has some further degrees. He could sit the DPH (Diploma in Public Health) while still in uniform, but life's too short to bury yourself in textbooks. Or he could become a GP. The government White Paper he has been reading suggests there'll be huge changes after the war, with the creation of a national health service and GPs brought under state control. Both his father and his Uncle Bert (a doctor in Southport) are against the plan, but it might give him an opening. He's noticed lately that blokes who come to SSQ seem more at ease with him than with the likes of Musgrave and Carslake. The role of GP would suit him, he fancies. If there were a way to set up a combined doctor-and-dentist practice with Ron, in some suitable country area, between Preston and Lancaster, say, not far from Windyridge (he's done with travelling, and doesn't want to be more than 50 miles from home for the rest of his life): how would that be? He puts the idea to Kim, stressing that she too could be included, but 'only as a dormant partner. Our clinic may be you and me and Ron *on paper* but only Ron and me in practice, while you learn to sew and relax.'

What does she think? How does the role of sleeping partner (and seamstress) appeal? On the face of it, not much. But she's exhausted and low in spirits, and appears surprisingly amenable to his plan. (But then, now you know my mother a bit, perhaps you're not surprised at all.) If GP is what he wants, fine, she wants it too. She even offers to go hunting for suitable practices. If need be she could get one started before he's demobbed, with a view to him stepping in when he gets home. In this she contrasts herself with Musgrave's fiancée Helen, who has cold feet about choosing between medicine and marriage: 'Can't understand her problem. I know I'd miss medicine for a while but I'd cheerfully give it up if that was what you wanted.' Or so she says. Since her concern is to show how flexible she is about this, as she isn't about religion, I take her amenability with a pinch of salt.

In fact, such is the unreality of Arthur's post-war planning, with hostilities (not least their own) far from concluded, she can say anything she likes. It's not as if he'll be able to hold her to it. A country practice, three kids, two cars, an oak table and a maid: sure, why not? It's a fantasy they share. Like something out of a film. Nothing more.

✳   ✳   ✳

*Arthur to Kim, Azores, 11.4.44*

Funny thing, but whenever I see a picture nowadays (like 'The More the Merrier' last night) or hear a story of any sort about a married couple, I always think of you and me. I mentioned it to Steve after 'Heaven Can Wait' – how you were like the heroine and me the hero – but of course just got my leg pulled.

*Kim to Arthur, 16.1.45*

Saw 'I Met Him in Paris' the other night, with Claudette Colbert. Marvellous skating and ski-ing scenes in Switzerland – want to go there. I loved the dancing scene, too, and thought of you all through. Ronnie Majd said it suddenly dawned on him while watching how like Claudette Colbert I was, and said he was quite amused putting me in her place.

WITH THE FUTURE on hold, they oodle at the movies. For him there's a brand new cinema on camp, the Azoria, 'magnificently fitted up (a waste of money – a plain large Nissen would do)'.

For her, there are the Odeons and Gaumonts of the cities she works in, as well as The Oisin in Killorglin, newly opened in 1939 and practically next door to Patrick's wool-yard. In two years, they see, between them, over 140 movies (which isn't to count those they saw together). And their picture-going is most intense in the latter half of 1944, when they average more than two films a week. Among hers are *Passage to Marseilles*, *The White Cliffs of Dover*, *The Hitler Gang*, *Rebecca*, *Pride and Prejudice* and *The Purple Heart* ('It would have made your blood boil – all about six American airmen who crash in Japan and their sub-sequent trial'). Among his are Powell and Pressburger's *A Canterbury Tale*, Sam Goldwyn's *The Kid from Spain*, David Lean and Noël Coward's *This Happy Breed* ('magnificent down to the last detail'), *Ministry of Fear*, *Double Indemnity* and *Holy Matrimony* (starring Gracie Fields – 'damned glad I was called out to see a sprained ankle after ten minutes'). In their letters they rehearse the plots and drool over the stars. Their reviews ('the makings of a damn good picture but just missed it somewhere', 'don't know what the hell people were raving about. There wasn't a laugh in the house') would win no prizes as film criticism, but they aren't trying to cut a dash. Nor do they see their film-going as escapist. The dramas acted out are their dramas. The characters are them: 'I love the part where they are dancing – when she wants to bite his ear. Ooh darling, I thought of you all the way through.'

In life, friends have often said how much they resemble two movie stars – he Mickey Rooney, she Claudette Colbert. He's insulted by the Rooney comparison, which makes him feel even less handsome than he is – short-arsed, bug-eyed, bulbous-nosed, unavoidably ridiculous. She's less insulted by the Colbert (Mary Galvin said it was the first thing that struck her when they met), though neither she nor Arthur can see it. The resemblance gives them a taste for being stars, if only in their own movie. *Love Story* with Margaret Lockwood reminds her of their time in Davidstow: 'it was set in Cornwall so you can imagine what I was thinking'. *Mr Lucky*, with Cary Grant and Laraine Day, has him clambering up onto the screen: 'she's lovely and the way she kissed him made me feel lonely and long for you. Later I dreamt about the picture with Kim and Arthur as the stars, and was pleased she waited for him.'

Other films they see remind them of their difficulties. They fall out over the Catholic piety of *The Song of Bernadette*. Then there's *Cover Girl*, with Gene Kelly and Rita Hayworth, of which he says: 'Quite enjoyed it. As usual you were the girl – when Danny (me) said "I've known her 6 months" and she (you) came in and said "No, 7 months, 6 days, 18 hours and 23 mins" I could have kissed her – really, I wriggled in my seat. Another thing that struck me was the comparison between her ambitions on the stage and yours in medicine – I felt you were superior in being ready to forgo your ambitions straight away. You are, really, aren't you darling?' Most discomfiting of all is *A Guy Named Joe*, about a pilot who comes back as a ghost to supervise his lover's new romance. Arthur likes it ('though I don't want to be a dead hero so I couldn't be Spencer Tracy'), but he doubts whether Mary should see it: 'she'll be thinking of Michael and Ron all the way through.' To which Kim replies, 'Mary has seen it and loved it, except the ending, which made her weep.' There are similar problems with a musical Kim takes Mary to at the Opera House, *The Years Between*: 'Very good but I didn't really enjoy it – nor did she, for obvious reasons. All about a husband who is presumed killed in an air crash and returns after two and a half years, during which time his wife has decided to marry someone else.' No, films aren't an escape from the present, but a reminder of its trials and tribulations.

After 1945, my parents gave up on films, as though they were part of the war they'd left behind. (Or rather, he gave up; she'd have continued going, given the chance.) They went to pubs, dances, shows in Manchester, but not the local fleapit. Only once during my childhood did we see a film together: *South Pacific*, the movie version of the Rodgers and Hammerstein musical about American Second World War servicemen on a distant island. My mother loved the music so much she bought the soundtrack, my father was taken back to his time in the Azores, and my sister and I were entranced by the Technicolor. It had been fun, everyone agreed, we must go to the pictures again very soon. And never did.

In 1944, though, films were part of their story. Even the titles mockingly echo what they faced, whether mutual infatuation (*He's My Guy, The Girl I Left Behind*) or separation (*Till We Meet Again, Thanks for the Memory*), whether intransigence (*Take It or Leave It*) or hope for better to come (*The Way Ahead*).

✶   ✶   ✶

*Kim to Arthur, Booth Hall, Manchester, 13.11.44*

Got here round 5pm. From Windyridge, it means taking two buses – very slow. The first person I met on arrival was a horrible man called Wilkins, a Manchester product and obviously a wartime medico (believe he was a chemist before). It's a very big hospital – takes ages to get round, so I won't lack for exercise. Went to bed round midnight and woke up with a start half an hour later to hear a mouse squeaking. Oh I hate the things. Left the light on and slept fitfully. Will set a trap tonight and hope to catch him. I'm on admissions today – which means from 10am today till 10am tomorrow.

ARTHUR, NEEDLESS TO say, is delighted. Working at Booth Hall, just outside Manchester, will bring her back within the orbit of his family. She sees it differently, as a post that just happened to come up; by the time Arthur's home again, she'll probably have moved on. Still, she's not unhappy at the thought of seeing Mary, who meets her off the train and helps carry her luggage back to Windyridge. Since the summer, little Mikela has shot up. At eighteen months, she's still not walking, but suddenly, on that first night, in the dining room, with Kim there, she does – lets go of Mary's hand and, elated, keeps on going right through to the kitchen. A lucky omen, everyone agrees: the war baby is finally on its feet.

Kim has come north again in order to get experience of 'Kids'. She feels idealistic about it. When children respond to medical treatment, you know it's not a brief reprieve but a whole new life, a Resurrection. But the sense of reward she's been hoping for doesn't materialise. She has barely put on her white coat when she's giving an anaesthetic to a girl with faecal vomiting and nearly loses her. Her colleagues are disenchanting, too. The surgeon, a Mr Tierney, is shockingly bad-tempered (damns and blasts all over the place) and his casual way with anaesthetics is frightening: in their first op together, on a boy who has head injuries and a ruptured spleen after falling off a bike, he tells her the dope's too light, and makes her double it, and the boy still hasn't come round three hours later. Worse is Tierney's leering predecessor and occasional stand-in, Dr Phelps, who, having established that she comes from Kerry, takes to humming 'The Rose of Tralee' as he wields his scalpel:

She was lovely and fair, like the rose of the summer,
Yet 'twas not her beauty alone that won me –
Ah no, 'twas the truth in her eyes ever dawning
That made me love Mary, the Rose of Tralee . . .

Mid-op, it's hard for Phelps to give the 'Ah no . . .' its requisite accompaniment – a little shake of the head, to indicate that the singer is overcome with rapture for his beloved. But she gets the message. Maybe it would work with someone else, but harping on her Kerry roots is the last way to win her heart. She hates Phelps's hairy ears, anyway, which show even when he's wearing a face-mask: old donkey, old goat. Another day, she arrives in a new tweed coat, and when a nurse compliments her on it Phelps says, 'Yes, nice bit of stuff.' She's relieved to escape to her room, despite the resident mouse. It's only a little mouse, but she's a caricature of the woman in all the jokes, up screaming on a chair when it appears. There are days she wonders why she ever left Brum. In theory, she works fewer hours here but in practice, as she might have guessed, there's little difference, and her salary is only £200pa, 50 per cent less than she was getting. Why did she do it? One morning, she sees 16 new admissions – 'can you imagine anything worse than 16 struggling, bawling kids?' Most of them have pneumonia. She has charge of skins too, on the days when Peach is missing. All these heartbreaking chronic eczemas, just like Kela's: is it something in the water or the atmosphere? The winter fogs of Manchester seep into the corridors – it's like swallowing buckets of soup. There are the bombs, too, less frequent than they were but always a risk. Even without the bombs, Manchester's no place to be alone in. One night she's due to meet Mary in Market Street, for a show. But Mary's late and she has to stand reading greetings cards in the window of Walker's hoping no one takes her for a tart. All this leering suddenly. It didn't used to happen so much.

'Is it the war that's driving men nuts?' she asks, when Mary arrives.

'You should be so lucky,' says Mary. 'They've stopped looking at me.'

'Nonsense,' she says, 'I've seen them.'

'Anyway, who needs it? Life's complicated enough.'

✳ ✳ ✳

*Kim to Arthur, Booth Hall, 9.11.44*

Mary writes to Ron every day. You'd think he'd be happy and content to wait till the war is over but no, he keeps asking if she's made up her mind yet. He can be quite awkward and moody at times. Today is her wedding anniversary but she hasn't been too bad.

*Mary to Arthur, Windyridge, 25.10.44*

You will realise it is very difficult for me to say definitely yes to Ron. I love Michael in such a different way and always shall.

*Ron to Arthur, RAF Dental Hospital no. 8, Belgium, 21.11.44*

I am hearing regularly from Mary but not really learning anything from her letters. This posting out here is a damn good thing, if only to enable me to get a more detached view. At the moment I'm pretty sure we shall never be able to make a go of it, because Mary has gone through too much for her ever to be happy with me and there are too many snags. Are you in a similar frame of mind? It looks as though we're in the same boat regarding our respective 'tie-ups', and may be setting up a joint bachelor apartment after all.

It would make things a bloody sight easier if we could talk about these things over a noggin at the White Horse or King's Arms.

KIM'S RETURN TO Manchester in November 1944 coincides with Ron's departure to Belgium, where he joins the dental division of the second front. If an army marches on its stomach, an air force flies by the skin of its teeth – and it's his duty to keep those teeth in order. It's a job like any other, he tells himself, and his new dental surgery's a damn sight better than any he's known, consisting as it does of captured German stuff. On the wall by his desk he sticks a photograph of 'Snip', Mikela, but so many erks say what a marvellous daughter he has (and him having to reply she's just a goddaughter), he wonders whether to pull it down. In his palm the Boche-made metal drills feel pleasantly weighty. To the patients in his chair, they're instruments of torture, but he admires the precision. 'Open vide,' he tells them as they fall pale and silent. 'Ve have vays of making you better.'

Ron never wanted to be a dentist, but he takes enormous pride in his work. Not that the patients appreciate it: for every ten he sees, two will refuse treatment and seven arrive with filthy mouths. One chap the other day said he 'didn't believe' in cleaning his teeth, as though hygiene were a faith you could opt out of. It's not that he expects any thanks, but it's a bind shoving decent work at rotten gnashers. Food rations are half the problem. The men are given biscuits by the boxful – he's never seen so many cavities. Sometimes he tries to drill some sense into his patients but most of them are too dumb to listen. At least in private practice they come because they *want* to. In the forces and in schools, dentistry's a thankless task; no doubt with the NHS it'll be thankless too. All this makes him unsure how to respond to Arthur's proposals for a joint post-war practice. Oh, he's grateful to be pencilled into the plans, but do they make sense? ICI has just advertised for a works dentist at £800 a year.

Not bad. Would a practice like Arthur Blakely's in Worsley – working like hell till eight or nine every night, having to fix up locums to get holidays, etc. – be worth the extra £300–£500 a year (half of it gone on income tax)? He may be lazy, but he'd rather cope on a reasonable salary and have time to enjoy life. He's more attracted to the type of practice he once worked at in the Lake District – the day's work done by mid-afternoon – but it wouldn't do for starting out. There's little choice in the matter, anyway. Several of his colleagues are already back on civvie street and, to judge by reports in the *British Dental Journal*, there's been so much wire-pulling and arse-licking that talk of fair play after demobbing is just cock. All he wants is a job, a home, his friends, and maybe a car. Oh, and a wife. Ideally, Mary. But probably not.

Meanwhile, he's in Belgium, and laddishly appraises the local talent. 'It seems you can muck around with a fellow's wife and he won't bat an eyelid,' he tells Arthur, 'but if you make any passes at his mistress then you're in trouble.' So far he hasn't been tempted – the women may be *très chic* but their looks are nothing to write home about and their legs are like matchsticks. But he can see how after a few months' celibacy his ideas might change. So he tells his old mate, whom he addresses not as a prospective brother-in-law but as a fellow bachelor unlucky in love. It's said that men of this era adopted a stiff upper lip – and couldn't or wouldn't discuss their feelings. But Ron and Arthur not only tell their *inamorata* how much they love them, they also tell each other their darker feelings – anxiety, cowardice, pain, terror, a sense of futility. Though Arthur (when arguing with Kim) likes to pretend he's a steely rationalist, in reality he's a gushing volcano, who can't help but pour out his heart. Ron's his closest male confidant, and Ron feels the same about him: 'It helps a hell of a lot to blow off now and then, and you, poor bugger, are the only bloke I can bind to.'

Back in Manchester, Kim and Mary club up together too, bewailing their difficulties with men. Having kept Ron at bay for over a year, Mary's now the one feeling cold-shouldered. Even before he left, Ron began calling less often – what with her being married (or widowed) and all the tongues wagging, they were seeing too much of each other, he said. Mary can see she deserved this, as a punishment for refusing to discuss marriage with him, but how else was she to play it? Whenever she asked him to wait, he'd say, 'Oh, well, I know I've had it then' and bugger off in a rage. She took it for granted he'd always be there: Reliable Ron, the good Samaritan and shoulder to cry on. Now he's gone, and doubtless the tarts he'll meet in Belgium will be more accommodating. His latest letters are the sort a brother would write to his sister – though he has stopped being sarcastic, which is something.

The irony, she tells Kim, is that she had begun to feel different about Ron. Or about Michael. Or rather, since she'll always feel the same about him, about Michael's family. Having borne them a grandchild, she'd nourished hopes of getting closer to the Thwaiteses and of them 'helping' in some way. How pathetic an illusion that was became clear when Michael's mother, Kay, recently came to visit, on her way home to Wales from a holiday in Yorkshire. Kay not having seen Kela for over six months, Mary expected her to stay awhile, but after *one and a half hours* Kay said she had to dash off to friends in Bury before carrying on to Ruthin – a lie, since Mary, out shopping next day, happened to see her at a bus stop in Bolton. She feels *very* bitter. Wouldn't you think Kay would cling to the baby as being part of Michael? It isn't money Mary wants from Kay, just kindness. But when she said to Kay how difficult it was to know what to do with Michael's clothes, her only reply was 'Yes, isn't it', as though she didn't give a damn. She sees now why whenever she's written asking can she and Kela come to stay in Ruthin, the house has always been full. She'd long suspected that Michael was the only one in that family worth anything. Kay she owes nothing. She'll remove the DFC ribbon and Wings, and send the clothes to Arthur. There's a nice warm dressing gown, too. What to do with all the pipes and tannery notes she can't imagine. Nor what the future holds, if Ron has gone for good. She feels so *alone*.

Kim does her best to console Mary. But depressed as she is by her own problems, she finds it hard to be optimistic. 'Leave it to Time and Fate,' Arthur keeps telling her. She'd say the same to

Mary about Ron, if only she believed it. Nine months ago, in London, the four of them were happily together. But what can Time and Fate do for women in the face of two such stubborn men?

✳   ✳   ✳

*Kim to Arthur, Booth Hall, 10.12.44*

Sudden fit of the blues tonight – I could say for no apparent reason but that wouldn't really be true. I got thinking after a letter of Ron's which Mary had shown me. He was discussing a pal who is in trouble, and said something about RCism's stupid attitude to contraception. It started me thinking, because I know that contraceptives would be a very important part of your married life – and not of mine. When I get like this, I feel like saying it's no use, I'm an RC and you're not. I want to be married in an RC church and you don't. I want to have RC children and you don't. You approve of contraceptives and I don't. It just doesn't add up, darling.

IT DOESN'T ADD up. Faith is greater than love. One and one don't make happiness. As 1944 draws to a close, that's the sum of things. The Catholic question has not gone away. For all the Xs and DILYs, the gossip and jokes, the weather reports and medical notes, they're no further on than when they started. Time and again, they bruise themselves on the hardness. *It's* like a boulder they can't get round. Their letters on the subject would fill a book. Better, pruned of repetitions, they'd make a play – a play of overlapping monologues, Two Characters in Search of a Denouement.

ARTHUR: Stop worrying. Leave it to Time and Fate.
KIM: Do you think Time and Fate will decide that we can be married in an RC church and have RC children, then?
ARTHUR: As far as I can see there are two possibilities. Either we decide now and finally that it will not work out, and remain pals, and hope that in a couple of years we can find happiness

with someone else. Or we can leave things as they are until I get home and out of uniform and we 'try it out'.

KIM: I don't know how I ever thought it would work out. I suppose only because I was so happy and loved you so much I couldn't bear the thought of not being with you. But now I know it's hopeless. This really feels like the end. Perhaps I've said enough to convince you that I'm not the one after all.

ARTHUR: I'm sorry if I upset you. But it's no use being like a couple of love-sick infants, is it? We must face facts – it's a very factual world.

KIM: For me the problem is simple: Is it better to be unhappy with you or unhappy without you?

ARTHUR: Remember me telling you about an orderly called Quinn? Well I was drinking with him last night, and he told me he was an RC who married a Protestant girl in a Protestant church and the children are Protestant. He had quite a row with his parents at the time but he is now very happily married and family relations are good. I just thought I'd tell you . . .

KIM: My brother Gerry was wanting to know what we were going to do about it, when I had a drink with him at the Queen's. Hearing your views, I'm afraid he wasn't cheerful. I didn't discuss it with him any further because I can't face up to the truth.

ARTHUR: I also met this Canadian pilot called Hubert, who it transpires once stayed with my Auntie Nan in Southport and is distantly related to her (and therefore to me). We had a few drinks and came back to the tent and had the wireless on. Then he got on to French-Canadians, and said how all the problems there boiled down to RCs, and how all the problems he'd seen on his travels through the world came down to backward peoples having that same religion. His own mother was a Catholic, his father too, but after she died his father started to please himself and told Hubert how much better he felt for it.

KIM: You think I'll eventually change *my* ideas, don't you? Well, I won't – ever. So where are we?

ARTHUR: We could choose to ignore certain things. There is an in-between, darling – if we changed our ideas a certain amount.

KIM: I'm terribly in love with you, but there's one thing I can't change.

ARTHUR: At worst we could always get divorced and start again.

KIM: I might as well live with you as marry you in a registry office – I'd feel just as married. Not a very nice feeling.

ARTHUR: You could get used to it in time.

KIM: I'd do a thousand things for you. But I can't marry anywhere but in my church.

So it goes on. They wear themselves out, taking refuge in drink and seasonal cheer. On Bonfire Night, Arthur watches rockets going off and warms his hands at a burning effigy of Hitler. On Christmas Eve, Kim goes to Windyridge, has a walk with Mary, helps put baby to bed, eats ham sandwiches, drinks a gin and lime, exchanges presents (a wallet cum purse from Kathleen, a brooch from Mary), and, after waiting an hour and a half at Worsley Courthouse for a bus, arrives shivering at Booth Hall and goes to Midnight Mass. The day itself she spends on the wards – though there's coffee and sandwiches in theatre at midday, tea with whisky at 4, then trifles, sweets and a panto for the kids. Arthur's Christmas Day begins in the mess at 10.30am with a beer (many men still half-drunk from the night before); then after the King's Speech the MOs serve the patients dinner; then it's more beer, laced with brandy, before their own cold buffet lunch and a couple of whiskies; more whisky in one of the huts; a game of squash and a shower; then a show at the Garrison Theatre, after which Arthur finds himself slaving behind the bar till 1am – but one of the lads has waited with a bottle of whisky for him, and then four orderlies turn up as tight as lords (he hides the whisky and gets out a bottle of brandy instead), and everyone's cheering him and booing Mac, and although he tries to stop them before they wake Mac up (and Carslake and Musgrave), off all the lads go up the hill cheering him and booing Mac – a satisfying day, though he'd rather have spent it at home. Ron doesn't get home for Christmas, either, but he does send a lavish present to Kela – a white wooden dog pulling a cart full of milk bottles, which when taken out can be used as skittles: such a lovely toy in these days of shoddy goods. The present enrages Arthur when he hears of it ('shows you what a terrible state of poverty and privation the Occupied countries have been in'), and isn't much consolation to Mary. Kind though he is to Kela, Ron's still being distant with *her*.

Will things pick up in 1945? It doesn't look likely. The Germans dig in for the winter. A good friend of Arthur and Ron is killed, Dick Strachan. V-bombs fall near Booth Hall. Then on 30 December Kim wakes to hear windows rattling and feel her bed shaking, and learns next day it wasn't a V-bomb but an earthquake. An earthquake in Manchester! (Not any dead.) Arthur has just read Kim's letter about this when, dammit, there's one in the Azores too, the floor quivering as he stands smoking at the bar. The earth beneath their feet is shifting, it seems. Both of them have terrible nightmares – Kim about dying in a plane crash, Arthur that the pinkish glow of his oil-stove is someone come to murder him. 'Happy New Year!' she writes, having spent the night round at Windyridge and, she confesses, 'kissed two men' – his father and old Mr Evans from next door. 'Wonder what 1945 will bring. I do hope it's going to be a happy one.' The mood at Windyridge is buoyant but she feels as though she's whistling in the dark. Sleeping in his bedroom is no comfort. On the door his dressing gown hangs empty.

Perhaps it's an omen. On 2 January, full of new-year decisiveness, he writes to her: 'I can finally say that under no circumstances will I be married in an RC church – or have RC children. That is definite and final – even if it should wreck my life.' The letter takes two weeks to arrive. 'I still can't believe that this must be the end,' she replies. Though she banters away in subsequent letters as if nothing had changed, with Mary she's weepy and depressed. 'Please don't think I'm interfering, but do you have to be so final?' Mary pleads with her brother. 'Poor little Kim hasn't been at all well lately and looks desolate. I hope you find some way not to ruin two lives like this. I speak from experience as someone who knows what it's like to lose everything.' Through Mary's mediation, they agree to go on writing, and to drop the subject of *it* till he gets home. But his message is an uncompromising No Surrender: marry him on his terms or not at all. She feels more despondent now than at any time in the past two years.

Her hope (against hope) is that he'll withdraw his ultimatum. His hope (a triumphalist confidence) is that she'll come over to his side. But if not, he won't despair. He has other fish to fry now. The seven sisters are about to arrive.

# CHAPTER NINE

# Love-Lines

I'M TEMPTED TO plot a graph. The love-line, let's call it. There's the landscape spreading out already, a range of valleys and peaks. The horizontal axis represents time, the vertical axis emotion, with indifference at the bottom, passionate intensity at the top, and attraction as the mean. Tracking the progress of my parents' love as measured on a scale of 0–10, I find them entering the chart round 3 in October 1942 (that party at Hope); climbing to 4 before he leaves for Iceland (she gets to meet his parents); holding steady at first, then dropping to 1 in the latter half of 1943 (she goes to Ireland, he talks of friendship, the letters become less frequent, both of them knock around with other people); rocketing to 9 in the early months of 1944 (the fortnight at Auntie's, the weekend in London); levelling out at 7 after he goes to the Azores (with a leap back up to 8 when he comes back for three days with his polio case); tailing off to 6 in the autumn as frustration and conflicts of faith set in; then sharply dropping to 4 and below after his ultimatum of January 1945. The line doesn't end there. There are more fluctuations to come before they marry. There are more after they marry. I could follow the line through to his death in 1991, or even, since she loved him all her life, to 1997. Only with her death does the line cease.

| OCT | MARCH | SEPT | JAN/FEB | JUNE/JULY | JAN |
| 42 | 43 | 43 | 44 | 44 | 45 |

A graph can help, but a graph can only show so much. The story of love isn't just a love story – other forces are at work. In the case of my parents, religious differences are a factor and make their love-line wobble, irrespective of other emotions and events. Work is another variable: my mother's flourishing career affects how my father thinks about her, and his lack of contribution to the war effort (his 'inactive service') damages his self-esteem, which in turn endangers his capacity to love. Then there's health, their own and that of their patients: a graph would have to show how flu, polio, menstruation, TB and perinatal death impact on the relationship. The variables make the line fluctuate in ways that are hard to track. That's if a single line is appropriate at all: shouldn't there be two lines, one for each protagonist, since their feelings for each other don't always coincide? If so, the blue (boy) line would almost certainly lead the way, with the pink (girl) line following a little behind: it was my father who called most of the shots. But my mother didn't live in his shadow; she had her own inner shadows as well, her moods and depressions and melancholy as well as her lack of faith in the relationship working out – so her love-line would, in general, be pitched lower than his. Two lines might make more sense. But should they start at the same side of the graph? Why not plot them from opposite corners, so they can marry in the middle? Even then a line wouldn't be adequate. How can a line register the doubts which lovers feel at the outset of an affair ('But I hardly know this person!') or later ('Is he/she right for me?'). Is love depressed or heightened or unbent by such self-questioning? And where would paradox figure on a graph? 'No one has ever felt this way before' lovers say, then in the next breath 'At last I know what love is'. Which makes no sense, but is impeccable heart-logic.

Graphs are a useful visual aid, but much of love remains invisible. Boffins in lab coats can measure heartbeat, pulse-rate, pupil-dilation, secretion of fluids and intensity of orgasm as indices of desire. But we doubt their methods and their motives, and they teach us only what we know. Poets are sometimes more help than scientists, but even poets can't be relied on to tell the truth. It was a poet, Yeats, who advised men to be strategic in love, to hold back in order to advance:

> Never give all the heart, for love
> Will hardly seem worth thinking of
> To passionate women if it seem
> Certain . . .

My mother, a quiet woman but a passionate one, wouldn't have agreed with Yeats. To her, the love my father offered was worth thinking of only because it *was* certain; she knew he loved her; any wavering and (given all the other difficulties) she'd have been out of there. But I'd be naive to think he told her everything in the letters. And certainly she didn't bare her heart for him. Honest though she was, she found it difficult to articulate all she thought and felt. She didn't *know* all she thought and felt. The love ran on, against the odds, but it didn't run plain or straight. Cross-currents troubled its path. They always do.

So much for love's vertical axis. What about the horizontal, progress through time? Can love be measured chronologically? How do you measure the wild fluctuations lovers go through within minutes ('I hate you', 'I adore you'), let alone hours, days, weeks and months? Is there a line at all? In retrospect, remembered at a safe distance, love appears as a series of squiggles and dots – vignettes, not a seamless narrative. Reflect on your own love-life and you'll see. A phrase, a hand, a birthmark, the beads of shower-water on her shoulder, the ferns we lay in as hikers passed along the fell-path, that day at the swimming pool, the amber slash in her left eye, the taste of her sweat, the tremor running under her skin just afterwards, the way she always eats the apple core, her laughter, her hair clogging the sink, her mispronunciations, the colour of Lake Louise as we stood gazing down, the evening she'll say the thing I've been wanting her to say, a hotel room in Stockholm, her right breast cupped in my palm as I sleep behind her nape, the secret night away we've been promising ourselves, paella and wine on the empty terrace restaurant, me washing her sleeping bag in the sea after she got sick from eating shrimps, that funny tooth, that dress, that other dress, the model in the Scottish Widows advert, my hand between her legs as she drove the car, the photo of her leaving the beach at Vai, the sudden thought (while out jogging) of the men she had before, that raffia bag she carried, the cards she sends, the e-mails, the phone call I'm still waiting for, the bump of her ankle, the curve of her leg, the shape of her mind. Love persists as an idea, the current under all we do, but these, the ways we remember love (or register it now, or anticipate it happening in the future), the palpable signs, have a separate existence. The in-love bits are just that: bits. Without them there'd be no line – no marriage, no children, no future. But on a graph the bits that matter don't show up.

Once I took home a girlfriend from university. We'd been sharing a house with other students, and my parents had met her twice. 'She seems a nice girl,' my mother said after the second occasion, adding when we were alone: 'I hope if you're sleeping together one of you is taking precautions.' I read this as acceptance and assumed we'd be allowed to share a room. But when we arrived my girlfriend was shown to the guest room while my father got me a drink. I protested: why the sudden prohibition? 'You can do what you like under your own roof,' my mother replied, 'but not under mine.' The night was humid and the house tense with static electricity. Upstairs, the spare room felt musty. Darkness leaned in from the moors. 'Like bloody Wuthering Heights,' said my girlfriend, sitting on the bed. She felt put out. The lack of welcome, the sleeping arrangements, my father conspicuously failing to offer her a drink – she wished she'd never come. We began to argue, in whispers. Come downstairs, I pleaded. No, she said, she was going home. At this time of night? I said, she must be mad. I was the mad one, she said, raising her voice. I clamped my hand over her mouth: what if my parents heard us rowing? She unclamped herself: so what, what if they did? Why not move back in with them if I was so bothered? As for her, she was off, she said, pushing me away, walking over to her suitcase and slamming it shut. There was a loud crack as the lid came down. A plastic bottle of suntan oil optimistically packed at the last moment had been wedged there, and oil exploded onto the grey flock wallpaper, leaving a pale brown stain in the shape of a tree: scattered leaf patterns up high, dense foliage in the middle, the drip of a trunk down onto the skirting board. Together we worked with tissues, toilet paper, towels, water, the acidic antidote of aftershave. None of it helped. We patted, we dabbed, we rubbed – to no effect. At last, reconciled by a hug and kiss, we went downstairs. There'd been a little accident, we explained. My girlfriend said she'd pay for any redecorating. My mum wouldn't hear of it. My dad belatedly offered a drink. We sat down and drank and ate and laughed, and my parents got to know my girlfriend better, and my girlfriend and I got to know each other better, and years later she became my wife.

The stain remained, despite all efforts to remove it. There it was, every time we visited, in full bloom behind the bedside cabinet my mother had bought to conceal it. A spot of time. A symbol of the muddle of sexual morality. And the site of an ancient battle. These days we bicker more than we row and often we don't do either: as an omen of marital discord the stain's beside the point. But I can't get it out of my head.

Where would the episode figure on a graph? Nowhere. Yet it seems important, for reasons I don't fully understand. It isn't romantic, and shows none of us in a flattering light, but it's there in my private anthology, alongside the more obvious pieces (first meeting, first sex, wedding-day, birth of children, etc). Perhaps it's no coincidence that my mother plays a part in the episode. In my Blakean-Lawrentian student phase, I saw her as an enemy of passion and sexual freedom. Yet I sensed there must be more to it, a story she wasn't telling, which had made her tense that day and eventually 'caused' the suitcase to explode. Who can say? I'll never get at the truth now she's dead; I'd never have got at it even were she still alive. Love's a dark and secret territory. We can make maps and draw graphs and assemble pie charts. But we'll never tell the half of it. We'll never know the heart.

My parents' love letters are a treasure trove. More prosaically, they're a resource. They help explain who my mother was, and how she lived, and why she acted as she did. There are things in them I didn't know. But I don't kid myself they tell me everything. And I'm happy for certain mysteries to remain.

CHAPTER TEN

# The Seven Sisters

*Arthur to Kim, Azores, 1.12.44*

Letter from Carina Tweedie, who was a nurse in Iceland – I never used to like her, but then her fiancé didn't come back one day after signalling he was about to attack a sub – to say that one of the seven nurses due to arrive here next month is a friend of hers, and very nice. So now you know what you're up against.

You say you 'can't imagine Ron wandering'. What about me? I think Ron would be less moody if he took several girls out, if only to test his will power.

*Kim to Arthur, Booth Hall, 20.1.45*

Shocking fog and ice again. The ambulances say they won't go out – at least the drivers do. Feel jolly glad I'm not doing GP in the country somewhere – it would be hellish.

Was at Windyridge the other day. At supper your dad said for the hundredth time that Pendlebury was the only decent children's hospital in Manchester. He's always rubbing it in – thinks Booth Hall is a dump. But I told him a thing or two. As if it would have any effect on him once he's got an idea. (Just like someone else I know.)

I don't agree that it's a pity Ron isn't taking girls out to test his will power. Would you like me to test my will power? Are you planning to test yours with the nurses? Please try to last out the remaining weeks.

*Arthur to Kim, Azores, 26.1.45*

Only one interesting news item today, but a major one: the seven sisters arrived at 1am. Needless to say, I was not there to tuck them in bed. My friend Carslake hadn't even had any beds made up for them – just left them some blankets and sheets on bare mattresses: 'Why should they be treated differently to airmen?' Presumably they're still in bed now – they had a rough crossing. I gather Miss Butler is really . . . [PART OF PAGE TORN OFF]. And I hear two others aren't at all bad-looking, either. Mac and Jim aren't going to tell their wives in case of jealousy. I ask you, what a way to be married. I'm glad you and I aren't like that, darling.

I do remember being jealous as hell when you went out with Billy in Manchester, even though Mary Galvin was there too. And who was that type who used to take you out from the Leigh area or somewhere? And then some guy from Bolton. When I think of it, I guess you are as full of wiles as any French girl.

*Arthur to Kim, Azores, 27.1.45*

Carslake brought all seven nurses down to SSQ to see us. I can't say I was all that impressed, but they do seem decent, pleasant girls, and are a better-looking bunch than the ones we had in Reyky. Carslake was in his element. They start their duties tomorrow morning – and I am up at the hospital all this week. Nice bit of timing.

What I meant about taking out a girl doing Ron (and me) good is that after a time when one can't speak to a girl one starts thinking about it more and more – then one feels hellish naughty and begins to wonder whether one would remain faithful – and in fact generally gets frightened of oneself, etc. It's hard to explain. But having seen all the other blokes slipping, I've actually wondered what I would do should a lovely girl present herself here. And surely if I couldn't go out with another girl after you and I were married without feeling unfaithful – well, I shouldn't have married you, should I? Not that I will ever want to take one out, but you see what I mean. It's the same with you – I wouldn't be at all happy if you were just a little girl who had not seen life at all, I would worry about how you would react after say a couple of years of married life.

6pm now, and we've got to go up to the Senior Officers' Mess for cocktails – they are entertaining the sisters. Poor girls, the great social round has begun. Must dash – toodle.

*Kim to Arthur, Booth Hall, 27.1.45*

Busy all day. Quite a few scalds. Still very cold and foggy. Think my bathroom is the only one functioning – burst pipes everywhere else.

Called at Hope and was persuaded to stay on to supper with the offer of a drive back from Mike Winstanley. He's getting married soon. You'll be glad to hear he didn't run out of petrol and dropped me at the gate without even stopping the engine. I know you don't trust him much, and I don't either, but it was a decent gesture on his part to give me a lift.

Ron said he saw a cartoon in an American SSQ which said 'Don't let VD spoil your V-Day'.

Daddie is still in bed in Killorglin: not too bad, but the doctor says he has to stay there.

Had the most amazing dream last night – that I was having a baby.

*Arthur to Kim, Azores, 29.1.45*

Last night had a look at a type who had tried to sever his carotids – unsuccessfully, poor devil – then on to a medical meeting, to which the nurses came. On my ward is Cousins (Lorna) – Guys-qualified, about 30, a decent type, but hardly seductive (you've no worries there). She has been on theatre work for the past 8 years so doesn't know how to treat sore throats, colds, etc, which is all she'll have to deal with here. Hooper (Audrey) – tall and sweet, about 27 – looks as though she should be engaged but I didn't see a ring. Rees (Molly) is the youngest and most attractive, dark, rather pale, and enticing – and she seems to flirt rather well. The others are Miss Byrne, the Senior Sister – Irish, plenty character, 35. Miss Williams – heavily built, about 34, very straightforward. And, probably the nicest of the lot, Dilys Palmer, small, nice figure, fair, blue eyes, rather sweet. Then of course there's Miss Butler – Carina Tweedie's friend, who has the biggest . . . [PARTS OF PAGE CUT OUT OR TORN OFF] . . . you've ever seen and supposedly . . . ready to do it with anyone . . . casting shy glances my way . . . well in there by the look of it . . . I was in bed by 11, alone.

*Kim to Arthur, Booth Hall, 30.1.45*

Don't know if I told you that Dr Crawford's wife had a baby in Hope – it died after 10 days of pneumonia. There was also a very bad outbreak of gastro-enteritis on the Mider block and they lost about 14 babies. They had bacteriologists up from Oxford to investigate, but it seems it was a virus infection and nothing could be done.

My letters are short and miserable, I know. The day you get this you'll probably go out and get drunk, and I don't blame you. And if there are any nurses about, you'll probably feel like saying 'what the hell' and taking them out, and I don't blame you.

*Arthur to Kim, Azores, 1.2.45*

The blasted Nazis have a ridiculous amount of fight left in them yet – damn their eyes – but I feel more cheerful now than I've done for the past ten months. Stood in the moonlight last night with Throne and Coffin imagining how we would hear of the end of the war – probably an announcement on the wireless. Whether it takes six months or is over tomorrow, I can't imagine what it will be like to live in peace again.

Later, went to chat to Charles in his tent, because he'd been out with Molly Rees. I'd suggested to him earlier that now the girls had finished their official social round we might take them for a walk – only to find he was already organised. He took her to the flicks, and after was surprised by his own virtuousness – they sat on the hill looking down on all the lights of the town and talked about lots of things – and then he took her back and she asked him to 'come in' to their mess, and there was no one else there – but he amazed himself by saying 'No, I had better go'. He feels wonderful now, confident in himself again, because he was worried how he'd react to a situation like that after being here 15 months – and he's a married man with two kids.

This morning talked to 'de goils' again till 12. Tonight am going out with Bugs and Hicks – with Cousins, Hooper and Rees.

Had shocking dream last night. It was that you arrived soon

after the nurses but I got drunk and spoilt everything, after being so good for so long – disgusting.

*Mary to Arthur, 1.2.45*

Kim has asked me to write because she won't be able to herself for a few days – her father is very ill and they've sent for her.

*Arthur to Kim, Azores, 3.2.45*

Collected the girls at 7 (amazingly they were ready and waiting). Got to Praia at 7.20, ordered supper and walked up the street to a little cafe where we had one brandy each. There were half a dozen drunk airmen there (it was payday) and three Portuguese with mandolins, and a piano, and singing, so the noise was terrific – after a bit Hicks took over on piano and we finally had to drag him away. At the Confienca, Audrey (Hooper) and Fifi (Lorna Cousins – or Cosens – anything less like Fifi I can't imagine, but it's what she likes to call herself) had half a chicken each, and the rest of us steak and eggs. Then fruit salad and at 10.45 we went down to the Miramar, where we sat on high stools at the bar and more or less paired off – Hicks with Audrey, Bugs with Molly, and Fifi with me . . .

You'd think he'd never seen a woman before. Six months on his dusty archipelago and the nurses are like water in the desert. It's not that they're glamorous or that he's looking for romance. But with relations back home at a standstill, he feels like having fun. Since leaving Kim on Swindon station back in June, the only good time he's been offered with a woman is the sort you have to pay for, and he's too mean or fastidious for that. On his two recent jaunts away – Gibraltar and Casablanca, then neighbouring Furnas – there were prostitutes on every street corner. But he resisted, unlike his companions, alluring though some of the women were. So he told Kim. And given the candour with which he recounts his enthusiasm for the nurses, there's no reason to doubt his word. Credit where it's due: Arthur is honest. Where his fellow officers omit to tell their wives and fiancées about the arrival of seven unmarried young nurses, Arthur refuses to play that game. Perhaps he's playing other games. I wouldn't put it past him. But he can't be accused of secrets and lies.

Doctors and Nurses is a game in itself, of course. In the Azores they play the adult version, not the one where children undress. According to the rules, doctors have the money and power, nurses the youth and beauty, and play follows strictly gendered lines. The object is for the doctor to make a sexual conquest and for the nurse to earn kudos by association. There are snakes as well as ladders – scandal, pregnancy, anonymous letters sent to spouses – but if the game's played sensibly no one need lose. The only real danger is of a doctor breaking a nurse's heart, *his* heart by definition being unbreakable. Whether Mac, Carslake, Coffin, Throne *et al*, are old hands at the game isn't a matter of record. But they, too, seem excited by the seven water-bearing maidens, and, to reward their fetching and carrying, organise a night out on the town. A slap-up meal. Then a bit of slap and tickle afterwards. Just what the doctor ordered.

To the nurses it's discomfiting to be fussed over so much, though hardly a surprise. Any woman in the forces can expect sexual advances. 'Lie to them and lie on them' is the principle: women in the ATS are treated as a groundsheet by the army and WRENs as a rubber dinghy by the navy. It's why some nurses choose to attach themselves to the RAF, since pilots are meant to be more respectable. The seven sisters would like to meet a pilot or two at Lagens, but they're not given chance. 'Come for a drink,' the doctors plead, monopolising them. 'A meal, a dance, a walk, anything.' It's a difficult business and the nurses don't intend to be easy. But a girl can get lonely too. And wonder why she's holding out when an attractive man takes her arm along the clifftops, and the air's warm, and the moon slips a band of gold across the sea . . .

Harmless fun: so Arthur presents it to Kim. A bit of mixed company for a change, that's all, pet – nothing so naughty that he can't share it with her. She's uncertain how to react. If they'd

broken it off irrevocably, he'd not be telling her. That he writes as often as ever is a sign of hope, hopeless though things seem to be. That he'd like to make her jealous, by banging on about the sisters, isn't wholly dispiriting, either: at least he's still *involved*. She finds it hard not to bite his head off all the same. Is this a fore-taste of what marriage will be like, him going out all the time while she's stuck on Kids' duty? And why should she feel good about him enjoying himself without her? When she hears 'Making Whoopee' played on the wireless – the woman who sits alone most every night, the man who doesn't phone or write – the words strike home. Arthur says he's innocently busy, but is he?

In one letter he compares British servicemen with GIs, concluding, 'All men are as bad – not a thought above the navel – except that we, unlike the Yanks, stop before rape.' All men are as bad and women, so she feels, aren't much better: she has just heard reports of a scandal back at Dudley Road, where an MO and nurse slipped into the empty ante-natal clinic during a party, prompting other doctors and nurses to follow suit – next morning cleaning staff found underwear strewn about the floor.

That's what happens when doctors and nurses socialise after hours. How can Arthur seriously pretend it's innocent? Even if *he's* innocent, there's no knowing the wiles of nurses. The determination, too, when they get their claws in. And the easy physicality: being around bodies all day can make them pretty uninhibited about their own. No, she doesn't like the sound of it. Heaven knows, she's one of six sisters herself – eight if you count the two that died – and knows what women are like. She'd tell him this and more. But he wouldn't listen and she'll not play the nagging wife – that's what he wants, and she won't give him the satisfaction. So the tone she takes with him is as gently teasing as she can make it. 'Just look the other way,' she advises, 'eyes right if the sisters are on the left, and vice versa.' It would be humiliating to admit what she really feels.

The only clue comes from Mary, who tells Arthur how desolate she looks. It doesn't dampen his enthusiasm for recounting his outings with the 'goils'. Nor does he seem to take in that her father's very ill (suspected cardiac failure), and that she has been feeling so under the weather that she went three days without food. Perhaps he *does* notice, but decides she must be exaggerating or playing the victim. Then, on the last day of January, her father takes a turn for the worse and she's summoned home to Ireland. When she sees him, on the Friday night, she gives him less than a day to live – he can't keep anything down, is fibrillating, and the family doctor says 'It won't be long'. But he survives the weekend, and by the Tuesday it looks as if he'll pull through. She'd stay longer, but the hospital has given her only a few days' leave, and that, as she tells Arthur, with very poor grace: 'Patterson didn't even say he was sorry, just asked, in a horrible tone, "How long will you be off for?" Now it looks as if I can go back with an easy mind. Daddie knows how bad he is and is very frightened and likes to have people with him all the time. Fortunately both nurses are very good.'

But are the nurses in the Azores good? Is Arthur? The letters he has sent in her absence, so she finds on her return to Manchester, are full of drinks and meals and late nights. On the 3rd, he 'more or less pairs off with Fifi'. On the 5th, the sisters are taken for a posh dinner, 'all in evening dresses – and what evening dresses, some marvellously seductive.' The dinner is followed by dancing on 'excuse-me' lines and once again he goes for Nurse Cosens, whom he christens Cosy ('better than Fifi – I'll see how she reacts when I call her it'). On the 7th, with the Allies just forty miles from Berlin, he reports the latest advances: 'Charles is doing a very strong line with Molly. He'll probably break her heart, apart from other things.' On the 10th, he has to stay in for once, as OMO, but doesn't mind, since Cosy is on night duty all month.

By now he has heard of her father's illness, and writes to console her, though the consolation is oddly tactless: 'I must admit I have a feeling that you were too late. I feel a miserable devil writing that but at least I'm being honest. After all, if he is fit and well you can laugh at my feeling. And if you were too late, it's probably a good thing – I'm glad I've missed the actual deaths of all my relatives up till now. What we want to remember is not the terminal part but how they were when enjoying life.' He could murder himself for 'carrying on as normal having a good time', he says. The bits he cut off the page about Miss Butler were only meant as a tease (she's fat, 40 and matronly). Chastened, he says sorry for pulling her leg – then happily resumes his narrative of who exactly is getting off with whom.

Does he expect her to love him regardless? Or has he begun to think of her as a boyish confidante to his escapades? Whichever, he finds it natural to tell her every little thing. Share and share alike: that's the principle. So even the meals and drinks he shares with other women, he shares, in writing, with her. It may be naive or narcissistic of him to think she won't be affected by it. It may be crass to go into such nudging detail. But it proves he has no 'side', and he doesn't know how else to be. At first, she takes it well. Even when she returns from Ireland she doesn't protest. But that's only, she tells him, 'because I was too tired and miserable to be jealous.' Once she has time to think about it, she declares herself 'jealous as hell. Up to now I've had nothing to worry about. But now I'm sitting here at night, wondering where you are and who with, etc. I also think you

took the very unhappy letters I sent you too lightly. And you
don't seem to have noticed that since I wrote them, and told you
how hopeless it all seems, my tone has been what you would call
"brittle and impersonal". Even the news that you're coming
home before too long doesn't thrill me like it should. But I'm
miserable enough already without getting on to that subject.'

At least when he's out as one of a crowd, he can fairly claim
there's nothing dodgy going on. What if he started cosying up
with one particular nurse, though? How would that be?

✻   ✻   ✻

*Arthur to Kim, Azores, 10.2.45*

Stayed talking to Cosy last night – about all the MOs and general
scandal. She lost her fiancé last February when he went down with
his destroyer. I asked her to go to a dance at Angra and she rang
back this morning to say OK, as Audrey will stand in for her. Basil
is taking Dilys and Charles Molly.

*Kim to Arthur, Booth Hall, 14.2.45*

Very shocked by Charles's behaviour. If he doesn't think of his wife,
shouldn't he feel a bit ashamed, especially with you and others
knowing he is married? Or is this sort of thing so common no one
takes any notice? Actually, quite a few of the married sisters and
staff nurses here talk glibly about men they've been going out with.
But to me it seems like asking for trouble.

*Arthur to Kim, 14.2.45*

It was 10.20 before we got to the Tennis Club. Even so we were among
the first to arrive, and all sat on high stools at the bar. We knocked
back a few brandy and oranges, and then the band started. In no time
at all the wolves moved in – I saw Cosy for about 10 minutes, and had
only two dances with her all evening. There was a lot of confetti
about, and everyone tried to catch everyone else with their mouth

open – the paper fell in our drinks and had to be picked out. I got
into wonderful form – just perfectly whistled. At 3am Carslake
suggested it was time to go, so we left – eight of us in his car – at 4.

### Kim to Arthur, 20.2.45

Eight in the car coming back from the dance? Quite a crush.
Someone must have had to sit in someone else's lap. Come on, let's
have it. You realise there is not an ounce of jealousy in my make-up
– though I hope Mr Tierney wasn't watching when I read your latest
letter and didn't hear me say 'hmm'.

Dreamt Daddie died again last night – that's twice in one week.

### Arthur to Kim, Azores, 21.2.45

Taking out other women has interfered with my letter writing again,
I'm afraid. On Wednesday, lovely weather, Harra and I went out with
Cosy and Audrey for the afternoon. We wangled lifts down to the air-
sea rescue base, and took two rowboats out, and went round to the
bathing beach and had a wizard bathe and general fool about on the
sands. Audrey was on night duty, but after dinner I nipped up and
collected Cosy and took her to the Azoria, for a stage show. Good
compere, contortionist (ginger-haired, female), concertina player
( female – blonde), xylophonist ( female – brunette) and card-trick
bloke.

Last night the band was playing in the mess – a damn good
excuse for a party, so we had one. That's 3 parties in 4 nights!
Harradence was damn funny imitating Bing Crosby by singing into
an empty jug of water.

### Kim to Arthur, Booth Hall, 22.2.45

Went with Mary to see 'The Thin Man Goes Home' at the flicks. We
got in just at the end of the previous showing and being a thriller I
didn't want to see the ending. The two couples in the back row
weren't watching either. I said to Mary 'There's a much better
picture on behind us.'

How is your Cousin? No, don't give her my regards. I once tried to tell you that human nature is very weak but you said that was ridiculous. At least you won't need me to darn your socks for you now. But don't get them done in your tent, and don't get too cosy, even with a Cousin.

### Arthur to Kim, 23.2.45

Yesterday I went up to the hospital and collected Cosy and walked along the cliffs, just the two of us – left at 2.30 and got back at 6. What do you think happened? I'll tell you. <u>We walked all the time</u>. There were too many airmen about to sit down. It would have been too cold anyway.

You shouldn't be shocked by married men taking girls out – it is more or less the done thing with 80 per cent of them. I agree you can go out with lots of males – safety in numbers, etc. – but alone it always leads to someone thinking it is the 'real thing'. I should know. So don't you start trying it out.

### Kim to Arthur, 5.3.45

Wizard day – very cold but the sun is pouring in as I sit here in front of a roaring fire. There is a field across from here where they play football. And at this moment I can see them bringing someone in on a stretcher so I guess here comes some work for me.

Wonder what you are doing now – talking to Cosy? This is one of those nights when I'd normally write you a miserable letter, but we seem to have given up that discussion. I still wonder what's going to happen when you come home. Anyway, you may have fallen for Cosy by then.

### Arthur to Kim, 5.3.45

Can just picture you chasing through my letters to see how far my latest spearheads to the sisters have advanced. I don't intend to let you relax. Mac is now starting a quiet line with Audrey and is most conscience-stricken. He gets damned annoyed when I pull his leg and threaten to write to his wife, etc. – crazy! I think Charles is still virtuous, with Molly, but only just.

I hadn't realised I only defined women in two ways – seductive or hand-picked – but I'll stick to it until I think of a better way. It's 2pm now and Harra and I are taking Audrey and Cosy walking along the cliffs – they're bringing tea and sandwiches. So will continue later. Toodle.

PS If I seem to be out a lot with Cosy and the others, don't forget there is very little to do here – I've really no work unless I look for it. Also, the island does seem more civilised – and normal – with girls here. Stops us getting blind drunk and swearing.

So *that* was where it came from. In the last months of the war, my father decided that a man could take a woman out and expect his *other* woman – the one back home – to accept it. Harmless fun, he said. Kim wasn't convinced. Nor Mary. He didn't care. Let them mither all they like, this was his notion of marriage. He got the seed from the Azores and when the war ended brought it home with him, in hopes of growing an exotic flower. It wasn't the flower of polygamy exactly, nor that of a *mariage blanc*. But he believed a man could blossom by having two women in his life, one for companionship and one for pleasure. It was a difficult notion to cultivate in the cold, thin soil of post-war England. For a time he forgot he'd even planted it. But in the late 1950s and early 1960s it appeared in luscious bloom. And loomed over my childhood. And for ten years or more overshadowed my mother's life.

If my tone's reproachful, that's because she suffered. But I don't judge Arthur harshly for his conduct in the spring of '45. He has TXitis. Tent life has begun to tire. His career, his hopes of marriage, the peace – all are on hold. There are only a few weeks till he goes home, and he might as well make the most of them. In his innocence, he tells Kim everything. He might have made life easier for himself by leaving bits out. But he can't help blabbing the truth. A man, he says, can see a bit of life and not get carried away: to take a single girl out now and then is 'more or less the done thing' among 80 per cent of husbands. A woman, on the other hand, being by nature weak and romantic, should go out with men only in a crowd; spend time with just the one man and she'll start thinking it's the real thing. He doesn't say how Cosy might be feeling after all the time spent *à deux* with him. His concern is to make a different point: that boys' rules don't apply to Kim.

What's revealing is how she reacts to this – or, rather, how she doesn't. Her tolerance is being severely tested. First, he tells her that 'under no circumstances' will he marry her in a Catholic church, even if this means the end of their relationship. Then he recounts his nights out with the nurses, which soon become nights out with one particular nurse, Cosy. Finally she is informed that, should they marry, he intends to go out with other women (whereas she has no such rights, since as a woman – so sweet, straightforward and emotional – she'd not be able to cope). It's enough to make anyone fly off the handle, or call it quits. Added to that is the sense of *déjà vu* she must feel about his christening games – rather than call Nurse Cosens by her given name (Lorna) or preferred one (Fifi), he invents his own (Cosy), which would suggest that he's far from indifferent to her. Several times Kim owns up to feeling jealous. But only once – on her return from Ireland – does she say it with conviction. For the rest her tone is teasing. Rather than nag or whimper or explode, she sends him up. Isn't it bad road safety to crowd eight into a car? Don't they say that mixing women (like mixing drinks) is bad for your health? Even when he posts her a photograph of the goils – a few months back he was complaining how unflattering photographs of her were: is this his idea of how women *ought* to look? – she keeps her temper and makes a cool appraisal: 'This is my honest, unprejudiced opinion. Audrey is very attractive, much more so than Molly, though she has a nice smile. Cosy looks quite nice too. But I'd pick Barbara Stanwyck as a pin-up.' Pique would be undignified. To put up and shut up is the only sensible course. Agnes-like, she takes it like a lamb.

Why? Because she trusts him? Because she reads his accounts as pathetic stratagems for making her jealous? Because she knows

he'll soon be home and what he does in the Azores is of no consequence? Or because she's already withdrawn from him, seeing that he won't compromise over her religion? Has she even begun to despair of marriage itself? Every marriage is unhappy in a different way, but those she has come across in recent months seem particularly wretched. Take Bill and Betty Strachan, newly married friends of Mary. When he came home on leave at Christmas Bill slept at his mother's house instead of with Betty, and now he's written to her wanting to call the whole thing off. There's also a staff nurse whose husband is away in the RAF and who has had several affairs in his absence. Now she's pregnant – maybe maritally, maybe not. They have a long talk, and at the end the nurse says, 'I do hope you get married soon, doctor.' Get married? To be promiscuous like her or abandoned like Betty Strachan? No thanks. But the nurse's argument is that she, Kim, is 'too cold and blasé' and that marriage would do her good. The comment knocks her back: she doesn't *feel* cold and blasé. But it's a mask she wears when feeling vulnerable. And with all she has had to face since January, she has instinctively slipped it on. Her letters to Arthur only hint at what's underneath. But Mary, for one, has seen it.

What keeps her going, as always, is her work. Doing too much of it stops her brooding, and coping with others' distress contains her own. New Year's Day sets the pattern – first a toddler DOA (dead on arrival: she has to break it to the mother), then a baby who's WR+ (tests positive for the Wassermann reaction – evidence of congenital syphilis): 'I had to tell that mother, too. Nice new year presents. I felt like a home-breaker.' (The baby dies within a week – a blessing.) Soon after, she assists with a tracheotomy on a kid with laryngal diphtheria; she'd always thought a tracheotomy a clean operation, done in minutes, but Tierney, to her fury, takes over an hour – and a fortnight later the child dies. One with meningitis dies, too. There's an outbreak of gastro-enteritis on the Mider ward, followed by an epidemic of tonsillitis. One week the police interview her about a child abandoned on a convent doorstep, the next they're crawling all over the place after another kid is found dead in a sandpit. She'd feel better if she liked her immediate colleagues, 'two Yids and three Irishmen', but only Winner, one of the former, earns her respect. The specialists are a waste of time, too – Ashley, for instance, swans in, asks 'What's this?', looks at her notes, doesn't bother to examine the patient and just gives back her own diagnosis, whether correct or not. Money for old rope. Whereas she earns barely enough to buy a ball of string – in February her take-home is just £11. 'Must see why the Income Tax people are taking so much away,' she complains to Arthur, and in the meantime tells the hospital that she intends to stick to her six-month contract and leave in May – perhaps before he gets home.

Depressed as she is, she's glad to spend any free hours with Mary, who's about to move into Red Lodge, the bungalow her father bought. One day they go to inspect the completed decorating, walking through snow across the park. Mary has lit an oil-stove the previous night to stop the pipes freezing, and as they approach the house there's an acrid smell. When they open the door, smoke rolls out to greet them. The oil-stove must have been smoking for hours, because the walls and paintwork are covered a filthy black – very upsetting, not least when they have to tell Ernest, who hits the roof. Two weeks later, the place cleaned up, they make plans to sleep there, but spend so long shoving unwanted stuff up in the attic – Kim standing on a shaky ladder, hauling up chairs and suitcases, the two of them in fits of laughter – there isn't time. At last Mary does move in, a week before her 25th birthday. Unsettled by bombs and fearful of burglars, she doesn't like sleeping there alone with Kela. But to go back to Windyridge would feel like failure. So they agree that Kim will stay over as often as her hospital duties allow.

The arrangement lets them pool their troubles. Not that Kim's the moaning kind, but inevitably, one night in early March, after a drink or two, the story of Cosy comes out – and Mary is suitably outraged. In a letter sent to Arthur the following day, she lets him have it:

So you're taking a nursing sister out and making Kim jealous and you say 'Goodie'. Well, I'm glad to hear you're enjoying life again but amazed that having women there can make such a difference, while we women at home are supposed to lead a completely manless existence. Why is it that men can do just as they bloody well like and women be jealous as hell, but let us go out with a man and that's wrong. My advice to Kim is also to go out with a man, but I can imagine what trouble there would be if she did. Why can't any of you see how damned unfair it is? One rule for men and another for women – my God. I don't care how innocent you say it is – it's just not bloody well fair. Not that Kim grumbles but it must hurt knowing that you're concentrating on one woman and thoroughly enjoying life because of it. I suppose men will always be the same but oh how I'd love to reverse positions and see what happened. I am aware there are some women today doing their husbands wrong, but good God when a man knows he's got a decent woman at home why does he have to take another one out?

Well, no more. I can quite imagine what a cutting epistle I shall get in return because it will hit you in the raw and you'll try to bluff it out by being sarcastic. But it won't wash, brother, and in your heart of hearts you know it's wrong.

The line Mary takes – 'One rule for men and another for women . . . it's just not bloody well fair' – wasn't as commonplace then as it is now. Most people, certainly the people she and Arthur knew, believed that men and women had different *urges*. If a man let himself go occasionally, that was normal. But if a woman did the same, she was disturbed, wanton, a nymphomaniac. Mary doesn't buy this stuff. Arthur needs standing up to, for his own good. For Kim's good, too – she, Mary, knows what it's like to have a man walk all over you, and though in the short term she tolerated that with Michael, in the long, if they'd been allowed a long, it would have been different. An unbalanced relationship is in no one's interests. Before Kim can resolve the great RC issue, she must fight Arthur on this one – and rein him in.

Mary wouldn't be so fierce but for a worry that Ron is behaving just like Arthur. Though his letters home suggest that life is a virtuous round of tooth-filling, she knows it can't be. Since January, he's been tootling round Normandy in his Mobile Dental Surgery, a converted three-ton Ford with 'Nobody's Baby' written above the windscreen. Life on the open road suits him fine: there's none of the 'bull and braid' you get in the mess, he likes cooking for himself ('soup, bully beef, toast and lashings of tea'), and you make some interesting finds: 'whilst we were stuck in a ditch the other day, I came across a human vertebra in the mud – a grim reminder of the last war.' ('A good Jerry' he later captioned the photo he took.) Unnervingly, his patch includes Minaucourt, the village where Michael was shot down – 'Funny how, of all the parts of the Continent, I should land here . . . Makes me think sometimes.' Already he has been to visit Michael's grave – a wooden cross in the corner of the village, with a vase of freshly-cut flowers beside – and sends photographs of what he finds. It sets Mary's mind at rest to know the grave is cared for, but the visit's a cause of friction all the same. Because she'd said, when he asked, that he mustn't bother about going, or go to the trouble of taking photos, he now infers she didn't really want him to go, and that she wished he hadn't taken photos, and that she thinks he only went to lay the ghost of Michael so that he, Ron, could receive due consideration as a marriage suitor. Such a touchy devil – he's always misunderstanding her. But perhaps it was naive of them to think a visit wouldn't cause trouble: seeing a shot of Michael's grave was bound to upset her. Whatever the rights and wrongs, Ron has now pulled back. 'I have started writing again to a very pretty WAAF,' he confides to Arthur. 'She was one of the blondes at Kirkham and so far things have developed into us spending a 48 together.'

So Mary's intuitions are right: fed up with not knowing how he stands with her, Ron has begun to stray. It's no wonder she rips into Arthur when she hears of *his* adventures. As a retaliatory measure, she encourages Kim to go to a Fancy Dress Ball at Booth Hall. 'Have yourself a good time there,' she urges, 'or at least make Arthur think you have.' Together, they kit her out as a little Dutch girl, in an apron, a cap, clogs, plaits and a frock that ends two inches above the knee. No one will believe the plaits are real (though they are, her hair having grown long again), and they all say she looks seventeen. There are prizes for the best costumes, and the feeling among the judges – who include the leering Phelps – is that the little Dutch girl must be given one. But then it's revealed that she's a doctor in disguise, and the policy is to give prizes only to nurses. Afterwards Phelps apologises for not recognising her. She sidles away from him, and spends the evening dancing with two brothers, one an RAF pilot, the other a naval type, both very nice. But she's not at her best (the next three days she spends in bed with flu) and lacks the will to take revenge on Arthur. Her letter to him about the ball is too mild to make him jealous. And when she drools over Paget, the dishy new MO, or tries to – 'I wouldn't say he's tall, dark and handsome – but he's dark, anyway. And he isn't married' – the tone is too light to be convincing.

Peace is only weeks away. Though Mary says she should be waging war, Kim lets things be and consoles herself with cheap music. Arthur mightn't deserve her love but how can she help it? She's got him under her skin. Night and day he's the one. Can't help loving dat man of hers.

\* \* \*

*Arthur to Kim, 20.3.45*

Shocking party to inaugurate the sisters' mess. It had begun as a cocktail party for the COs, and by the time we got there at 8.30 the band were all drunk, any remaining COs were out on their feet, and numerous other bods were whistled. I'm glad to say only one of the sisters was – Audrey. We had some quick drinking to do to catch up. It broke up round 10.30 – at which point 10 of us (including Cosy) went along to the Jappes place, had a fry-up (toast, bacon, scrambled eggs) and drank bourbon and coffee.

No more news except good war news – the Rhine bridgehead's rapidly enlarging. I think at this rate Germany might cave in while I'm on leave.

*Kim to Arthur, 22.3.45*

Glorious spring day again. Windows wide open. Half-expect you to appear any moment. Think I'll go stockingless from now on. Did an appendix last night, because Tierney is away in Ireland and Pattison asked if I'd like to. It felt good to do some cutting again – really enjoyed it.

Have talked to Paget a lot lately. He's very nice. I haven't worked on him yet. With you coming home in April it might be too complicated. But then again . . .

Nice of Harra not to come with you and Cosy to Praia. He must think it's the real thing if he felt to be intruding.

*Arthur to Kim, 1.4.45, Easter Sunday*

Perhaps I've not explained I only exaggerate about Cosy (who, as I've said is about 32) to pull your leg. If I wanted to make it 'the real thing' I couldn't: she is out with other males (in groups, usually) on other nights. If I wanted to make it a sexual relationship I couldn't. <u>I just go out for something to do</u>. Got that? If you only meant to tease me, please in future put exclamation marks to make it clear.

Everything is going to finish together – my tour, your job, the war. Today, after tea, practised bag-packing for half an hour – then got annoyed with myself for wasting my time like that. Musgrave has been packed nearly a week and sits in his tent all day doing nothing. Jim Flitcroft has closed his surgery, and spends his time with an ENSA actress, Esther Coleman (he apparently knew her in London). Mac Russell wanders round like a lost sheep when he isn't talking to Audrey. Charles is restless, too – and only takes Molly out twice a week.

*Kim to Arthur, 1.4.45*

Daddie is not so good again. I should be very upset, but I have got used to the idea that it is only a question of time. Sounds cold-blooded, but he is one of these people who hates not being on his feet – and I realised when I left home last time I might never see him again.

*Arthur to Kim, 2.4.45*

Squadron party the other night. Shortly after arrival I was shaken rigid by one of the boys getting up and making a most complimentary speech and then presenting me with a wooden desk-set (blotter, ink-wells, pad, calendar, etc.), which must have cost at least £4. Honestly, from a small bunch of airmen it was magnificent. When I stood up to try to thank them, I had a pretty effective tremor on, I can tell you. Later they tried to get me drunk and more or less succeeded – I eventually poured myself into bed about 1am.

I think I'm taking Cosy out tomorrow night. And Audrey reminded me about a long-since-promised walk along the cliffs so I said I'd take her on Friday afternoon. Quite in demand. Not bad, eh.

*Kim to Arthur, 6.4.45*

Letter from Sheila who, after all the time she's spent in London has now, with the war nearly over, gone and got herself a job somewhere near Leicester. She says they have started victory celebrations in London already.

SO THE WAR drew to a close and the cosiness with Cosy came to nothing: that's what his last Azores letters suggest. Or was he subtler than I'm giving him credit for? Was his denial of 1 April – 'If I wanted to make it a sexual relationship, I couldn't' – just another of his April Fool jokes? His letters break off on 8 April, though he may not have flown home for another week. On the 5th he took Cosy to a show. On the 6th he got 'beautifully whistled' at a cocktail party, though – untypically – he claims not to have bothered with the sisters. There was still that walk he'd promised to Audrey, and the time allotted to Cosy. Warm winds, white sands, vertiginous cliffs, the feeling of spring in the air. The empty seats at the back of the Azoria, in darkness after the film, with everyone gone. Who can say what happened? He was young, she was young, next day he'd be going home, what more natural than a memento of their time together, if only a kiss . . . I don't know. It's not my place to know. People die and you're left with the holes where their lives were. My parents are aching voids now. I'd like to body them forth. But their lives belong to them, not me. I've been trying to tell the story their letters tell. Archivist, editor, biographer, novelist – I'm a little of all of these. But also a son. Filiality needn't stop me speculating. But curiosity should stop short of prurience. What my dad did with Cosy isn't important. I know that, because I know the ending. But the role she occupied was important. I know that too.

If my mother had known the ending, would she have played it differently in the spring of 1945? I think she would. Confrontation wasn't her style, but she'd have let him know that girlfriends were out of the question. Instead, she clammed up and hoped the problem would go away. She tried falling out of love with him, too, and was tempted to end it, to call the whole thing off by air-mail. But that was too painful a prospect: if they called the whole thing off, then they'd have to part, and oh, if they had to part, then that would break her heart. The denouement would have to wait till he got home. Why berate him for carrying on with Cosy, jealous though it made her, when the prospect of marriage (open or otherwise) looked remote? Why force the issue of other women, when the hopelessness of their situation – the religion dividing them – made it superfluous?

That spring, their letters reach an *impasse*. Reading them, I found it impossible to see how my parents would resolve their differences. And yet I knew they did resolve them – or buried them deep enough for marriage to become a possibility. Was it my mother giving in? My father offering a way out? Or something else? I needed to know. My life depended on it.

# CHAPTER ELEVEN

# Home At Last

*Kim to Arthur, Booth Hall, 3.5.45*

My darling,

Just got your phone call. Can't get used to the idea that the MG isn't going to come roaring up the hill at any minute. I didn't feel you were really going away this morning – knowing I'd be speaking to you tonight and seeing you soon. But it will be an awfully long week.

Round 3, Mary Galvin came and drove me to the motoring school. Quite enjoyed it but not as much as the other lessons I've had. The instructor said I had quite good points about driving, and liked the way I always moved my leg from the accelerator to the brake when necessary. My main weakness is going round corners, I gather.

This time last week we were at the Black Dog. Wish we were there again.

*Arthur to Kim, Pitreavie Castle, Dunfermline, Fife, 3.5.45*

Hello my own little darling,

I feel a bit whistled – mainly excitement, I think, but also I'm tired and the fire here in my room is terribly hot and making me woozy. AND I STILL LOVE YOU. I've actually had 6 pints of draught since seven pm, but you know me.

I gather I'm going to be very busy with medical boards for at least six weeks, and after that with more medical boards for the crowd being demobilised. But there is no future for me living in at this place, even if you weren't coming up – it's dead. The majority live out. It's apparently hellish difficult finding a place but I'll fix it. In fact I'll do some hunting round tomorrow.

If you're anything like me you'll have slept with a smile on your face six feet wide.

ARLY MAY 1945 and Arthur, uprooted again, treks the
streets of Edinburgh in search of a hotel room for his wife.
Hitler is three days dead, but there's still a war on, and rooms
aren't easy to find. He has no luck at the posher establishments.
But at the newly opened Royal Stuart Hotel in Abercrombie
Place he finds a double at £5 5s 0d a week, and the manageress,
whose son is in the forces, says she'll see what she can do about
a discount. Edinburgh isn't exactly convenient. He is working in
Rosyth, an hour away, and will be busy till 5.30 each day – far
from ideal when the last train back is at 8.30 and the last ferry
an hour later (in those days there was no road-bridge across
the Forth). But the camp doesn't have room for wives. The hotels
in nearby Dunfermline are too expensive – £7 7s 0d a week,
and him on a meagre £3 10s 0d. And though the local GP,
Dr Campbell, has offered a room in his house, Arthur would
feel inhibited about coming and going, with Campbell and
wife, as dour a Fifeshire couple as you'd ever find, monitoring
every move. So Edinburgh it is till they find something more
convenient. He can meet her after work, and maybe, now and
again, stay over. There's good shopping, which should suit her.
And it's a city they can lose themselves in, as lovers will.

Back at Booth Hall, winding up her duties on the children's
ward, Kim's not happy with the proposed arrangement. The
three weeks since Arthur returned have been euphoric: picnics
in clovered grass, outings to country pubs, Sunday lunches at
Windyridge, driving lessons in his MG. After a year of fretting
and separation, it all happened so fast. But now he's been posted
north again. And though Edinburgh isn't Reyky or Lagens,
which means she's free to join him, she worries how she'll cope
there. 'Remember, I'm your husband,' he tells her. Well, yes. Easy
to say. But how to *behave* like a married couple is harder.

For she isn't yet Arthur's wife, and worries about wearing
his ring. Oh, she's a pragmatist too, and can see the argument.
The Scots are puritanical. 'No gentleman callers' is the rule.
Unless it's believed they're man and wife – by the Campbells,
hotel receptionists, landladies, whomever – every visit he pays
will arouse suspicion. No, a ring makes very good sense: slipping

one on – third finger, left hand – will put a stop to awkward questions. All the same, she can't help thinking it a mortal sin. To wear a wedding ring without exchanging holy vows! She knows what her brothers and sisters would say, what her mother would say, what her father would say if he weren't so terribly ill. She also worries that Arthur will take her for granted – not grow bored and abandon her (he's not the Don Juan type), but assume she'll now marry him on his terms. Once pretend to be his wife, and she'll end up becoming it in reality. Which is impossible, as she has told him till she's blue in the face, unless they marry in a Catholic church. No, she can't let it be thought that her crossing the border signifies a victory for him. Their war's not over yet. On the phone to him each night, she nags, natters, takes offence where she used to shrug and laugh. He's used to her being miserable on paper, but not in person or down the line, and it gets to him. Life's simple, why make it difficult? Why are bloody women so perverse? Irked, he writes a spoof letter to her, the kind he normally keeps for April Fool's Day, as though seeking help from an agony aunt:

Dear Doctor,

I am writing for your advice. Nearly three years ago, I met a girl who I fell in love with at first sight. Since that time I have taken her out on every possible occasion – to the extent of gross neglect of many old friends. I have left her at various times between 11pm and 5.30am, and she has always seemed to want me to stay, telling me she doesn't mind what other people think. In the usual selfish way of most types in the service (the 'here today, overseas tomorrow' attitude), I have always made the most of these opportunities.

However, now I find myself stationed in this country, I've noticed a change in attitude. Whatever I want to do she queries. Where I once adopted a rather irresponsible, devil-may-care attitude while on leave, I'm now asked to remember what any passer-by might think, discouraged from staying late, expected to keep my eyes open when kissing, etc. I wonder if there's been a change of heart – I've had my way and now she wants hers.

All this probably sounds very silly but I would be glad of your opinion.

Beneath the jokiness is a real worry – that she's too preoccupied by 'what people will think', and that the power struggle between them has subtly altered. In the past she let him be boss. Now she's the one wanting control. It doesn't bode well for married life.

On the same day he writes his spoof, she consults a priest. She has long intended to do this, in order to clarify the position, and Arthur has encouraged her, while also hoping she'd let it go. Father McDermott is young and Irish. They know each other from his visits to the wards of Booth Hall. He couldn't be more sympathetic. But his answer is discouraging, as she explains:

It's not that he disapproved of it all, darling – on the contrary he didn't see why it couldn't work out quite well, with the usual provisos. But I'm afraid there is no way round those.

To get married by an RC padre, we must have a dispensation and to get that you must make three promises – that there won't be a double wedding (meaning we will be married in an RC church only); that you won't interfere with my religion; and that the children will be RC. I talked to him for a long time and he really was very nice but that's how it must be. Please believe me when I say I love you very much but I won't marry you anywhere except in an RC church, and nothing will make me change my mind. So I am asking you, do you still want me to come up? I promised I would. But do you still want me to, knowing all this?

Looks as if I won't get out of here before VE Day.

Those are the rules. (They continued to be the rules till 1970, when Roman Catholic regulations concerning mixed marriages, and the children of mixed marriages, were relaxed.) Knowing how things stand, she asks, does he still want her to come? Of course, he replies. He's relying on it. The moment she's

finished at Booth Hall. On VE Day if she can make it. If not, asap
– the day she comes will be their own V Day, he says, 'the first of
hundreds we shall have together'. He'll meet her off the train,
and they'll walk to the Royal Stuart and lie together. Name?
Morrison, Mr A and Mrs K. Place of residence? The Red Lodge,
Walkden, Manchester. The address is Mary's, she won't mind. As
to the lie about their status, they *feel* married, so why not?

In the event, still anxious he'll think of it as *his* Victory, not
theirs, she isn't ready to come till 13 May. VE Day itself scarcely
impinges on them. She spends it quietly, at work, then in the
evening calls on Mary: there are great goings-on in town, they
hear, but neither is in the mood for celebration – she's sick with
nerves, and Mary's fed up with Ron, who's incommunicado (and
doubtless loving it) down in Cannes. Arthur's VE Day is similarly
unfestive: he's busy with sick parades, and anyway it pours with
rain. His boss at Rosyth is a S/Ldr Gimson. Together they run
medical boards, which means checking the health of every RAF
man between Gretna and John O'Groats, not just the hundreds
who've suffered war wounds of some kind, but the thousands
due for demobilisation. Arthur has been looking forward to these
boards as a chance to do something useful at last – not winning
the war exactly, but hastening the peace. His role turns out to be
routine, though (blood tests, urine samples, paperwork that could
as well be done by a clerk) and he's quickly bored. Kim's arrival
is his only excitement. On Saturday, V Day, he'll be working, but
hopes to be through in time to catch the 5.59 to Edinburgh, due
in just before her train.

Come the hour, Gimson lets him off early – quiet day,
newlyweds, 'passionate leave', it would be unkind not to, etc.
He's in Edinburgh by 4.30, combing the streets again, this time
for a ring. Though she promised to bring one, it's as well to be
on the safe side. Just something to brandish should a landlady
prove nosy (he has felt 'quite a frost lately' whenever he mentions
his wife, as though no one believes him). Later, when they *really*
marry, they'll buy a pair of rings in 18-carat gold. But in the
meantime there's nothing wrong with tin. He finds the answer –
not cheap-looking at all – in an alley off Princes Street. The

jeweller, hurrying to close, knocks a couple of bob off, which he spends in a pub round the corner. The train must be across the border by now. He'll be at the station in good time. But in case something goes wrong, and she gets in late or early, he has drawn a map for her, showing the route to Abercrombie Place. Does he still want this, given all that divides them? Of course. What other future can there be?

As he sips his pint, she sits on the train with her one suitcase. Her fingers tensely clutch the handle, coiling round and back on themselves, eating into her palms. Is that a ring she's wearing? Is it as good a bargain as his? She feels apprehensive in her new uniform – the shoes, the blouse, the specially bought suit – like a girl starting at senior school. The one comfort is the thought of him waiting on the platform. 'Oh, I do long for Saturday,' he said, 'and the months and years after that.' He will meet her off the train, and they'll walk to the hotel, and register as Mr and Mrs. They're grown-ups, and it's a grown-up thing to do. Their V Day. The first of hundreds. The beginning of the post-war age.

✶   ✶   ✶

To be honest, I've no idea if my mother tensely clutched her suitcase. She may have stowed it in an overhead rack. What I do know is that she felt nervous about coming to Edinburgh, and that these nerves expressed themselves, in the days before she left Manchester, in confusion about what that suitcase should contain. How much would she need? How long would she stay? Would the weather be cold, wet, windy or humid? How smart was the hotel – would she have to dress up for breakfast or could she slum it even at dinner? How many sensible shoes, how many high heels? Arthur had already spoken to Campbell, the local GP, about taking her on part-time, and it looked hopeful. But what sort of outfit would suit a locum in a small Scottish town over the summer? A long-sleeved dress? A woollen two-piece suit? A knee-length skirt and high-collared blouse? Unsure, and getting no useful answers from Arthur, she repacked her suitcase several times. She was still dithering when Mary Galvin came to collect the trunk she had arranged to leave behind. A silk scarf or a woollen? The blue suit or the grey? 'Stop fussing, Agnes,' said Mary. 'There'll be shops in Edinburgh.' Only then was the lid of the trunk closed, and the matter laid to rest with an 'Ah, well, I suppose you're right.'

My mother always had trouble with suitcases. Felt oppressed by how much to put in. Couldn't be sure, unless visiting relations, what to expect. Wanted to blend in, but unless she knew the habitat couldn't tell which chameleon skin would be required. 'Packing the right clothes' wasn't a decision but an identity crisis, never more so than in May 1945. Which self would be travelling up to Arthur? The eager lover? The furtive mistress? The new bride? The young doctor? The economic migrant? The rose of Tralee? There were certain garments of hers, especially undergarments, which Arthur liked. Taking them would please him, but was it also playing into his hands? No suitcase was ever more fretted over. It would contain all she required for the foreseeable future. It was her. But who was she?

Her packing agonies were something I observed as a child. But the special way she clutched a suitcase handle is something I remember from meeting her at King's Cross towards the end of her life. She had trouble walking by then, had been helped into her place at Leeds and told to stay there, carriage F, seat 23. The train was late: I had to wait behind the barrier. Beside me, young men with flowers were discovering the romantic agony of railway stations. Even I felt a thrill of anticipation, as though there to meet the new woman in my life, one whose face I was afraid of not recognising. At last the train nosed in. The young men raced ahead to sweep up their lovers. I walked the grey platform against the throng and found my mother in the door of carriage D. 'You didn't have to come,' she said, clutching her handle. 'I could have managed.' I kissed her cheek and helped her down. A porter brought a wheelchair, into which we eased her. Though she was coming for a week, her suitcase felt as light as air. It floated beside me down the platform and out into the boot of the car. Back home I helped her unzip it: a nightie, a skirt and blouse, seven days' worth of tights and knickers, three bags of sweeties for the kids, a toothbrush – and a Maeve Binchy novel laid on top.

She had run out of parts to play by then, and didn't care what the suitcase contained. She wasn't dressing up for life, but simplifying herself for death.

✳    ✳    ✳

*Kim to Arthur, Rosyth, June 1945*

Don't forget to lock the door darling, when you go out. Make some tea if you want – wish I were here to make it for you. I'll try not to be long. I love you.

THE TRAIN PULLS in the station and there he is to greet her, with a ring: V-Day, peace and happiness, the dawn of their post-war world. Six weeks later her father dies. The news isn't unexpected – he has been ill for months – but she cries when the boy brings the telegram. The funeral's fixed for 29 June, a Friday. She packs a suitcase again. By now they've found lodgings in Rosyth, close to his camp. She has a job with Campbell (who pays her part-time but uses her full-), while he cycles back and forth to his medical boards. Well rehearsed, half-convinced by it themselves, they've been playing husband and wife. In the long evenings they walk to the pub or sometimes, since it closes so early, stay home mooching to songs on the wireless: they thought that love was over, that they were really through, but they (in unison) 'just couldn't say goodbye'.

The landlady, whom they nickname 'Auntie' in memory of her predecessor at Davidstow, worries are they eating properly and having any sleep: these newlyweds, you know. She serves them Spam, lettuce, tomatoes, boiled potatoes and huge chunks of bread, to stop them getting run down. In truth, they have never felt better. Until the telegram comes and Kim packs her blackest clothes. Wangling a day off work, Arthur travels down with her as far as Manchester: from there she changes trains for

Preston, then Holyhead. Next day, they scribble letters to each other. She slept badly, she says, unused to spending nights away from him. The view from Auntie's window, he tells her, just isn't the same.

She makes it in time, though only just, reaching Killorglin at 2.15 for the funeral at 3. It's a big event, the church in Mill Road packed to the rafters. Her father would never miss such an occasion. 'Ah, but he's here,' she tells herself, seeing the coffin, but it isn't a presence that counts. She marches with her siblings behind the coffin, arm-in-arm, as wide as a street. An ancient aunt is scattering salt from her pocket, 'to keep away the *other people*'. Ghosts in the cortège? Kim shudders to think of it. At last, they reach the cemetery, on a hill overlooking the Laune. The priest mutters his prayers – 'Sacred Heart of Jesus, let one drop of that Precious Blood which fell from Thy wounds be applied to the soul of Thy servant PATRICK, if he is still detained in Purgatory, since it was shed for him . . .'. Familiar rituals, but today they feel alien to her. Is that Arthur at work, making her see them as if through the eyes of a stranger? Or her own doing, from having lived in England for four years? She stares down at her shoes – ankle straps with buttons, shiny black leather, low heels, bought at Kendals' in Manchester – and feels suddenly lost at being home.

During her absence Arthur gets cracking on his car. It's the best part (Kim aside) of being in Britain again: sticking his head under a bonnet, diagnosing, tinkering, finding a cure. He feels more like a doctor in that posture than when examining blokes for demobilisation. They have a holiday planned for the end of July, a tour of highlands and islands, and he's been saving his petrol coupons for the purpose – his allowance is a lavish 13 gallons a month. Though the MG has been playing up, he knows the parts he needs to fettle it, and while in Manchester, after putting Kim on her train, in the hour before catching his own train back north, he collects a catalogue from Cockshoots in Roseburn Street. Now he has the code numbers, he can order the parts by phone, and ask his father to collect them, and then get Kim – passing through Manchester on her return – to bring them up to Rosyth. Once that's done, he'll have the car working in no time. Next day, between listening to pilots' chests, fiddling with the cylinder head and playing snooker, he fixes things over the phone, first with Cockshoots, then with his father, then with Kim in Killorglin. She, it's true, doesn't seem to be paying attention when he explains the arrangements. She has that resigned, hopeless tone in her voice again, as though since going home she'd lost her faith – her faith in marrying him. But he knows she has suffered a terrible loss, and patiently goes over the details. Collecting the MG parts from Ernest may delay her an hour, but surely, for the holiday, their first great peacetime jaunt, it's worth it.

Next day, a letter arrives from Windyridge:

Dear Arthur,

I have been to Cockshoots. They only had 1 oil filter, 1 induction manifold gasket and 1 exhaust pipe gasket, for which I paid 12/. For the rest, they advise you to try the MG agents in Edinburgh or Glasgow or to wire direct to the works. Sorry I cannot do more at this end.

Cheerio and all the best, Dad.

PS I have been going to ask you for some time but keep forgetting when I see you: of what religion is Agnes? I should as you may guess be very worried if she happened to be Catholic.

Like the death of Patrick O'Shea, the letter comes as a shock but not a surprise. For over a year, Mary has been warning Arthur this was bound to happen. Only a month back, she mentioned it again: 'Daddy is on at me practically non-stop about Kim's religion, and said again – not in rage this time, but very calm – that he'd commit suicide if you married an R.C.' During the three weeks in April that Arthur was living at home, neither father nor son broached the subject. Now the burning question has been put at last, as a PS in a letter about car parts. It's not clear why Ernest chose this moment. Perhaps the news of Kim going back to Kerry for her father's funeral brought it home. Perhaps he suspects the two of them are living in sin. Or perhaps he feels he has to pop the question to Arthur before Arthur pops the question to Kim. Whichever, the tone is bluff and to the point. But he isn't as plain-dealing as appears. Slyly, in the context, he refers to Arthur's *inamorata* as Agnes, not Kim. And the question is put casually, as an addendum. The car parts are in hand. And by the way 'of what religion' is your fiancée?

Ernest's letter throws everyone in a tizz. 'I told him that as regards a daughter-in-law there was nobody I would welcome more,' Kathleen writes to Arthur, dissociating herself from her husband's inquisition. 'Kim has been brought up in her way, and we in ours, and considering the small place religion has in our lives (particularly Daddy's), it's hard to understand why he's so bigoted. I do know, though, it's your happiness he is considering.' Arthur begins drafting a reply. In the meantime, he breaks the news to Kim over the phone and tells her not to worry, he will deal with it. All she need do is collect the two gaskets and the oil filter from Windyridge on her way through. The next day after supper, he revises his letter to Ernest till he's satisfied and cycles down from Auntie's to the postbox. After a pint at the local, he returns, amazed, to find Kim there, a day early. Hot, tired and dirty, she intended it as a 'lovely big surprise', and so it is, till he discovers she's partless. He can't believe it. He'd set it all up. Why has she failed to do the thing he asked?

'I wanted to get here as fast as possible,' she says. 'That's all.'

'It would only have taken an hour,' he says. 'They were expecting you.'

'But what if your Daddie had asked me? I'd not have known what to say.'

'Well, I've told him now.'

'But you didn't tell me what *I* should tell him.'

They argue in the humid July evening, with the window open and Auntie doubtless listening downstairs. Both feel badly done by, Kim all the more so since she's grieving. An apology duly comes. It is she, though, who makes it. Next morning, while he's out at work, she appends a plaintive note to the letter she sent him from Ireland, which is lying there on the table: 'I'm sorry darling. I know you're disappointed, and I'm ashamed for being so stupid about it all. But I'll make up for it.'

Reading their letters, and between their letters, I feel myself tugged both ways. My Dad and his bloody MG: can't he see why car parts aren't my mother's first priority just now? Her father dead, and all that Father McDermott said made rawly painful again by being back in Kerry – it's a lot to bear without having to collect gaskets from Ernest the Inquisitor. How could he ask it of her? And all just to save on postage. It's unfair. Insensitive, too. If he can't see that and won't apologise, she should pack her bags and leave at once. There must be other men who'd treat her better. Go on, I urge her, let rip, walk out of there if need be. I'm willing to forgo my life, Mum, to see you make a more suitable match.

But then again . . . Why does she stand for it? Need she be so bloody supine? I want to shake her. Put up a fight, woman. Give him what for. There's a lightbulb joke about the deference of women of her time and place – 'How many Irishwomen does it take to change a lightbulb?' 'Ach, sure, I don't mind sitting here in the dark' – and I want to tell it her, in provocation. But if she were capable of rage and self-assertion, wouldn't she be someone else? At work she stuck up for herself. But she couldn't stick up for herself in love. Or rather, what she stuck up for was the love itself, and willingly paid whatever price was asked in order that love survive. If my father's feelings for her were in question, she might be less accommodating. But spoilt, callow, selfish and stubborn though he is, she never doubts him – and therefore apologises when (as here) she's not to blame. I'm a beneficiary of her capacity for surrender. I owe my being to her being amenable. And yet I mourn her suffering and feel driven half round the bend by her passivity.

Did it come from her religion? Was her willingness to endure my father a product of the very faith he was seeking to expunge? Surely not. Catholicism doesn't demand weakness of its adherents. Yet the Protestant (and father's son) in me is tempted to link her passivity to a part of Catholic worship – the (unthinking?) obedience demanded by the Mass. Perhaps that's why, as a teenager, I found Holy Communion, the C of E version of the eucharist, hard to swallow — not the wine and wafer themselves, nor even the symbolism of flesh and blood, but the words preceding them: 'We do not presume . . . We are not worthy so much as to gather up the crumbs under thy table.' Oh, please. All that humility. *Do* presume. *Do* feel worthy. Don't let yourself be walked over by a God.

Once, at the Church of the Holy Sepulchre in Jerusalem, I saw how low religion could bring someone. She was wearing a tweed coat and brown stockings, her face was European, and she crept along the ground like a worm. From the church entrance, among the legs of tourists like me, she crawled 10 metres to kiss the stone, then crawled another 20 metres to the sepulchre, finally standing to join the queue of pilgrims waiting to enter, but then immediately, once inside, sinking to her hands and knees. That day I'd seen Copts, Jews and Muslims in postures of self-abasement. But none had stooped so low as the woman with the knee-worn stockings, crossing her heart before her Maker. Was my anger with her, or with her religion, or with the image she evoked — that of my mother prostrating herself before my father? I don't know. I can't even be certain she was Catholic. All I know is I had to walk away, to avoid the urge to kick her.

My mother wasn't the woman in Jerusalem. I've no right to feel angry. I just wish she'd walked a bit taller and felt less apologetic for who she was.

✻   ✻   ✻

*Ernest to Arthur, Windyridge, 14.7.45*

I must confess your letter gave me a shock . . .

WHEN KATHLEEN SEES the envelope on the doormat, she knows exactly what it is. Her heart drops just as it did a couple of days ago when Ernest let slip he'd finally *asked*. She takes the letter up to him in the bedroom where he's dressing for work, then joins Mary and Kela for breakfast. The toast burns under the grill as they listen to the silence upstairs. A worryingly long silence. If they hear him walk to the bathroom, the agreement is to run up fast. At last there's a creak above, then the sound of footsteps on the stairs. He enters the kitchen a little pale and stands with his back to the Aga. 'A letter from Arthur,' he says, and hands it over for them to read. 'Now I know,' he says, drinking his tea.

'Of what religion is Agnes?' She's RC, that's what. Arthur meant to tell him before. He and Kim weren't being deceitful: if asked, they'd have answered honestly. But it's been a great worry to them for the past two years, and they wanted to resolve it themselves. How exactly it'll work out remains to be seen, but he'd like to reassure his father that his views on the Catholic religion haven't altered one bit. Yes, he's in love with Kim and intends to marry her. But not in a Catholic church. Nor will any children of theirs – any *grandchildren of his* – be taught by priests or slyly indoctrinated by Kim's relations. The two of them have had this out. She knows where Arthur stands. Her religion is a primitive and superstitious one, unsuited to the modern world, and he has told her so. Catholic priests lord it over a craven people, keeping them in the dark ages, and he has told her so. Naturally, given her upbringing, she finds it hard to agree with him. But he has no doubt that she will come round, and marry him on the rational terms he is proposing. That's really all there is to it. Now Ernest has been put in the picture, he, Arthur, trusts the matter can rest. Sensible criticism of religion is well and good, but bigotry should have no place in any discussion. Kim is insecure and easily upset. Were anything said at Windyridge to drive her off, Arthur could never forgive it. Marrying Kim matters more to him than anything in the world, and surely that should govern his family's opinion. Are they not of one mind about Kim? Have they not had two years to get to know her? Is she not kind, loyal, intelligent, a girl any man would feel proud and lucky to have as his wife? Well, then, why should her being raised RC matter a jot? It belongs to the past. No future in making a meal of it. If he, Daddy, can't see this and act in a spirit of tolerance, then he's not the man he took him for, the one who raised his children to allow other people their opinions, however fatuous those opinions might be. Let that be the end of it. Or if there's more to say, then let them say it over a pint one day, man to man. But he trusts that won't be necessary. Trusts his father will embrace Kim as a daughter-in-law. Trusts that he himself can be trusted not to become RC.

'Now I know,' says Ernest, drinking his tea. Then adds, seeing the heads of his wife and daughter bent together conspiratorially, 'But I suppose *you* knew already.' They deny it. He accuses them further. They stick to their guns. Just for a second he complains about Kim: 'Oh, I like her well enough, but she's been sly about not going to Mass whenever she stays here.' Well, perhaps she isn't so devout as to go every week, they tell him. Or perhaps Arthur made her promise not to go. Or perhaps she was being respectful, not wanting to throw it in their faces. (Or perhaps she did go but concealed it.) He's unconvinced by their arguments. But he's already ten minutes late for work and, shocked as he is, feels oddly appeased. Always better to be told the worst, he says. Especially when the worst isn't so bad.

'I am very glad indeed you share my views on the RC religion and the power of the priests,' he writes to Arthur later that day. He is, he says, exceedingly sorry for their trouble – 'It seems such a pity you should have to worry' – but at least they are both mature enough to find a solution. Heaven forbid that Arthur should think he is 'intruding' (Mummy's view) or 'naggling in the most bigoted fashion' (Mary's), but he hopes 'for both your sakes that you face the facts and don't think verbal promises or measures of agreement are going to meet the situation. These sorts of arrangements have been tried many times before but always fade out or break apart and both lives become one of misery. There are too many pitfalls in marriage without the parties holding directly opposite views on religion. It *is* a very vital question.'

Up in Rosyth, over a lunch of Spam and lettuce, Arthur shows the letter to Kim. With her father less than a week in the ground, she's not in the best of spirits when she reads it. She wasn't exactly happy with Arthur's letter, either (he kept the draft for her), since it rehearsed old prejudices and would concede no ground to her. But at least Ernest finally knows, and can accept the designation 'Catholic' provided it's preceded by an ex-. For this relief, much thanks. The only opposition now lies in Killorglin, with her mother and siblings – and in her own head.

✳    ✳    ✳

*Mary to Arthur, Red Lodge, 15.7.45*

Good show! Am I glad you've told Daddy and, boy, what a wizard letter – you told him off very nicely. He's taken it extraordinarily quietly. At any rate he asked for it and now he's got it. Do grasp your happiness firmly – life is so fleeting and full of needless misery. I'm resigned to never being completely happy again, but I thank God that I was, gloriously, for a short while.

IF MARY'S PLEASED to see her father put in his place, it isn't just sisterly solidarity. Her own problems with him get worse and worse. Though officially based at Red Lodge, she feels exposed sleeping alone there with Kela, and spends much of her time at Windyridge. Which would be fine, but for Ernest's interference in her affairs. Her social life, her clothes, her nail varnish, the treatment of Kela's skin (on which they're using calamine now) – he tries to control them all. He even stuck his nose in when she sold her car – the RAF laddie who offered £50 would have paid £70 if she'd held out, but Daddy said to play safe and take his money. Christ knows, she should be able to run her own life by now. He'd regulate her bowels if he could.

It would help if Ronnie were around but he's still in France. She has suggested a weekend in Edinburgh with the four of them next time he's home on leave. But she doubts he'll come to see her, let alone make the effort to go to Scotland. Of course, he's punishing her for having told him that she won't consider marriage – to anyone – for at least another year. But if he thinks by being moody he'll make her change her mind, he can forget it. In her heart of hearts, she has decided he probably is best second-best. Or *had* decided, till he virtually stopped writing. It's her loss if he's taken up with a WAAF or some tart from Cannes. But what else could she have done? It was only this year she heard for sure about Michael. And the effects recovered from the aircraft, including the 9-carat gold signet ring with the plain octagonal bezel, still haven't been returned to her. Until she has his ring back, and holds it in her palm, and sees the hole where Michael's wedding finger went, she can't think of wearing another man's. It feels too soon. Why can't Ronnie accept that?

In France, Ron is trying to accept it – but he can't allay his suspicion that if she won't commit herself now she never will. What's going to happen when all the other chaps are demobbed? She's a good-looking woman, and once RAF pilots with their stripes are swarming round her like bloody bees, a wingless wonder like him won't stand an earthly. Frankly, he feels to have been buggered about. Bad enough to know he can never take Mike's place in Mary's heart, but to be strung along for two years is even worse. Lucky sod, everyone said back home when told of his latest posting. But they can stuff the Riviera as far as he's concerned. The climate might be pleasant but, streuth, the pong. One day the French will learn about health and hygiene. But meanwhile the place is a stinking dump. As for all these voluptuous, sex-hungry women about the place, there's no future with them except a penicillin drip. He has begun a weekly bitching campaign to be demobbed. The dental surgery is being run down, and he ought by rights to be first on the list. He's all the keener to go since the arrival of two new MOs, one a Fl/Lt 'trick cyclist' (that's to say, a shrink) who's himself utterly bats, the other a nancy with a floppy handshake. The only consolation is having charge of a group of Jerry POWs, who've been repairing walls, putting up doors, fixing sinks, etc. Good workers, he has to give it to them. But that's the job of Jerries now, to pay for their crimes and help get the post-war world in order. As a dentist, he's in on that. Jaw-jaw reconstruction. Decent teeth, equal treatment and a working wage for all.

In August the H-bomb is dropped on Nagasaki and Hiroshima, and Japan throws in the towel. Ronnie spends VJ Day with an army DO – champagne, mousse, beer, whisky and gin, finishing up with bastard French aperitifs. Quite a do. Quite a hangover too. If every day were like that, he wouldn't mind so much. But nothing is changed by it. The autumn brings no sign of demobilisation. Nor of Mary being ready to say yes. He is, he tells Arthur, 'well and truly fromaged'.

✻   ✻   ✻

THERE ARE NO letters between my parents – not yet my parents – from the day of her father's funeral, 3 July, until the day she left for Ireland again, 28 December. They were living together, and could talk: why write? It leaves a gap in the story. But I don't complain. It's their private time. I know they both worked for Dr Campbell (he in odd hours between medical boards, she virtually full-time) and felt aggrieved to be paid so badly, the old miser taking the view that £12 a week was fair for a locum, though the going rate was nearer £16. I know they played golf and squash, and when the winter came took up skating. I also know that he began using a UVF sunlamp – after the Azores, in pallid, gloomy Britain, he liked to keep himself tanned. But the rest is silence.

In letters home, they skirted round their domestic arrangements. He was living on camp, he told his parents, while Kim rented rooms in town. His fellow officers heard a different story, that he had lodgings out with his new wife. To my sister and me, years later, there was no word about this phase of their life. It would have meant them admitting that they'd lived together before marriage, a practice which, like most parents in the 1960s, they condemned. Perhaps they took this line to save the world, or their teenage children, from promiscuity. Or perhaps they disliked the overtness of 1960s pre-marital sex, when they, in 1945, had had to be so secretive. Their disingenuousness – hypocrisy, I'd have called it then – isn't much to resent. But I'm sorry they weren't more candid. They might have spared themselves (and me) unnecessary guilt.

If they couldn't marry in a Catholic church, she'd once told him, they might as well live in sin. By her lights, that's what they were doing. She must have felt bad about it, like a mistress. But it was better than betraying her faith.

✳　✳　✳

*Kim to Arthur, Ormond Hotel, Dublin, 27.12.45*

Isn't it terrible? You there, me here.

*Arthur to Kim, Rosyth, 28.12.45*

I keep trying to think of the name of the hotel in Dublin where you usually stay, and all I can think of is the Sherborne – or is it the Shelbourne. Silly, isn't it – not 33 hours apart and I am pining. I keep thinking I should have kissed you longer, shouldn't have nattered at any time, oh and a thousand things. Hope that doesn't sound soft.

SHE RETURNS TO Ireland for two reasons: to look after her mother, who's ill with God knows what, and to give support to Kitty, who's getting married. It won't be a long stay. There's been no rift with Arthur. The irreconcilables remain, but she plans to follow him to his new posting in Thornaby, near Middlesbrough, and take it from there. He is due some leave before it starts, which will work out nicely. Kitty's wedding is being held in Dublin on 16 January (a Wednesday), and he can come over for it as a guest, Kitty's sister's young English *beau*.

After a Christmas spent at Windyridge, with a chastened Ernest on his best behaviour, Kim finds it bleak back in Killorglin. Bereaved, black-weeded, inconsolable, her Mammie has taken to bed. Already she's down to six stone, 'mere skin and bone', and won't be coaxed into eating. Worse, she wants someone to sit with her day and night, preferably her doctor-daughter. It's usually two in the morning before she drops off and Kim can creep away to bed. The first four days feel like four years. 'You will come back to look after me after Kitty's wedding?' her Mammie pleads one morning. Arthur has talked of them driving back down from Dublin, so he can see Killorglin. But if they do, she tells him, they'll not escape her Mammie's clutches. 'You've seen where I live,' he protests. 'Can't I do the same? After all, you're going to be my wife.' Well, yes. But *is* she? He seems to forget there's an insuperable difficulty.

In odd moments away from her Mammie's bedside, she shares some of her worries with Kitty. They're close in years, and have always been able to talk, and it helps to have someone who understands. But when Kitty, in return, asks for medical advice about 'married life', she finds it hard to reciprocate freely. 'Someone had been giving her a pretty grim account of the first night,' she tells Arthur. 'I tried to reassure her without giving it a personal note. I don't know what she suspects about you and me but I haven't enlightened her any. I've still dysmenorrhoea, and if I weren't so early this time I would think I was aborting, to judge by the loss.' Her awkwardness is made worse by envy: though Kitty's younger, she's the one getting spliced, leaving Kim and Sheila as the spinsters of the family. 'Why don't you marry me, darling?' she asks him. 'I get so jealous of Kitty fixing it all up so easily. I went to Killarney with her yesterday while she was arranging something and I was very near to tears. I'm not even "happily lonely" as you are. I love and miss you too much – that's my trouble.'

'Happily lonely' is how Arthur has described his state since she left. In other letters he doesn't put it so buoyantly. 'If I weren't able to write I'd be miserable as hell,' he says in one. In another (he sends them thick and fast, a letter a day, and there are also nightly phone calls) he describes life without her as 'terrible. I'm like a dog without a tail – a man without a personality – a woman without a husband.' The tailless dog seems fairly bois-terous, none the less. To relieve the boredom of the journey back to Rosyth after Christmas at Windyridge, he takes Ron with him, who's over from France and (glum about Mary) needs cheering up. The drive north is an epic of speeding and drink-ing. Their first stop's just down the road, in Eccles, at the Cross Keys. A nifty pint each and they're en route to Kendal, which they reach at 12.45, where they stop at the Fleece, have a couple of pints and leave by 1.10. Then they steam on over Shap – no trouble, car running beautifully – eating lunch en route (steering wheel in one hand, leg of goose in the other), and get to Penrith by 2pm. Ron knows a man who owns a pub there, so that's another two pints and a lot of chin-wagging, before they leave at 2.35. They arrive in Carlisle on the dot at 3pm, too late for a drink, but get petrol instead. So to Hawick, where Ron takes over. At Galashiels at 4.30 Arthur rings his base – all quiet, needn't have bothered, but it costs 2/- to find out. The phone's opposite a grocer's, so he checks the water and finds the car's thirsty and borrows a large jug from the grocer to quench it –

and buys 4 bottles of beer to quench *them*. Ron then drives on at a leisurely pace and they arrive in Edinburgh at 6.50, stopping at the North British to shave, ring Mary and have dinner. They stop for one at the pub by the ferry, where Arthur's detained with colic in the gents, and – damn! – when they dash out at 8.58 the ferry has just pulled up the gangway, but they roar down and the gangway's lowered again and all is well. In Rosyth they go straight to the club for a last slow gill, before retiring at 11 and nattering on past midnight. That makes eight pints each at least, by my count. But they're young, and no one has yet thought of breathalysers, and next morning Auntie sets them up with a hearty breakfast: cornflakes, grapefruit, fried egg, bacon and dippy, two rounds of toast and marmalade with tea.

Auntie feels sorry for Arthur with his wife away. He has such trouble coping on his own. First, lighting a fire in the living room, he nearly burns the place down. It's partly Auntie's fault for keeping him chatting in the kitchen, but mostly his for using a sheet of newspaper to draw the fire. When he walks in, there's one blaze in the hearth, and another in the coal scuttle (which he puts out with his tea), leaving holes in the lino, blistered woodwork and wallpaper black for about three feet up. Equally troublesome is the damn writing he has to do at work, towards *A Medical History of the War*: young Halliburton's supposed to type up his jottings, but because he came back late and canned on New Year's Day, and Arthur reported him, the bugger is sulking and dragging his feet. Then there's a row Arthur has at the bar with Gillies and his wife Ila (both of them doctors) about women practising medicine in the new NHS. They're strongly in favour, Arthur wildly against, and it gets heated. In short, without Kim around, he's lost, and Bournvita and a hot water bottle are no comfort. 'Remember when I said it might be a good thing for us to be away from each other if only to show that we're meant to be together always?' he asks her. 'Well? Don't you agree now?' He's relieved to see the back of Rosyth, dropping his bags in Thornaby and saying a quick hello to his new colleagues before driving west to catch the ferry from Holyhead.

In Langford Street Kim is also desperate to escape. What's

wrong with Mammie no one knows, but to ease her undiagnosable achings the local GP has prescribed morphine. In Kim's view, she's too fond of it – is all right when under sedation, of course, but worse than ever when she comes out, cross and obstructive and full of complaints. Her latest trick is to go wandering in the small hours, so that Kim has to get up and put her back to bed. Eating makes her feel worse, she says, and the most they get down her in a fortnight is a bit of liver and potato. They'd been hoping Kitty's wedding might produce a miracle recovery, but the doctor says she isn't fit to go. A nurse is hired from Dublin to spend three days with her while everyone's away. They break it to her gently. She says she won't be looked after by a stranger. They plead with her: what else can we do, Mammie? do you want us to miss the wedding? She simmers down. Then when the nurse comes, flares up again – insults her, won't have her in the house, begins putting her clothes on and threatens to leave. Even the nurse, who's red-haired and used to difficult old ladies, looks a little abashed. But Margaret O'Shea (née Lyons) has neither the strength nor sense of balance to get herself downstairs, and is persuaded back to bed. An hour or two of sulking (with the nurse defiantly sitting by the bed), and she relents. Soon enough they're getting on famously. Kim, hearing their chatter, keeps a wide berth.

She has her own dramas to contend with. In two days she'll be seeing Arthur. More to the point, he'll be in the Republic for the first time. What will he make of her relations? And how will they find him? She hopes he'll be quick to put his hand in his pocket. But she doesn't want him getting drunk, either: who knows what bigotry might come out? She wonders how he'll cope with talking to priests at breakfast. And how he'll look wearing his RAF uniform (the smartest thing he owns), which is bound to stand out in church ('Sure and who to God invited the English fighter pilot along?'). How marvellous if the wedding ceremony so moved him that he agreed to marry in her church; if Dublin proved to be his road to Damascus. But the Pope was more likely to become a Prod than Arthur to convert. At least her brothers and sisters have been forewarned.

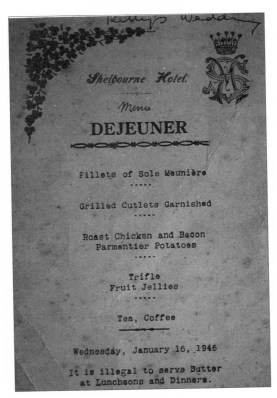

The wedding lunch is to be held at the Shelbourne. Kitty has been planning it for months. Fillets of sole meunière, garnished grilled cutlets, roast chicken and bacon with parmentier potatoes, trifle, fruit jellies and coffee: she's chosen well, says Kim. It might be France in the 1920s but for the small print on the menu to remind them this is Dublin in 1946 ('It is illegal to serve butter at luncheons and dinners'). Tomorrow Joe will drive them up. Killarney, Mallow, Tipperary, Thurles, Kildare: it's a long way, but she'll doze through the beating of the wipers, and dream of another wedding, the next wedding, the one where the woman marrying Arthur is a woman she's happy to become.

There's a photo of them taken on the day of the wedding, as they sit in a Dublin cafe with Joe and his girlfriend Bridie (within a week, Joe and Bridie would become engaged). But after that

the letters run out again. No news is good news. My parents – not yet my parents – are together, and have no need to write. After the Ireland trip, Arthur starts work in Thornaby. Kim continues as his camp-follower, and becomes a locum at the Royals Hospital in Stockton-on Tees. For three months they share lodgings – no need even to phone. But then in March he's posted back to Scotland, to East Fortune, the other side of Edinburgh from Rosyth, and with her still based in Stockton the letters resume. The story's nearly over now. The carrier bags are all but empty. There's only the one small brown envelope left. I'm desperate to remove any impediments, to get my parents to the altar. I know they made it. But I don't know how and I'm looking to this envelope for an answer.

☆　　☆　　☆

*Kim to Arthur, The Royals, Stockton, 4.3.46*

12 hours since you went – seems more like 12 years. When I took my reports along to Miss White this afternoon, her secretary said she'd

been looking for me on Saturday and this morning. Just then Dr Elder came on the phone and asked me where I'd been – I said doing NSPCC cases at the Maternity Hospital. Don't know how much he believed but he said I must contact the office every day, etc., and that Dr Hughes wants to see me at 4pm tomorrow.

*Arthur to Kim, RAF Station, East Fortune, East Lothian, 6.3.46*

This is b-awful – I'm lonely as hell, hate everything and everyone around here, and am just dying to get the hell out. This is what anywhere is like without you now – grim! Wrote to Wilcox asking to go back to Thornaby for two reasons, 1) You 2) To be in reach of home. Hope I hear something before I'm much older. Will probably be posted to the Hebrides or something. I suppose this isn't a bad station for a single man but that doesn't apply to me. They can keep it – I want you, and you alone, and the sooner the better.

I'M DISAPPOINTED. There are several more letters where those came from. But the answer, if there is an answer, isn't given in so many words. Arthur's still embroiled in medical releases, and very tedious it is too. Kim's back on maternity wards: forty mothers in one morning at the ante-natal clinic – almost as bad as Birmingham. Though her colleagues are welcoming – 'went to see a play with Tewk and her friend, who's Irish, but quite a nice girl, and we mustn't hold these things against people' – it doesn't feel worth getting to know them when she'll not be staying long. Both of them live for the weekends. He drives down each Friday night, then returns on Mondays at dawn. During the week, in letters or over the phone, they can make plans, negotiate, sort out their differences. And yet there's nothing on paper to suggest they did. It's as if they're coasting. As if there were no problems left to solve.

Her letters are short and unrevealing – either terse accounts of her work or 'natter-natter and glooms'. His letters are longer, becoming animated only on the subject of his car. Each Monday at crack of dawn, as he drives the MG back from Stockton to

East Lothian, he tries to beat the record of the week before. The journey takes 4 hours 35 minutes the first time, then 3 hours 45 (could have been quicker but for the mist, 'thick stuff drowning me one moment, thin stuff skimming the roof the next'), then 3 hours 33 (with a five-minute stop at Newcastle), then 3 hours 3 ('In time for breakfast, after which I beat that sissy Sq/Ldr I can't stand at snooker: not bad, eh?'), and finally 2 hours 56 ('a record – would have been faster but as I crossed the bridge the silencer fell off'). He's sorry his letters are so poor but really there's no news: 'Completely demoralised otherwise. Can't stand this useless existence stuck in this bloody hole with completely superfluous patients for much longer. The whole camp could close tomorrow and nobody would know the difference.' At SSQ he parks his car next to the mortuary, which seems appropriate. Kim's mood is sombre too: the days are 'mouldy', she says, and she misses him 'like nuttin on earth'.

Then everything changes. Her mother dies. At home, quietly, seventy-two years old, much missed by her ten surviving children and many grandchildren. Cause of death: according to the family, grief. Nine months of mourning and malingering and then she expired, or as she would have seen it was reborn. That Henry Wotton couplet from the seventeeth century might be her epitaph:

> He first deceas'd; she for a little tried
> To live without him; lik'd it not, and died.

But then Mammie *didn't* try, just turned her face to the wall the minute Patrick went. So her daughter thinks. At least she, Kim, has no guilt to carry, except the memory of feeling bored at her mother's bedside. All done with now. No more getting up at night to attend her. No more Christmases in Killorglin and summers at Ross Beigh. Already Joe has the family wool business; now he'll inherit the house. In September he and Bridie will be married – yet another wedding – and soon enough Langford Street, now so barren, will fill with family again. 'Well, it's all over at home,' Kim writes to Arthur, on the day of the funeral. 'Must be quite an empty house. I'm glad in a way I'm not there – I suppose it will be easier – and glad anyway you're near: I'd be lost without you. I told Miss Smithson not to light my fire tonight, as she is short of coal – I will get a heat at her fire and go to bed early. If I don't write any more you'll understand, won't you darling?' It's not like my mother to miss a family funeral. Did she feel less close to her mother than she had to her father? Perhaps. But it was, in any case, a long journey, and hard to get time off work, and she'd seen her mother only recently, and there were black-clad relations enough, and it all seemed so utterly *pointless*. Her home lay elsewhere now. Next year she'd be thirty. It was time to start afresh.

She can't have put it to herself so brutally, nor did it happen overnight, but the death broke my mother's ties with Ireland. (She later told my sister that she'd come to England after her parents' deaths – a fabrication, yet an emotional truth.) Becoming an orphan cut off the roots of her Catholicism, too. Her Mammie had been fervent, even fanatical – the embodiment of Mariolatry – and even away from home my mum felt constrained by maternal example: in any quandary, Mammie's was the voice whispering *This is how a good Catholic behaves*. Now that voice fell silent. After March 1946 religion makes no further appearance in my mother's letters. Never again does she tell Arthur 'I'll only marry you in my church'.

But she isn't ready to marry him yet, not even when Ronnie and Mary announce that *they're* getting married. The announcement comes as a surprise: everyone (including Ronnie) had begun to think his cause was doomed. Ironically, it's after spending a weekend together in Stockton – all four of them – that Mary's mind is made up for her. Arriving back in Worsley on the Sunday evening, she rings Windyridge to ask her parents to hang on to Kela overnight, because she is tired after the journey and intends to sleep at Red Lodge. Ernest, aware that Ronnie's there with her, insists she come home to Windyridge. There's a row over the phone, Mary raging at her father's nasty, interfering bloody-mindedness – can't she be trusted to behave? Ronnie, pacifying, says not to worry, he'll drive her over, best do as the old man says. But the episode's a turning-point. She's fed up with having to hide her love-life. The wedding-day is set just weeks ahead, at the end of May, when he'll be demobbed. 'Why not a double wedding?' a chirpy Ron asks Arthur, the four of them pledging their troth on the same day?

Why not? It's an obvious thought. There's nothing to stop them, except Kim. And Kim would happily marry Arthur in a double, triple, quadruple or however-bloody-many ceremony. But it's too soon. Her conscience still says no. She's depressed by her parents' deaths. There are practical reasons against it too. Unlike Mary, they don't have a home. Unlike Ron, Arthur won't be demobbed until the autumn. More sensible to wait and, if he really wants a double wedding, have one with Joe and Bridie in the autumn. Knowing what *that* means but ignoring the provocation, he keeps pushing. But then she has appendicitis, and spends a week convalescing in hospital, by which time it's all too late. They go to Ron and Mary's wedding not as doubles but as guests. In the event, Arthur is glad of that: it's enough being best man, and seeing his oldest friend become his brother-in-law, without getting in on the act.

In July he's posted to Oakington, near Cambridge, a place with unhappy memories. It was the airfield Michael took off from the night he died. Arthur's only previous visit there was to take his stuff away. Superstitious, he feels he has to be 'hellish careful', and spurns all invitations to fly. He's in charge of passing airmen for release, frustrating work when the only release that interests him is his own. There are 2,000 men on camp, and only one MO apart from himself, a 'frightfully flah' twenty-six-year-old, with a house of his own and a ticket to join the Colonial Medical Service in Hong Kong, the bastard. The work keeps Arthur busy during the day, but during the long evenings he goes hunting for suitable practices, certain that's his destiny now, to become a GP. One possibility is Ely, and Ernest, as his backer, motors down to see the place. Useless, he says: the doctor selling the practice is in debt, the house filthy, the surgery in poor repair, and anyway these are the Fens, a low-lying and unhealthy part of the country. Where else to look? London's a hellhole at the best of times, the south-east is overrun with County folk, the south-west and Scotland are too remote. Then there are the costs to consider. When the war began, the average GP salary was £1100 pa. It might be a little higher by now, but, even so, if Arthur means business he'll need £200 a year to keep a car on the road, and at least another £500 for food, clothes, etc. – it's important to look prosperous in order to attract patients. Money spent with the right people *makes* money, says Ernest, whereas loan repayments can ruin a man. Unless Arthur finds a suitable practice, a going concern which he can afford, he'd be better off working for Uncle Bert in Southport at £15 a week.

Kim isn't party to this man talk. It's assumed she'll be a sleeping partner, supposing she's a partner at all. 'But surely you'll give up work now the war's over,' people say, as though medicine has been a stopgap, something to pass the time till VE Day. Is there a future for hen doctors now the cocks are back? She feels rather sidelined and passive. Then on her last day up in Stockton she falls and twists her ankle, and is forced to recuperate at Mary's. With her leg as it is, and him due to be demobbed, it doesn't seem worth following him to Oakington. 'You relax, pet,' he tells her, but she, frustrated not to be working, is restless as an eel in a basket. 'The sooner I get a job,' she writes, 'the better.'

In the archive of their letters, her last words to him are 'Sweet dreams' and his to her 'I've just seen the new moon through glass.' Afterwards they fall silent. The courtship's over. The rest is (family) history.

✳    ✳    ✳

TUESDAY 30 OCTOBER 1946. The triumphal entry of my parents into Earby, a mill-town on the Lancashire Yorkshire border. Form of dress? Arthur, a blue RAF uniform; Kim, a two-piece suit, raincoat and headscarf. Mode of transport? A red MG sports car, its roof defiantly down despite the drizzle. Purpose of visit? To take up occupancy of a dank and depressing house situated next to a level crossing. Kim, who's seen the house only the once before, had forgotten how ugly it was. 'Never mind,' says Arthur, as removal men totter past with beds, sideboards and other Windyridge cast-offs. 'Now you're not working, you'll have bags of time to do it up.' She smiles, not taking the bait. The struggles of the past three years have worn her out, and here's this man raring to go and desperate to take charge. Work? It's hard to imagine going without. But she's not going to fight about it with her husband. Which for the past six days is what he has been.

Photos of the wedding show a modest affair, post-war -austere. Matching rings (18-carat gold this time). Carnations. Two-piece suits. Sensible shoes. A row of windswept faces against a pebbledash wall: Ernest, Kathleen, Arthur, Kim, Mary, with Auntie Winnie (Kathleen's sister) and her two daughters out on a limb. No Ron: maybe he's the one taking the picture. No confetti. No limo. No vicar or priest. And none of her relations.

So he had won. They married on his terms, in a register office, down the road from Windyridge. But when I look into my mother's eyes on her wedding-day, I find no trace of sadness or defeat. And when I imagine them arriving in Earby, I sense no resistance, except to the drabness of their new house. If this is surrender — her names, accent, religion and identity scattered to the Pennine wind — it is a willing surrender. Peace at last. She lays down her arms and puts her hand in his.

Why? Because she loved him. It mightn't have been wise or right. And it's not the whole story. But there's the answer she'd have given. Love.

✳   ✳   ✳

A CODA. In the five days between the wedding ceremony and their arrival in Earby, my parents spend a honeymoon in London. Three nights at the Strand Palace Hotel. Pubs, shops, cafes, a slap-up meal each night, and an evening at the Duke of York's Theatre, to see E. Vivian Tidmarsh's farcical comedy *Is Your Honeymoon Really Necessary?* Is theirs? They've lived together, worked together, holidayed together, and know each other as intimately as any bride and groom can hope to. Still, if Ernest's happy to stand them a weekend in London, and a trip to a West End theatre, why not? They sit in the front stalls and let laughter pour over them like confetti.

HUSBAND: You were incapable.
WIFE: Darling, I had only one glass.
HUSBAND: I know, but – my word – how you kept filling it.

The play opens with a couple arriving at a country house after their wedding. He has been married before, and the honeymoon's a chance for her to question him about his first wife ('I had two faults that annoyed her very much – everything I said and everything I did'). On cue, the first wife then turns up, with the news that the divorce he fixed in California isn't legal. The husband hides his first wife from his second wife. Complications follow. A pair of pyjamas is produced, and there's much toing and froing between bedrooms. When the curtain comes down, Arthur enthusiastically applauds. 'Damn silly,' he beams, 'but a good night out.'

Kim, as they leave the theatre, is subdued. He puts it down to tiredness, but next morning she's just as bad. Though she isn't the crying kind, he can see she's upset. That line at the start of the bloody play didn't help (was it the maid who said it or the butler?): 'I don't like these register office weddings myself. They don't seem the real thing.' Kim's sentiments exactly. No wonder she didn't laugh much. They're married, but she doesn't feel married, not really. It's why, this morning, she lingers in the bathroom for nearly an hour, hiding her upset while she prepares a smiley face for him, the kind honeymooners are supposed to wear.

The solution – the necessity of their honeymoon – comes to him in a flash as he sits waiting on the bed for her to emerge. It's something he remembers from a conversation he once heard as a junior doctor in Charing Cross Hospital in 1941. A thing you can do, a place you can go. Why didn't he think of it before? He says nothing when she emerges from the bathroom, only kisses each eyelid in turn. They go down to breakfast. Over its dregs, he tells her he's taking her somewhere, 'a little surprise'.

Outside on the Strand it's drizzling and there are queues for all the buses. No matter. Five minutes' walk and they are there. The building's grey and uninspiring, but the priest understands what they are after. It's common enough with people in their position. Have they a witness? A man loitering by the door is persuaded to do the job (discreetly, afterwards, Arthur slips him a ten bob note). Fifteen minutes is all it takes, twenty at the outside. The barest of ceremonies. No hymn, no incense, scarcely any prayers. But an exchange of vows. A joining of hands. A pair of signatures. And, most important, the blessing of Rome. They thank the priest and step outside. Sun has broken through the clouds. So she marries him twice, first in his way, then in hers.

My mother told me this story just before she died. Where did they go? St Anselm and St Cecilia's on Kingsway? Corpus Christi in Maiden Lane? St Patrick's in Soho Square? None of the registers has their names. My mother described the ceremony as a 'marriage'. Beaty said it must have been a 'blessing'. Experts tell me my parents were having their marriage 'rectified'. Since my research hasn't unearthed any records, I've no way of knowing if the story's true. It could be that my mother invented it to feel better about her surrender: 'Your father could see I didn't feel right about the register office,' she told me, and her version of events shows him meeting her halfway. Given his general inflexibility, and particular resistance to Catholic churches, it doesn't sound wholly in character. Yet I'm inclined to believe her: my father was an impulsive man, and in the safe anonymity of London, where no one (meaning Ernest) need ever know, he might easily have made this gesture.

Even if fictional, the story's important. It's what my mother died believing: that my father, for all his bigotry, was willing to do this, because he loved her. And that's the truth.

# CHAPTER TWELVE

# A Brief History of What Happened After That

1946–97. FIFTY-ONE YEARS. The rest of her life. I'm tempted to duck out and end the story here. That's what I'd do if this were a nineteenth-century novel – leave the heroine at the altar, her married future shining up ahead. But we've moved on a century or two, and this is non-fiction, and it feels wrong not to tell the rest of the story. How happily did things work out for Kim? What kind of wife was she? What kind of mother? What kind of doctor?

✳    ✳    ✳

THE PLAN WAS: she wouldn't work. This was Arthur's practice – bought with Morrison money – and Arthur's Pennine turf. It was also 1946, the year of the returning hero. Women, having held the fort, reverted to being wives and mothers, while the men got back their jobs as a prize for having won the war. In some professions, such as teaching, married women weren't allowed to work. There was so much to do at home. 'Have his dinner ready and freshen your make-up,' the rule-books said. 'Never complain if he is late. Don't pester him with your troubles. Show you are concerned about his needs.' When they rolled up in Earby that autumn, my parents were carrying this baggage. It was the baggage of the age. He'd hunt and gather while she played the little wife.

She couldn't do it. To sit at home was bad enough. To sit at home when home, the Crossings, was also the workplace – the surgery the other side of the kitchen door – was torture. Did he intend to keep her like a squirrel in a cage? It was agreed she 'help', if only part-time. The practice was small, and to make a go of it they needed more patients. Without her assistance in the surgery he'd not have time to woo recruits. The rival GP was close to retirement and they hoped to pick up some of his list. As a young husband-and-wife team, they were the face of the embryonic NHS: forward-looking, new broom, breath of fresh air, all that. He wore his RAF uniform and drove an open-top MG. She won the hearts of expectant mothers, though still not one herself. Patriarchal middle-class pride said a man should earn enough to keep his wife, but logic said two salaries were better than one. Even Ernest could see the point of Kim working, 'if only in a small way'. 'Hire a middle-aged woman to look after you both,' he told them. 'Far better to earn £5 a week and pay out 50 per cent of it than to do all the dirty work yourself.'

The winter of 1947 was the worst of the century. Local roads were snowed up for weeks. To visit patients on moorland farms meant finding a way through ten-foot drifts. The Crossings was a cold and ugly house, its front gate abutting the level crossing where the Colne–Skipton railway line intersected with the A56. Not a time and place for newlyweds. But they dug in through the big freeze and once spring came began to get out a bit, driving up the Dales or popping over to Manchester to see his parents or Ron and Mary. They also made friends with several pub-going couples like themselves: Stephen Pickles, heir apparent to Pickles Mill, and his glowing young wife Val; Charles Shuttleworth, a businessman from Nelson, and Selene; Gordon and Edna Parkinson, who lived in nearby Thornton-in-Craven; Stanley and Doreen Mason, Arthur and Florrie Wallbank, Bobby and Myra Dickinson, John and Ann Barratt; and Bryan and Hilly Thackeray, who ran the Cross Keys, where everyone would meet. They were an affable young crowd, demob-happy and post-war-bright. She felt like a sore thumb nonetheless – because she was Irish (which she underplayed), because she was Catholic (which she hid entirely), but above all because she worked.

In 1946 most rural GPs ran their practices from home, and

took money in the traditional way, three bob here, six bob there, depending on what the patient could afford. But on 5 July 1948 the National Health Service was born: free medical treatment for all. GPs had fought against its inception, for fear they'd become lowly state functionaries. At Windyridge the Health Minister, Aneurin Bevan, was seen as an enemy. 'Dirty in the extreme,' Ernest called him. 'Tub-thumping, playing to the gallery, vote-snatching, and full of lies. I should like you to be Mr Bevan's doctor for a week. He would not make many speeches after that.' But Arthur didn't share his father's hostility. As he saw it, there were benefits to the new system. Instead of scrambling round for fees, he and Kim had secure salaries, based on 'capitation' (15 shillings for each patient on their list, giving him around £1200, and her half that). Instead of struggling with difficult cases, they were encouraged to refer them to hospital specialists. (And why not? They knew their limits and had enough work on as it was.) Instead of holding surgeries at the Crossings, they were helped to set up new premises elsewhere, with a receptionist and, in due course, a third partner, Gordon Dick. People liked them, it seemed, and didn't mind that they'd not been born locally. They were family doctors, who'd listen to your grumbles as well as your pulse. The practice grew; the money in the bank grew too. They bought an Alvis and found a live-in maid, an Austrian refugee called Rosa. As yet, it was true, they'd no great need of her, except for taking messages. But once children came along . . .

At the start of the next decade, they did. First me, then fourteen months later my sister Gill. There would have been a third, as my dad had predicted in 1944, but my mum miscarried, after which she called it quits. They were in their late thirties by then, which in those days was thought old to be having babies. Already they'd outgrown the Crossings and were looking to move. An alluringly empty rectory was spotted, just up from Gordon and Edna's house in Thornton, and Arthur and Ernest laid siege to the Church Commissioners, who in time were persuaded to sell. Two years were spent restoring the place – much of the work done by my father at weekends. All that

digging and scrounging in the Azores had given him a taste for DIY. His involvement and the help of friends helped to keep costs down but the toll was heavy: purchase price £2500, builder £1458, central heating £626, plumbing £267, electricity £206, decorations £596, billiard table £108 – getting on for £6000 all told. Still, the sale of the Crossings brought in £3600. And by now they had their new surgery, in a terraced house in Water Street. You crossed a bridge over a stream to enter it. The Pennine rain made the stream run strong, even in summer, right beneath your feet. It flowed like time did, faster each year.

By June 1955, Thornton Rectory was ready to move into. My father rechristened it the Grange, purging it of religious associations. My mother must have been glad of that. It had lapsed, and she had lapsed, but there she was, a Catholic in the house of Protestantism. How long they'd stay was doubtful: a practice in Cheshire was their dream and they also flirted with emigration to Canada. But as it turned out they didn't move again till they retired – and then only 50 yards away. The Grange was spacious: five bedrooms, a billiard room, a barn, stables and outbuildings, a front lawn sloping to woodland, a back lawn almost big enough for a tennis court, a granny cottage, two greenhouses and two paddocks. My father couldn't believe his luck: for him to own all this! My mother delighted in his delight, but for herself felt more ambivalent. The O'Sheas had been comfortably off, but she wasn't used to so much space. She felt dwarfed by it, a little ghost flitting from room to room

\* \* \*

WHAT KIND OF mother was she? A working one. As well as her GP duties in the Water Street surgery, she'd become attached to Cawder Ghyll maternity hospital, in Skipton, where she ran an ante-natal clinic and delivered her patients' babies. It gave her independence from my father, allowed her to specialise and – being women's work – made her feel less freakish. (Only 15 per cent of doctors registered in Britain in 1951 were women; of those women, fewer than a third – around 2000 – were GPs. Women GPs in rural areas were rare. As to an Irish Catholic woman GP in a rural northern practice, it was unheard of.) The new Welfare State put great emphasis on children's health: free milk and orange juice, eye tests, regular checks of weight and height, tonsillectomies. We might not have seen it that way, queuing for jabs, but kids had never had it so good. Fanning the wind of change kept my mother busy. Gill and I weren't the only children in her life, it seemed: there were all these other babies mopping up her time. Rosa turned nursemaid as well as housekeeper. The two family labradors, Gunner and Terry, became my source of daytime warmth. I lay with them under the kitchen table, my head buried in gold, or sat on the floor, my back to the Aga. I didn't feel unloved but I sometimes felt unmothered. My mum's mum hadn't mothered her, preferring to tend the Virgin's lamp in church while maids took charge at home, so she had no model for it. The mums in the ads on our walnut-cased television had blonde hair, gleaming smiles and armfuls of washing. My mother didn't resemble them. Dark-haired, cerebral, angular and often absent, she cared more for paediatrics than for Persil. She had a live-in housekeeper.

She drove a car (unless my father was in it). There was no longer any question of her giving up work. It was a very un-Fifties set-up.

Yet I saw her as 'ordinary' and she encouraged this. No matter how limited her interest in domestic tasks, she wasn't going to skimp. Rosa might be there to clean, take messages and babysit, but the rest she considered her domain. Unless she had an evening surgery – and she tried to avoid them, so as to be at home when my sister and I returned from school – she always cooked and served supper, dealing the men of the house the larger portions. She did the mending and ironing, too, duties considered too demanding, or too effete, for my father, who took on the expected male roles, washing the car, mowing the lawn and paying the bills, as well as playing golf and going to the pub. However steely on the Maternity Ward, my mother was happy to defer to men (including me) at home. It was easier than doing battle.

There were days – or evenings – when I loved her intensely, times I had her all for myself. Mostly these were bathtimes, when she'd soap my neck and sing 'Smoke Gets in Your Eyes'. But it's her absences I remember. I'd sit at the dressing table, splaying the legs of a Kirbigrip or rescuing strands of her hair from the spongy hedgehog of her hairbrush, or I'd snoozle down in her vast wardrobe, among the scents of a fur coat or ballgown. My father was the one in charge of games, who rode us in the wheelbarrow, put up the summer tent, lay down on the floor to whizz the Scalextric racing cars round their figure of eight, built a swimming pool from polythene and oil drums, and taught me how to catch a ball. My mother wasn't into play. Perhaps her parents had never had time to play with her. Or perhaps it was just the times – in the 1950s, a mother might provide improving pastimes for her children but wasn't expected to sit on the floor with them, among wooden blocks and fluffy toys. I noticed it later, with my own children: she was sweet with them but hadn't a clue how to keep them amused. Amusement wasn't her thing. She cared too much about her work. To my dad, work was a necessary evil, to be offset with beer, golf, DIY, stock-market gambles and sleep. For her, it was life — or would have been, had she pursued it as vigorously as she wished.

It wasn't just my father who discouraged her. The era was against her, too. Work was for headscarved wives in mill- or mining-towns, whose households needed the extra shillings, or for professional women too brainy or lezzy to get hitched. A middle-class lady with young children was allowed out only on a part-time basis. In terms of qualification and experience, my mother ought to have been the senior partner in the practice. And many women patients, or men who needed sensitive handling, preferred to make appointments with her. But when people turned up at the house asking for the doctor, we knew it was my father they meant. He was the The, she merely an A; Gill and I felt ourselves to be the doctor's children, not the doctors' children. On holiday, kids on the beach would ask 'What's your dad do?' No one ever asked about my mum.

Was she unhappy with this state of affairs? Not that she'd have admitted. She didn't read the Stoics, preferring Jilly Cooper, but would have agreed with Seneca: 'That which you cannot reform, it is best to endure.' The age was unreformable (Conservatism ruled from 1951 to 1964), my father was unreformable, and she herself was unreformable, too much the quietist to assert herself except through work. Had she been taught in church and school that femaleness was a condition of endurance? Or did she arrive at this conclusion herself? Was her stoicism a virtue or a weakness? Whichever, she got on without complaint. If my father did something she disliked, or if I did, the most we got was a look, a silence that let us know. She would not say what she felt in so many words. Only in so few words. The fewer the better. Best, no words at all.

Yet a child can't miss what a parent is feeling, and from the moment I saw my mother as someone separate from me, what I sensed was disappointment. I heard it when she sang 'Smoke Gets in Your Eyes', a song of hope betrayed. I saw it in her sad, distracted eyes. Sometimes those eyes would prick with moisture, but I don't remember seeing her cry. She was never a 'performer': in company she chose self-effacement. But the withdrawal into herself, the quietness, the reluctance to be noticed: this was a kind of performance in itself. Those make-up items in her wardrobe – the powder puffs, lipsticks and mascara brushes – were for concealment not beautification. Let others display themselves. She preferred to cover up.

Among her unspoken feelings was a dislike of village life. The green hills, sheep-farming and busybodiness of the Yorkshire Dales made her feel at home, but it was a home she thought she'd escaped. Killorglin, she'd told him back in 1944, was a dump: she'd 'go nuts' if she had to spend time there because of the pressure to 'go around and say hello to everyone'. What she loved about Manchester and Birmingham, as well as the shops, was knowing no one knew you. Yet here she was back in Lilliput, among little people spying on each other's little lives. My father thought the Dales a good place to raise children, and she accepted that. But given the chance, she'd have lived somewhere more urban (the sigh of trains in crowded stations, waiters whistling as the last bar closes, cigarette butts on the pavement with lipstick traces – these foolish things gave her great pleasure). When we walked through the back fields in wellingtons she rarely joined us. And she looked too much the lady to be visiting farmers' wives up muddy tracks. One Saturday she hit a puddle on the back road between East Marton and Gargrave and skidded into a ditch. My sister was in the front seat and banged her face against the dashboard: I remember her bruised cheek and swollen top lip. My mother escaped without damage, but the crash summed up her discomfort. The country was no place for her. If it hadn't been for Cawder Ghyll, and the busyness of its labour ward, she'd have gone mad.

\*　　\*　　\*

IF ASKED, GILLIAN and I would have said we were happy, though between us we had problems – tantrums, encopresis, obesity. I exaggerate about the last. But both of us were fat, and got teased for it at school. Our parents didn't consider it a problem: it was chubbiness, that was all, and we'd grow out of it.

Perhaps, subconsciously, they even felt relieved. The ration books and other wartime skeletons had finally gone. Look, our flab said, We Have Come Through.

IN THE POST-WAR English provinces, anti-Irish prejudice was rife. Did my mother encounter it? If so, she never let on. By now her accent was barely discernible: no one need know and unless asked she didn't say. Effacement wasn't her only way of coping. She also told jokes against her tribe. The Irish as stupid, feckless, drunk, poverty-stricken – the thing was to get in first, before the English did. In letters to my father during the war she had gently made fun of fellow Irish doctors. In retirement she kept a book of Kerryman gags by her bed ('Have you heard about the Kerryman who got a pair of water skis for Christmas? He's still looking round for a lake with a slope'). There was no anti-Irish crack too scabrous for her, and like many other Catholics from the Republic she loathed the IRA ('Jesus, Mary and Joseph,' she'd say, as news came in of some new bombing or sectarian murder, 'hasn't the world Troubles enough without theirs?'). When good friends clumsily alluded to her origins, she behaved

with perfect grace. 'I've found this wonderful little man,' someone would say, then throw her a meaningful look. 'Actually he's
Irish, Kim, a Mr O'Sullivan.' To which she'd reply in mock-
amazement, 'O'Sullivan! We're probably related,' the tone so
charming no one felt the edge.

Only once do I remember a humour failure. It was
Christmas 1960 or so, and my cousins – Auntie Mary, Uncle
Ron and family – were over from Manchester. By now Uncle
Ron was established as a dentist for Tootals, the shirt and tie
manufacturers, having finally abandoned all thoughts of a share
in general practice (a wise decision, the Morrisons said, since
Ron was neither pushy nor much of a mixer). The Astles were a
growing family, Richard, Edward and Jane having been added to
Kela. With six of them, four of us, Granny Morrison, and old J.J.
Duckworth from Elslack and one of his daughters invited too,
we had to shunt two tables together (one rectangular, one oval)
to accommodate everyone for lunch. Cold rain beat against the
dining room window as we took our seats. The air was already
darkening. 'Thirteen,' said my father, counting heads, 'my lucky
number.' He carved the turkey at the far end of the room, while
we children, down the other, pulled crackers. Novelties and
paper hats spilled out, and as the adults drank red wine and sized
up the turkey we read aloud the mottoes.

'How many Irishmen does it take to clean an upstairs
window?'

'Cooked to perfection, Mummy, love.'

'Don't know, how many?'

'It's been in the bottom oven since 7.'

'Two, one to use the cloth and one to hold the ladder.'

'Breast nice and white, and lots of succulence.'

'How many Irishmen does it take to clean a downstairs
window?'

'I was worried it would be too dry, even with the foil on.'

'Don't know, how many?'

'Dark meat lovely and juicy. Anyone for stuffing?'

'Twenty. One to use the cloth, and nineteen to dig the hole
for the ladder.'

Not many laughs. The jokes in crackers got worse each year. But something prompted Auntie Mary to ask after my mother's family.

'Oh, they're all fine.'

'Do you never think of spending Christmas there, Kim?'

My mother, busy with roast potatoes, ducked the question. My father, a glass or two to the good, laughed and said, 'What, Christmas with peasants? In the peat-bogs?'

My mother being my mother didn't react at first – the merest flinch, that's all. But my father continued laughing, as though expecting her to join in. Perhaps it was this that did it. She departed pale and silent from the room. He was still chuckling after she did. The rest of us were shocked. A show of emotion from my mother was unprecedented. 'Poor Kim,' said Mary, dispatching my father to fetch her. There were whispers among the remaining adults. It was said she'd been working too hard, was suffering from a headache, that cooking Christmas lunch could be a hell of a strain for any woman. Silent, the spirit gone from the occasion, we ate her soft white breast. Even my cousins seemed subdued, though they were used to marital tiffs. Once, staying at their house, I'd walked in on Ron and Mary fighting over a frying pan in the kitchen: seeing me, they'd stopped and laughed and sent me off – the little peace-maker, who sensed they'd be at it again once I left the room. With them there was lots of spark. And Mary knew how to stand up for her-self. But it was unheard of for my mum to stand up to my dad. They had no differences. None they'd acknowledge. Or none that couldn't be solved by her giving way.

Soon, with an 'All's fine now', he returned. Taciturn, she emerged shortly after, newly made-up. By the time the pudding flamed blue with brandy, the incident was closed. But something had opened inside me – a sudden vista of a woman among aliens, orphaned and nostalgic for home. And though my mother was quickly 'herself again', she never was, for me.

✶   ✶   ✶

MY MEMORY OF that Christmas is one of the few with my mother in a principal role. In the rest, my father is the main protagonist, while she plays a minor, often non-speaking, part. It was an age when women didn't have their own narratives. Remembering her, what comes to mind is not a story but a mood. An expression. A feeling. A certain something in the atmosphere. But nothing so dramatic as an event. I find this frustrating. I see her clearly for no more than an instant. Sometimes trains at night catch the rail at a certain angle, sparking a phosphor-flash of whiteness that lights the surrounding trees and buildings for half a second; my memories of my mother are the same, brief flashes, nothing more. She isn't, like my father, a 'character' (larger than life). She *has* character, but that's a subtler thing to evoke, a matter of shading not colour. In the mirror I sometimes see him but never her. I carry her inside me – a way of thinking and feeling – but detect no outward sign. She is my mum, my DNA, my secret sharer. But I can't find her.

Is the problem that I'm a man? Is it gender-blindness? Would my sister be better equipped, as a woman, to decode her? Should she be the one writing this book? Perhaps. But if sex is such a prison, if men can't even begin to understand women, if the only genres open to blokes are the blokeish ones – buddy books, adventure tales, war epics, father-son memoirs . . . no, it's too depressing.

I used to think of my mother as the Woman Who Was, married to the Man Who Did. But given her workaholic instincts, her inability to relax beside him on a sunbed or in an armchair, I see that's wrong. It wasn't that she didn't do things, but that she hated to be *noticed* doing them. To be invisible was her objective, and she succeeded with a vengeance. I look at photographs, in the hope they'll dredge some memory from the swamp. I talk to friends and relations, but nothing they say brings her nearer. It's as if she has gone without a trace.

My father left letters, diaries, tapes, notebooks, a family tree, even a message on my answering machine. She left bric-a-brac and furniture, but nothing uniquely hers. That's how she wanted it. What began as a secretion of her otherness became a talent for self-occlusion. After the erasure, in life, of Agnes, the oblivion, in death, of Kim.

✶   ✶   ✶

CHRISTMASES WERE IMPORTANT, the one fixed family occasion, though none of the family was hers. In earlier years there'd been fourteen for lunch, but Ernest, my father's father, died in November 1958. 'Don't let your waistline grow like I did,' he wrote just weeks before his death, his last piece of advice to his son. 'Believe me, a big stomach is a nuisance beyond repair.'

Obesity was probably a factor in the coronary. He woke complaining of chest pains and, by the time the doctor came, he was dead. His death was no surprise to Arthur, who'd written to consultants about his father's heart problems five years before. But he'd not expected to feel such grief. There was also the problem of where Kathleen should live, since Ernest had left a letter in his desk, asking his children to 'take care of Mummy and under no circumstances allow her to *live alone*, not even for one night.' In time, a solution was arrived at: Ron and Mary would move into Windyridge (a more suitable home than Red Lodge for their growing family), while Granny would come to live in the refurbished cottage next to us. A sensible arrangement, but nothing could allay my father's sense of loss. A year or so before the coronary, Mary, rather than just phone, had sent him a letter. 'I wish you could manage to slip over for a weekend as I feel that in his quiet way Daddy is missing seeing you and hearing from you,' she wrote. 'It's getting on for three months since you were here, isn't it? I understand how busy you are, and you shouldn't panic or worry – I just think it's time you popped over.' That time he had seen him. But in the three months before he died, there'd been no visits. Most unusual. And a guilt he never got over. I remember him saying, when I moved to London, how important it was we keep in touch. It was meant more for my sake than for his.

✻   ✻   ✻

THERE WAS A reason my father hadn't seen his father. He'd fallen in love. In 1957, Beaty and her husband Sam had arrived to run the bar at the local golf club. For the next decade the nineteenth hole was where my father's heart lay. He adored Beaty and, being the man he was, brought his family along so we could adore her too. At quiet times my sister and I would be allowed in the clubhouse. More often, on Sundays, we played out back among the drinks crates, a bag of crisps and bottle of orangeade to keep us quiet. My mother sat smoking on a high stool and watched. As though she was used to this. As though, as a wife, this is what you did.

My father mightn't be tall or handsome, but his smiles were winning, his energy was prodigious and he looked much younger than his years. He wasn't sly or predatory, but out there in the open, an innocent. Beaty had this innocence too. With her Marilyn blonde hair and pointy big breasts, the golfers at the bar liked to flirt with her, but she considered herself a good Catholic – and made a point of being friendly to my mum. In time Beaty and Sam became regular visitors at our house – or rather Beaty did, since Sam, as bar and catering manager, had few hours off. Though easy-going, he sometimes wore a scowl and knotted brow. He was bigger and burlier than my father, and could easily have taught him a lesson or two. But like my mother he felt powerless to act. They could see the chemistry between Arthur and Beaty, but were told it wasn't dangerous. If anything funny was going on, Beaty reassured Sam, why would Arthur bring his family with him? He wasn't just their best customer but the local GP, a useful man to have on your side. Sam should take a lesson from Kim, sitting there benignly. He shouldn't make a fuss.

Whether she really felt benign is doubtful. My memory of her on that barstool is of someone careful not to drink too much or drop her guard. And even if she wasn't suspicious, she would certainly have felt bored and resentful – all that time wasted at the golf club bar when they could have been together at home. But it's true she didn't kick up – not even when my father began going out with Beaty each Monday night. She was feeling low, he said, and needed 'taking out of herself'. With Sam on duty every night, who else was there to cheer her up? My mother would have been welcome to tag along. But three was a crowd, and she didn't share the interest in pubs and clubs. To judge by Beaty's smiling face in photographs, the restorative measures soon worked. But the Monday outings stretched on indefinitely – and when Ernest died, my father was the one who needed comforting. Their excursions became more adventurous. He began coming home in the small hours. Soon there was gossip. A patient spotted them together at a nightclub in Bradford. Two married people going out without their other halves – it couldn't just be harmless fun. Sod what the world thinks, my father said. Easy for him to say: wasn't he the one doing the doing? For my mother, stuck at home with her jealousy and humiliation, it was harder.

It became harder still when Josephine was born. Beaty and Sam had been told there was little chance of them having children, but suddenly, miraculously, a daughter. Stranger things have happened: couples lose hope and adopt and then find themselves conceiving. Still, at some point in my teens it occurred to me that Josephine might be my half-sister. She was born at Cawder Ghyll, where my mother delivered her patients' babies. Beaty being a patient, she delivered her baby too. I remember, on the day of the birth, my father taking my sister and me along, and a nurse holding up a tiny face in a blanket to show us. He doted on Josephine – as my mother, otherwise so discreet, sarcastically observed. I look at old photographs now and her resemblance to him still seems unmistakeable. But if she was his, he never said so. Nor did my mother or Beaty say it, even much later. She was not there in his will. There were no death-bed confessions. Perhaps the aim was to protect Sam or Josephine. Whatever, I have to accept it's not my business. It goes against the modern spirit, operative in adoption agencies, that children need to know the truth. It adds to my genealogical bewilderment. But I don't expect ever to find out.

✻   ✻   ✻

My mother did her best to tolerate the relationship with Beaty, but there were times her quiescence reached its limit. One day I found her at the foot of the stairs, her coat on, her suitcase packed, announcing that she was going away for a few days. I wasn't to worry, she said, but how could I not? She never went off like this; her only trips away alone were to Ireland, and wherever she was going this time it wasn't there. She went to the Midlands, I think, to stay with her sister Sheila, and came back to fight another day (which meant continuing to surrender). Her departure chastened my father, but not so much as to give up Beaty, who – he now admitted – he loved, 'but in a different way from how I love you'. She needn't worry he'd stopped caring. Let him have his head a bit, that was all he asked.

*Why did she put up with it?* Because she believed him when he said he loved her. Yes, she resented Beaty being his bit of fun: why couldn't *she* be that? why couldn't he be kind to *her*? But he showed no signs of wanting to leave home or end the marriage. Yes, he was having his cake and eating it, but so what? If Beaty was just the icing did it matter? The advice columns said that women in my mum's position should put their foot down – retaliate with a flirtation of their own, run away with the kids, threaten divorce. But she had no appetite for an affair, knew if we ran off he'd follow, and, as a Catholic, lapsed or otherwise,

297

regarded divorce as a mortal sin. Nor could she face going back to Kerry, fearing what she'd meet there would be *Schadenfreude* – hadn't they warned her about marrying out? For the same reason, she resisted returning to her church. In theory, there was nothing to stop her. She could go headscarfed to Mass six miles away, in Colne, and with luck none of her patients would spot her. But she had left all that behind. Having made her bed in Arthur's kingdom, she must lie in it.

In that bed, for a time, she turned cold on him. But outside, around the house, in surgery, at the pub, on the surface, their life went on unchanged. No one could make sense of it. She was too intelligent to be walked over. If she'd had close friends to confide in, she might have been angrier and more defiant. But her friends were all *their* friends, and she was too proud and private to own up to her distress. There were no feminist groups to join, no Relate, nothing for someone in her condition. She stuck it out.

In photos from those years, she looks slim and elegant. In shorts and a blue-ribbed sweater pulling weed from a fishing net; blue-suited (with a white handbag) by a drophead Triumph;

yellow-anoraked and knock-kneed as she learns to slalom in Glenshee; green-jacketed raking leaves from the garden lawn; fur-coated by a winter hearth; blue-suited (again, but a paler blue this time) as she poses with my father in front of the house – she looks different in each snap, a chameleon, only half present, alone with her thoughts, neither laughing nor scowling, the intelligence of her eyes the only constant. Whereas Beaty grins and glows. I'd forgotten till looking at the photos again – the glossy prints, the hundreds of Kodak and Agfa transparencies – how often Beaty featured in our family activities. It wasn't enough for my father to take her out at night, or invite her over at weekends. She joined us on our holidays, too. It wasn't sex she offered so much as unconditional acceptance. She mightn't be a soulmate like my mother, but nor did she frighten him with cleverness. She was fun, too: before becoming a barmaid, she'd been a nurse. Cosy: that was the word. It had taken him fifteen years and it wasn't the Azores, but my father had his Cosy after all. I warmed to her myself. There's a photo of us all swimming together on a beach near Kircudbright. Everyone but my mother, that is: she was the one taking the picture.

Later, Beaty stayed at the Abersoch caravan we bought – usually while we were there, but sometimes alone with Josephine. Once, by mistake, she arrived early, when Auntie Mary (another regular visitor) was still packing up to go. Mary made a point of being cold – didn't offer a cuppa, cleared off smartish, virtually refused to speak. Kim might put up with Beaty, but that was no reason for Mary to do the same. By then the affair was waning, and any damage had already been inflicted. But it was Mary's way of showing sisterly solidarity. And a rebuke to her brother, just like the one she'd sent him by letter in 1944. 'I don't care how innocent you say it is – it's just not bloody well fair.'

*　　*　　*

FIVE FEET SIX inches tall, barrel-chested and with two black pouches under his eyes, my father was an unlikely charmer. But he put women at ease: there was no rakish leering or hulking power to make them fear for their virtue. The husbands felt at ease, too, and over the years there were several married women whom he captivated. Two or three he met on holiday and, if only temporarily, made part of the family. The pretext was usually that he felt sorry for them – A's husband was working away from home, B had been having tests for leukaemia, C's nerves were so bad the night winds kept her awake, etc. He'd meet these women out walking the dog or drinking at the bar and then invite them back, feeling sure my mother would like them too. Often she did like them, and they always liked her, but the electricity was all with him. In my lurid adolescence I imagined more to these relationships than was there; I don't now think they were sexual (even Beaty went on denying it had been sexual with her). But there was a pattern of acquisition and an excitement that went beyond friendship. Once, when he wasn't around to hear, my mother spoke wryly of my father's habit of 'bringing home strays'. He was like a cat that carries a baby bird into the kitchen. Or like a wagging gun-dog, eager to please its mistress. Did I say my mother spoke *wryly* of this? *Sardonically* might be nearer the mark. *Bitterly* might have been in it too – but she'd not have allowed herself the word, and won't allow me it either.

No, bitterness was reserved for Beaty, without whom my father's relations with these other women would have seemed blameless. And even with Beaty, my mother's bitterness couldn't be fully expressed. At first she was told she was 'imagining things'. And once it became clear she wasn't, she was made to feel she was 'blowing it out of all proportion'. Deferential by nature, stripped of her name and identity, overwhelmed by his protestations of innocent fun, she felt unable to fight back.

Part of the problem was that his boundaries were so different from hers. Though both were doctors, and unillusioned about the body, she was shyer and more reserved than him. He liked to go as naked as decency allowed – the merest hint of warmth and he'd strip down to a pair of shorts, no matter who was around. He liked others' nakedness, too: not pruriently or voyeuristically, but because flesh, he thought, not clothing, is what makes us human. A few women found this intrusive or just plain rude: one friend of theirs was put out when he brought her a gin and tonic in the bath. But others took it in good heart: Arthur was a bit eccentric, that's all. And some women warmed to his candour. I'm sure my mother did, despite herself. And certainly Beaty did, as Cosy had before her. Where was the harm?

☆　☆　☆

THE HARM TO my mother came out as migraines. She'd had them during the war, when overworked, until her rotten teeth were pulled. In 1948, in Earby, they briefly re-emerged, along with diplopia, double vision. But it wasn't until the 1960s that they really hurt. Irons would clamp her head and pain sear her eye sockets, and she'd feel nauseous and have to lie in the dark. My father urged her to ease off in surgery and do less at Cawder Ghyll. But she could hardly stop her patients having babies. And meanwhile there were just the two of them in the practice, and my father refused to bring in a locum. Free weekends disappeared: one or other of them – meaning him – would be on call. Family holidays became the three of us, while he stayed home. My mother suspected – or I suspected on her behalf – that the reason he wouldn't come on holiday was Beaty. The holidays felt empty. Back home my mother's migraines raged on. Cheese, chocolate, alcohol – all were given up, without improvement. It was agreed she was suffering from stress. But the stress didn't come from work (which she loved and would happily have done more of) but from brooding on what she had come to. They were midlife migraines. Brought on by the conflicts of identity. And by my father's ten-year crush on Beaty.

The migraines reached a pitch one summer Saturday. It was the village fete, and my father let the parish council use his paddock. The day was thundery. Between showers there were races – running, sack, three-legged and egg-and-spoon – and my father served black sausages from his barbecue. During a lull, I don't know why, I drifted back to the house. From above I heard vague moans, which, as I climbed the stairs, grew more intense.

My mum was lying on the double bed – or rather rolling her head and thrashing about. What scared me wasn't the noise she was making, or the drawn curtains, or her being in bed mid-afternoon, but to see her so unrestrained for once, writhing, kicking, out of control. 'Get Daddy, quick,' she said, her eyes tight yet open wide. I ran back to the paddock, faster than I'd run in any of the races. He, too, moved quickly when I called him, slammed down his tongs and charged back to the house, like a man sent to put out a fire. Later, a black car sat in the driveway. I took it for a hearse at first, a mistake compounded when some-one in the kitchen said, 'Your mother's at peace now'. But the man whispering to my father carried a little black bag and, death-suited though he was, had the voice of a doctor not an undertaker. I walked in on them in the billiard-room – two whiskies and a conspiracy. A look from my father sent me quickly back out again, and then the door was closed so their murmurings wouldn't be heard. But I knew my mother was safe now. And though she slept that day and half the next, she came back again, order restored, her brow unbraced.

Tests were done, to rule out a tumour. New pills were tried. Soon enough, the headaches returned, never with such intensity but enough to knock her out for a bit – a couple of days of darkness and Veganin. I know what they feel like, having inherit-ed them from her: they come round every month or so, like periods, though I don't suffer as she did. I think of the fete as the day her stoicism ran out. Might she even have been a little theatrical? If her screams and gyrations were a cry for help, they did the job. Later, her head brought her other problems – anxiety attacks, dizzy spells, lapses of memory and tinnitus, with its hum of melancholy and piercing whistle of despair. The demons of the cortex. But back then the demon was Beaty. And though I don't blame Beaty for the migraines – I don't blame Beaty for *anything* – for a time her existence was a blight.

\* \* \*

I DON'T REMEMBER having sexual feelings towards my mother. Perhaps it helped that till twelve or thirteen I didn't know what sex was. But not knowing didn't stop me, at eleven, being fascinated by Marjorie Malina's breasts (which I spied on while on holiday in the south of France) or by Beaty's breasts (which she exposed when feeding Josephine in our bathroom) or by the breasts of our various housekeepers. Why did these middle-aged women excite me, while my mother, whose dark nipples I'd once glimpsed in the shower, did not? Why no fantasies about her? 'Most men have slept with their mothers in dreams,' Jocasta tells Oedipus: isn't it abnormal to feel no incestuous desires? I loved the scents she left about the house. But theirs was an erotica of absence: they stood in for her when she was out. Her physical presence didn't stir me because it *wasn't* physical. Her thereness was her not being there. And the evidence that she'd gone – the empty rooms, idle brushes, untenanted clothes – was to me more sensuous than having her there. I luxuriated in fantasies of orphanhood. I liked being a lonely child.

Did she like being lonely too? Though she didn't bath me any more, she still hummed 'Smoke Gets in Your Eyes'. Its sadness had seemed generalised before, but now I knew it was specific: something inside had changed; she felt herself to be an object of derision; her true love wasn't true. She'd married thinking love would be enough. And with a job, two children, and a house as solid and spacious as the Grange, she had enough and more than. Yet she carried this tumour of sadness, this spot on the heart. She didn't regret loving my father, but life might have been easier had they never met. Habit, children, work and domesticity took the edge off any marriage, she knew that. But theirs had been special. She'd surrendered so much to make it happen. And now look.

There were no cells of melancholy in my father. His only disease was unbounded optimism. He didn't care when the weatherman said that it was raining, he was certain the sun would shine. 'The man who has everything' he sometimes called himself. But if you have everything, *can* you fall in love elsewhere? He told her yes, that it was possible to love two women at once. It didn't seem that way to her.

I shouldn't overdo her sadness. I may be confusing it with my own sadness, which is the sadness of no longer having her here. When I look again at those old photos, I find she's sometimes smiling after all, even with Beaty at her side. But smiles are easily put on; they're only frowns reversed. Underneath lay feelings of loss and uselessness which would send her into troughs of depression. Moods, she called them, and hoped by keeping her head down to spare the rest of us. It didn't work. These periods of her lying low upset me. How low might she sink? Why wouldn't she say what the matter was? What if I lost her for ever? When others I've loved since have suffered from depression, I've become mildly hysterical. It's no excuse, but perhaps their depressions trigger memories of hers, and of how afraid I was she'd die or disappear. ('Ach,' I hear her saying, when I try out this theory, 'stuff and nonsense.')

✳   ✳   ✳

MISFORTUNE BROUGHT ME closer to my mother. She was a victim, and as a teenager I thrived on victims. The dead of Passchendaele, Auschwitz, Hiroshima and My Lai sang in my head like elegies. The tortured, the exiled, the disenfranchised, the abused, men and women with famished bodies and bursting heads – they were the ones in all my dreams. I numbered my mum among them.

Had she been living at home, my sister might have offered my mother some same-sex solace. But Gillian was at a boarding school in the Lake District, having botched her 11-plus. My mother felt ambivalent about sending her there. Though she'd enjoyed being a boarder herself, and thought St Ann's preferable to the local secondary, she worried that Gillian might feel punished. For the sake of fairness, pressure was put on me to go away too. But I was two years into grammar school in Skipton, and dug my heels in, and when even the head at Giggleswick – the nearest boarding option – said he thought it better I stay put, my parents gave up the struggle. So I was allowed to live at home and be a day boy, while my sister was banished. We were a house divided by the pass-fail exam system. Three years on, Gillian became so miserable at St Ann's (she always had been, but now her letters home expressed it with greater eloquence) that she was rescued, taken out, brought home, and (her academic standards having been raised by exile) admitted to Skipton Girls' High School. But in the meantime, holidays aside, I had my mother to myself.

With my father, I was made to *do* things (play tennis, wash the car, mow the lawn); with her, it was permitted to sit. His lessons in car maintenance went over my head, but I listened attentively when she talked, and debated love and fashion with her. At thirteen I sang alto and lacked facial hair, and my left ball had only just dropped – so it was all right to be an honorary girl. Together we closed ranks against my father, whose bullish peremptoriness – so our silent sorority let him know – was a deep affront. Thick-skinned he might have been, but he got the message. I remember one summer holiday when he joined us for the weekend at a rainy Welsh caravan and – exasperated at our silent resistance – told us what miserable sods we were and disappeared to the pub. He'd have gone to the pub, anyway, but denouncing and running out on the family wasn't his style. He came back a bit hangdog. Next day we made more effort – he'd be leaving at the end of it, anyway. Outwardly, harmony was restored. We made up. But sides were taken, and my mother had me on hers.

The high point of our intimacy came when I was fourteen or fifteen, the time when boys feel closest to their mothers, or when certain kinds of boy do, those intimidated or repelled by their fathers. I was off school, recovering from chicken-pox, and rather than leave me at home she drove me round while visiting patients. I had an Illustrated Shakespeare with me, a naff picture book with potted narratives of all the plays. She would disappear inside some house in Kelbrook or Foulridge while I made my way through another history play. Then she'd come out again through the rain, and we'd exchange stories – Falstaff's girth, Mrs Cowgill's haemorrhoids – while she drove to the next patient. My mother wasn't a great reader, but there was an aura of bookishness and ideas; I dreamt a girl somewhere would have this too, but I hadn't met her yet, and until I did . . . In Colne we stopped at a baker's and she brought back a warm yellow loaf in its sheaf of white parchment. 'For lunch. Won't be long now,' she said, as we pulled up outside a large semi in Trawden. 'Just this last visit.'

Rain snare-drummed on the roof. The loaf sat warm in my lap and I tore one end away, a crust. I was on *Richard III* now (and, if I'd known it, the Lancs–Yorks border) and it was hard to follow who was whose relation. I thought of Paddy Rogers, the Irishman who taught us English, an exile like my mother. When he read Shakespeare (and Joyce and Hardy and T.S. Eliot and Wilfred Owen), it was easier to follow than when I read by myself; he made books seem close to our lives, close to hand, things we could *hold* in our hands; even the tundish and pandy-bats in *Portrait of the Artist* were like objects we might find at Skipton Grammar. Lately, I'd been reading a novel by Heinrich Böll, *Das Brot der frühen Jahre*, set in post-war Germany at a time of privation and food shortages. In the book there's a scene where the hero hungrily devours a loaf of bread. In the car, frustrated by my mother's absence, I began doing the same. Not that I was hungry, but it made life much more interesting to copy what people did in books. I tore another chunk from the loaf, not crust now but the soft white flesh beneath. What was my mother *doing*? She'd been gone twenty minutes at least. I imagined an old lady etherised on her bed, stretched out like the evening sky. My mother would have asked her, first, to undo the buttons of her blouse, please, and would be kneading the white flesh in search of lumps. I yanked some more bread into my mouth. Now my mother would be shining her pencil torch into various orifices – ears, nose, throat, perhaps even 'down below' – in search of cysts and polyps. Beneath the mounds of white flesh, the woman's nerves would be like cheesewire. I dipped my hand into the loaf again: the centre had gone completely, so I began to peel the flesh from the inner walls, clawing at the swooshy lining of the womb. Half an hour and still no sign. Maybe the patient was not an old lady. Maybe a pre-natal check had turned into a mid-natal crisis, and my mother would be out in a minute asking me to get sheets and boil water on the stove, the contractions coming faster now, her hand feeling for the baby's head, me ready with scissors to cut the cord . . .

Then she was there, under the rain, slamming the door and laughing – 'God, sorry, she was wittering on' – and, taking in the ruins of the loaf, 'There goes lunch,' she said.

Were we ever closer than that day? There were odd intimate phases later – her comforting me by the mantelpiece after my first heartbreak, the girl by the bonfire who'd gone off with an older boy; and then the letters I wrote from my summer job as a barman in North Wales, intended to amuse her while we were parted, full of the foibles of my clientele. But the day with the loaf was our high tide. Part of it was seeing her working. At home, it was easy to miss how much more she was than Mum. Work wasn't just a comfort or 'something to take her mind off' her marital troubles. It was challenge, stimulus, graft, guile and social interaction, and she did it on her own terms. Medicine confirmed her. It made her feel useful. More important, it made her feel *her*. In the car, I caught a glimpse of that. There we were, each in our way working together, a book in my hand, an auroscope in hers. A partnership. Such as she'd had with my father until Beaty.

I saw too, when we called at Cawder Ghyll, how much at home she felt in hospitals. The Water Street set-up was small, with only my father and a receptionist for company. Hospitals were bigger and more fun: she'd got used to them in the war years, and had grown up with a sense of thronging (the huge family in Langford Street, the bustling dormitories at the Loreto Convent in Killarney). Was going into general practice a mistake? Would she have been happier as a surgeon? Or would that have meant a life of sewing and sawing, no better than a seamstress's or butcher's? Much later, during a convalescent fortnight at Gisburne Park, my mother took to calling on her fellow patients at night, talking to them and checking their charts, as though still a doctor (in her distraction, perhaps she thought she was). She loved the company – the nurses, doctors, thermometers, swabs and medicine bottles. Even the smells were reassuring: iodine, bleach, the waft of the sick ward (and never mind that she was the sick one). Hospitals were institutions. And my mother, nineteenth of twenty, was an institutional soul.

That day thirty years before, I'd glimpsed this – or seen her in ways I'd never seen her at home. It cemented our relationship. And made it easier for us to shut out my father.

✻　　✻　　✻

IT WAS THEN I began sleeping with Sandra, our new house-keeper – the third or fourth we'd had since Rosa left at the end of the 1950s. I was fourteen and technically a minor, but she was only four years older and scarcely more experienced herself. I didn't love her, but I was fond of her, and liked breaking down her resistance. The resistance didn't go deep, and nor did I. We were kids excited by our suddenly adult bodies, but uncertain how to use them for penetration. 'I shouldn't be doing this,' she'd say, thinking of her position, which was under me but also that of trusted servant. Conscience-stricken, she'd fight me off. But then I'd kiss her neck and stroke her breasts and be allowed to go on unhindered. I don't remember kissing her on the mouth much. This wasn't passion or even intimacy. But we were friends without our clothes on, and in the process discovered orgasms. Our games in bed fostered an illusion which the era, the sixties, fostered too, a dream of sex without consequences. Intercourse was a teenage experiment. The fun and games happened on Friday evenings, when my parents were down the pub. Come closing time, we'd keep our ears open for the car. The furtiveness seemed perfectly natural. My father and Beaty were furtive too, disguising desire as platonic friendship. This was the house rule: that things must look innocent and familial. The chief dupe in it all was my mother. Not that she *was* duped: I'm sure she knew but, as with my father, turned a blind eye. Once she walked in on us in the dining room. Sandra was getting some cutlery from an alcove, and I came up behind her and slipped my hands round her breasts. We were struggling and swaying there, my mouth on her nape, my chest on her spine, my erection against her coccyx, when my mother appeared in the doorway. 'What's going on?' she said, more intrigued than accusing. 'Just mucking about,' I said, pretending to fight Sandra for the right to lay the table for supper. Not for a second could my mother have believed it. But she shrugged and left the room.

Looking back, I see my father and I leading parallel lives – acting in concert with our consorts. There's him sleeping with Beaty and me with Sandra right under my mother's nose. Both of us, put to the test, would have sworn it was her whom we loved best (we'd even have called her by the same name, 'Mummy'). But both of us betrayed her. And though in time she forgave us (her teenage son easily enough, her husband with difficulty), for a season or more she must have felt to be living in a hothouse, a stew of hormones, a den of masculine vice.

✻   ✻   ✻

Her sexual history? Easy.
There was no one before him.
There was no one during.
There was no one after.

✻   ✻   ✻

HER LIKES? Elegant clothes, babies, collecting antiques, Frank Sinatra, Bing Crosby, Alan Bennett, Victor Borge, the humour of Dave Allen, the art of conversation (with her in a listening role). Dislikes? Swear words, weeding, beer, long walks and scruffiness.

She held herself back, and I understood this was the right way to behave. Extroverts might be fun but they were vulgar. Rather than flaunt what you had, best keep it in reserve. Blushing and stammering through my teens, I adopted her aesthetic of shyness. What lay behind it – her great fear of declaring who she was – never struck me. Her chameleon skin rubbed off on me, too: I was all things (and therefore nothing) to all men, the quiet one at the back of the class, a blender-in.

Did she instruct me at all? Give me advice for later life? Tell me how to behave with women? In *The American President*, a not very prestigious Hollywood film, the titular hero (Michael Douglas) is advised by his young daughter that the way to a woman's heart is to compliment her on her shoes. 'Did Mom tell you that?' he asks (her mother, aka his wife, having died some years before). She did, of course: it's what moms are supposed to do, tell you things to store away for future use. But my own mother wasn't like that. I can recall no conventional wisdom dropping from her lips, no list of Dos and Don'ts. Buy her flowers, flatter her beauty, look fascinated by what she's saying, tell her you love her three times a day, don't criticise her clothes and never ever mention her weight: she'd have thought such stuff silly and soppy. It was her job to help me through childhood. But as to relationships, let me find out for myself.

✳   ✳   ✳

IN 1950 MY parents had been adventurous, travelling for six weeks through Austria and Switzerland, a £50 travel allowance in his wallet and a foetus (me) inside her. After that they holidayed in Britain. There was a fortnight in Majorca in 1960, but for the rest it was tents, caravans and rented cottages on western coasts. In the rain and wind, beside a gloomy emerald sea, my mother must have felt at home. But Scotland and North

310

Wales were as close as we came to Ireland. We had the one holiday in Kerry when I was five, then never again. I didn't know what I was missing and yet I missed it. For my mother's siblings, leaving Killorglin hadn't meant breaking ties: Eileen and her children, for example, would go back there every summer, all the way from Africa or the USA. But for my mother that wasn't an option. Her family would visit us, but we didn't visit them. If she was nostalgic, there were no signs: the TV ads for Kerry Gold butter didn't tug her heartstrings and when tourists from all over Europe began discovering the beauty of the Ring of Kerry she exhibited no local pride. She preferred not having to think about where she'd come from and who she'd been. I regretted this scorched earth policy. But it was how she wanted it – her choice, or martyrdom.

For ten years, where to go on holiday (and whether my father should accompany us) was a vexed question. Then in 1967 we bought a 'chalet' – a glorified caravan – overlooking the Warren Beach at Abersoch. My father had a special feeling for the place – the Llyn Peninsula was where he'd holidayed as a child – and, having forked out 'a small fortune' (£2700) for the chalet, he made a point of using it as often as possible. The Warren had a club, with table tennis and Sunday opening, and my parents made new friends there. At closing time the friends would be invited back – afternoons to sunbathe on the terrace, nights to swim in the phosphorescent sea. My mother sat out the swimming. She also sat out water ski-ing when my father bought a speedboat and wetsuits, though if no one was around she sometimes drove. She was content to stay on the margins. 'I'll make the tea and sandwiches,' she'd say. 'So long as Arthur's happy – that's the main thing.'

By now his relationship with Beaty had lost its heat and after the chalet it cooled still more. My mother told herself she had been right to stick it out, though the effort had left her wounded. She had him back, not tail between legs exactly but undivided in his loyalties. She counted her blessings, or rather he counted them for her. So it was all right then? No. There was still the loss of faith, the sense of a God that had failed her. And the depression underneath – the little shadow, looming larger now, that pre-dated Beaty and even him.

*   *   *

WOMEN ENVIED HER waistline. Her breasts might be too small, and her hips too wide, but she was slim. She didn't count her calories or take exercise, and I assumed this slimness came naturally. Looking back, I see it more darkly, as a loss of appetite for life. She eats no fruit and little meat, and left to herself would live off toast. Only celery seems to delight her – or perhaps it's me who's delighted, watching her dip the pale green stalk in salt and hearing it crunch between her teeth. Her whole manner when she eats is of someone in discomfort, afraid of enjoying herself or putting on weight. Indulge herself, even for a moment, and the ugly truth will come out.

She cooks, of course, because that's what a wife must do, but gets no pleasure from it – and since my father thinks them pointless never holds dinner parties ('The Joneses asking you round, and you having to ask them back, and everyone stuck at a table for hours when they could be playing snooker or darts'). For herself, she wouldn't mind the company. But in other ways it's a relief. Food just doesn't interest her. If she could, she'd be an astronaut, getting all her nutrition from pills.

*   *   *

AS THOUGH TO anchor herself in the English middle classes she became, if only mildly, a snob. At first she didn't mind me hanging out with the working-class kids. She hadn't much choice in the matter: there *were* no middle-class kids in Earby or Barnoldswick as far as I knew. One friend was Graham Jagger – bony as a whippet, easily injured, but a star at games. Once, after football on the rec at Sough, he and I had a bath at his house in Kelbrook – a tin bath in front of the fire. My mother liked the Jaggers. And approved of me 'mixing'. I sensed no snootiness at all.

312

By my mid-teens, though, it was different. Because he drank with farm-hands and mill-workers in the taproom, preferring their company to that of businessmen and lawyers, she called my father an inverted snob, and took pains to ensure I didn't follow suit. My broad Yorkshire accent discomfited her – as did my asking, when I was ten or so, what the word 'fuck' meant. Her worry was I'd get in with the wrong crowd. So-and-so was rough, she'd warn me – and if I disputed it, she'd point out that the family were all patients, so she *knew*. Rough girls were a particular problem – what if I became too involved? what if one of them fell pregnant? In birth control matters, she was a liberal. Best be safe and prescribe the Pill was her attitude. But she didn't intend her son to be a beneficiary of such largesse. Even with the Pill, mistakes could happen, and a girl might refuse the offer of a hush-hush abortion. I'd be off to university soon. And with luck would meet someone nice there. How terrible to miss out through embroilment with some wild or wily local lass.

She needn't have worried. To a teenage boy, the template of femaleness is his mother. So when I began going out with girls, the quality I looked for was deference. In the sixties small-town north, it wasn't difficult to find. Girls would put up with a lot, it seemed, so long as you were occasionally nice to them. In fact they'd do more or less anything you asked, except be touched in certain places (which was allowed only if you'd been going out together for a decent interval – anything, depending on the girl, from a fortnight to five years). Sex aside, we boys called the shots: life at home, a patriarchy, was mirrored by life out there. Though not the forceful sort, I got used to being the boss in relationships, the one who drove the car, chose the film, arranged the tickets for the dance – a chip off the old block. For a couple of years I had an easy time of it. Later I had a harder time, encountering things for which the maternal template hadn't prepared me. I was used to intelligence in women, but not to self-assertion. It hadn't occurred to me that men don't always get their way.

✳    ✳    ✳

MY FATHER WANTED me to be a doctor — to take over the family business and live nearby. My mother didn't care what I did, so long as it was respectable. Children left home — you couldn't stop them. It was part of growing up and becoming independent. I felt guilty leaving her, all the same. My father cried when I went off (to university, a two-hour drive away), but I knew he'd be all right. My mother I wasn't so sure about — who'd keep her company and give her solace if things with Beaty hotted up again?

Work, as ever, was her solace. She had no hobbies, and though she was more of a reader than my father this wasn't saying much, since he read nothing but the *Daily Mail* and *Sunday Express*. In later years, I sometimes passed on literary novels to her, and once, playing the Irish card, a book of Seamus Heaney's poetry. But she was happier with easy reads — Jilly Cooper, Dick Francis, Maeve Binchy. 'Ach, it's piffle,' she'd say when I asked her about her latest library borrowing, but she preferred relaxing with piffle than struggling with high art. Severity she reserved for linguistic matters. '"At this moment in time"!' she'd mock, when some politician said it. 'It's not "disoriented", it's "disorien*tated*",' she'd chide. A woman journalist I know still remembers my mother berating her for using the word 'actually'. Her own use of language was spare. She trimmed and pared, as though back in theatre with a scalpel.

\* \* \*

IT WAS MY father's idea they retire at sixty. Though he still got along with most of his patients, his interest in medicine, never extensive in the first place, had long since disappeared. At the farewell party his friends plied him with whisky till he was legless (I have the photos of him being carried out). Next morning, clear-headed, he was up early, dying to get on. His new project, building a house in the paddock at the back of the Grange, reignited old passions and DIY skills. He was happy, unburdened, free to do as he pleased.

My mother was less happy. Left to herself, she'd have

carried on working indefinitely. But he talked her into making a clean break — no more medicine, not even Cawder Ghyll. She missed the work immensely. All the time on her hands felt like imprisonment, not liberation. Though she helped with the new house, it was his project, not hers. The days stretched greyly ahead. Unlike him, she had trouble sleeping. Dawn would find her awake and worrying — about her husband's heart, her daughter's eyesight, her son's lack of a proper job. Why was the house taking so long to finish? Where would they put all their furniture when it was done? Who'd buy the old house, given its disrepair? Were their pensions large enough? Who'd look after the dog when next they took a holiday? What were the odds of them being burgled? Was it fair asking Sandra to hoover round now she had that job in the Nelson dress shop? Should they ask her to start paying rent? What would they do if taken to court for those trees Arthur had so brutally lopped? If she went through to Skipton today, would there be less traffic morning or afternoon? Where should she park? Did the car have petrol? Was it worth trying to get an appointment for the hairdresser? Should it be the same perm as last time? Would they be able to disguise the grey . . .? There was no disguising the grey. Work had kept off her sense of futility, but retirement let it pour in. She had, she complained, too much time to think. The little worries were the worst. *Weltschmerz* she could cope with, but not this flood of niggling minutiae.

She hid her depths of depression, for fear we'd become alarmed. But sometimes she'd own up to 'feeling low', or my father would report that she'd been 'fretting and mithering'. He'd expected her to bloom, now she was a woman of leisure. Instead of which she creased and shrank.

✳   ✳   ✳

THERE WERE FRACTURES, too. Twice she broke her wrist in minor falls. They seemed unlucky accidents at first, until the word osteoporosis came up — brittle bone disease. She was still in her early sixties when it struck. Stress and poor eating habits are known to make it worse, and here she was spreading herself thinly: a slice of toast for breakfast; cheese and cream crackers for lunch; meat and two veg (but she might miss the veg) for supper. Doctors neglecting their own health: *that* old story. But my father was fussy about diet. Why, pushy in most things, didn't he push her on this? Or was this the one part of herself she clung on to, telling him where to get off, that she would eat, or not eat, as she pleased? Perhaps decline was in the genes, and her bones were simply programmed to break up. Once five foot five, she seemed much shorter now – as though the inner shrinking, into depression, were affecting her physique. When Gill and I were children, she used to measure us against the side of the door, in ruled lines, to see how we were growing up. I imagined doing the same with her, to see how far she was going down.

✧    ✧    ✧

THEY HUNG ON to the Abersoch chalet as long as they could, but also bought a Dormobile, for touring. The most spectacular tour (which meant shipping the Dormobile across the Atlantic rather than rent an American equivalent) came in 1973, when they spent five months travelling through the USA and Canada. My being there as a student was the excuse but the real reason was itchiness. The Dormobile eased the itch. Later, they upgraded to a Hymer, the Rolls Royce of camper vans. 'So many places to see,' my Dad said, 'and now we're retired we've all the time in the world.'

All the time in the world still wasn't enough to get them to Ireland – until September 1988, when my mother was over seventy and all her siblings bar Kitty and Eileen dead. From the overnight Holyhead ferry, they drove to Dublin for breakfast, called on Eileen at Crumlin, had lunch in Wicklow, passed through Glendalough, and went on from there, sleeping at assorted camp sites. It rained most of the time. The headlights kept failing, the engine wouldn't start, the exhaust snapped when he reversed into a wall and had to be tied with wire. But they visited both her sisters, and saw several nieces and nephews.

Their 1988 diary records every step of the journey. Each name and place-name is underlined. For the rest of that year (and every other year) they took turns to write the entries. But for the fortnight in Ireland, all the handwriting is his. She has nothing whatsoever to say.

✻    ✻    ✻

'There is a moment in each day that Satan cannot find,' wrote William Blake. For my parents, post-retirement, that time came round six in the evening: a gin and mixed for him, a G and T for her. Preferably outside, in the dying sunlight, York stone warm beneath their feet. The Dales rolling west beyond the garden. Friesians chomping the meadow. Swallows chittering overhead. A lens of moon rising. Marvellous.

✻    ✻    ✻

In 2001 a woman was discovered lying next to her husband's corpse. She'd been there for three years, and the joke was she didn't know the difference – the sex, the conversation, the contribution to housework were just the same. When my mother lay next to my father's corpse, a decade earlier, it was because her life had been snuffed out with his. She got up after a day or two, for the cremation, but her heart had joined his in the fire. Had she no autonomous being, then? No identity of her own worth preserving? Of course. But what they'd had together was larger. He'd had his faults, to say the least, but when she was with him she felt alive. Now she felt half-dead and very small.

For the sake of her children she hung on, but for herself had little interest in survival. She drove a car for a few more years, till hitting the accelerator instead of the brake and ploughing straight across a roundabout. She kept a dachshund called Nikki. She collected commemorative plates and snuff boxes. She attended the Mother's Union, went to stay with old friends, and babysat her grandchildren. But her sense of purpose had gone up in flames with my father.

317

I too was griefstruck when he died, and wrote a memoir of our relationship as therapy. When it appeared, people asked how my mother felt about it. 'She feels OK,' I said, which is what she'd told me. But she also informed my sister, just before it came out, 'I could top myself because of that bloody book.' Pre-publication nerves, we thought: she'd feel better once it was out. And when a couple of friends of hers read the book and reassured her it was 'well-meant', she rang to tell me, sounding relieved. But whereas the other books I'd written were proudly displayed in her living room, this one never made it there. After she died I found it in her wardrobe, at the bottom of its deepest drawer. By the look of the pages, it hadn't been opened. Reading the draft had been enough.

We'd often talked about the book, and she never complained, except to say that she hoped certain passages would be read as fiction. But perhaps her letting me publish it without protest was a mother indulging her only son. Or perhaps it was capitulation. Now I accuse myself of exploiting her quietist nature just as my father did. What right have I to criticise him, when guilty of the same offence?

✤    ✤    ✤

HER FRACTURES BECAME more frequent and healed more slowly. The worst of them came from that crash on the round-about (just outside Skipton, on an August Bank Holiday week-end – a miracle she'd not hit anything, witnesses said). My sister and I were on holiday at the time, and from her hospital bed my mother made friends promise, at pain of death, not to call us: she didn't want to spoil our time away. Her customary response to all offers of help was similar: she wasn't going to be a burden.

After the crash, I asked if she'd ever thought about moving house. It couldn't be easy on her own, I said. And she admitted to being low in spirits. Might she be happier living elsewhere?

'Dad built this house for our old age,' she said, 'and now I'm old. Gill can have it after I'm gone, but I'll not be budged till then.'

'I'm not trying to budge you, Mum. I just wondered. Some people do move – or even go back to their birthplace.'

'Me go back to Ireland? Not likely.'

'I don't want you to get lonely, that's all.'

'My friends are here. And Gill. And people call – a sister from Cawder Ghyll was round just the other day.'

'Is Cawder Ghyll still open, then?'

'No. It's a home for the elderly now – that's people like me, remember.'

The crash put an end to her driving. Left to herself she'd have gone on, but the doctors wouldn't allow it. She'd depended on cars – MG, Alvis, Metropolitan, Triumph Herald, Mercedes, Fiat, Renault – the models varying in status according to the money in the bank, but invariably with a soft top or sunroof. She'd needed them to visit patients. Now the patient, increasingly, was her.

✳   ✳   ✳

Without tights on, her legs looked pathetically thin. Pins, she called them. Bones with a sheaf of clingfilm round. She was becoming, as it were, steadily wobblier. Despite the wobbliness, when I arrived one July day during a heatwave, she insisted on making me tea. Stumbling about the kitchen in search of milk, mugs, teabags, she confessed that she'd cancelled her meals on wheels. These were the hot lunches we'd organised to be delivered each day, when it became clear she wasn't eating. How long ago did she cancel them, I asked? Oh, about Easter. Why? She was *sick* of them, that's why, and wanted the pleasure of cooking for herself. 'What else is there for me to do?' she asked. 'Anyway, I feel better.'

I was angry. The reason she felt better enough to cancel the meals was that she'd been eating them; now she was getting worse again. As to cooking for herself, there was no evidence of it. 'Is this blue Stilton?' I asked, not ironically, about a piece of blue cheese she was offering. 'No, it's Lancashire.' I pointed out the mould. 'Oh, I've gone off cheese,' she said. Gone off everything else too, by the look of the rotten half-lettuce and bottle of milk turning sour in the fridge. The fridge, otherwise, was empty. She said there was plenty in the freezer but I found only a single single-person meal. Her hands lived in the freezer, by the feel of them: 'poor circulation,' she said. She admitted she couldn't be bothered any more – wasn't in pain but had a sense of living only to live, 'days and weeks and months with nothing to look forward to.' I found it hard to argue with this. Her depression seemed entirely logical.

Next day, I took her back to London with me – an excuse to feed her, a chance for rest. She was a little better for the change of scene. Kathy and I were working all day, but she liked the evenings *en famille*, indeed thought them an extraordinary indulgence. After a week she said: 'You're spoiling me to death.'

✳   ✳   ✳

Three diary entries.

*11.11.96, Remembrance Day*

I take the train to visit her in Gisburne Park. Bad start, at King's Cross, when a man my age gets in the carriage to see off a mother my mother's age – he cheerful, she lucid and uncreased, me left sullenly brooding on the injustice of the ageing process: till my father died my mother looked young, but lately she's put on a couple of decades. Depressing journey, which includes the guard asking us over the address system if we'll kindly observe the traditional two-minute silence at 11am but the train then stopping at Retford at 11.01, which means admitting new passengers unaware of the request and disgorging old ones unable to observe it. In the cab from Skipton station, the air grows dark. Black clouds spread like bruises. In the distance Pendle Hill has the shape of an ancient burial mound. Down the long drive, I realise this is the place to which my parents used to come for their great annual shebang, the Craven and Pendle Harriers' Hunt Ball. I can remember my mother bending her perfumed cheek to kiss goodnight, then disappearing in her air-blue gown. Left to the mercies of a babysitter, I couldn't sleep for imagining the time she must be having – the buffet and chandeliers and dance-band polkas. Thirty years later, I can finally see the place for myself. The entrance hall where she left her fur now throngs with wheelchairs; instead of belles and beaux there are Zimmers in the corridors. It isn't what the place has come to that makes me sad but what my mother has come to to revisit it. Six croquet hoops rust outside. The peacocks on the lawn can't summon the energy to shriek. Memento mori are all around.

But my mother, in her bed, is feeling perky, and tops my story of the Intercity Remembrance Day fiasco with one of her own. She too tried to observe the silence, she says, but at 11am 'two nurses from physio came in, and I couldn't not talk to them, it would have been rude'. I suspect her of making this story up to keep the conversation going. In other respects, she seems confused. She asks me if I noticed 'how amazing the light was at eight yesterday evening: I must have fallen asleep – when I woke it was still bright sunshine.' Evening sunshine in November? The world of times and dates is slipping from her. It's as if she has lost some thread. As if she can't remember what day it is.

### Boxing Day–New Year's Eve 1996

To Suffolk for a few days. I drive up to Yorkshire to fetch my mother down, while Kathy and the children go ahead. I arrive to find them cowering in front of a paraffin stove, the central heating having failed. Outside, it's snowing and six below. 'Miserable for you,' we say to my mother, but she seems oblivious to the discomfort – her body's so racked by other pains a touch of hypothermia makes no difference. Once the heating's fixed, we have a good few days. But on the last, New Year's Eve, she gets up at dawn to have a pee, misses her footing and falls on the hard stone floor. I find her lying there some time later. Her elbow is gashed and, though there's little sign of blood (her heart too faint for vigorous pumping) her arm's a mess of bone and gristle. The doctor in Halesworth doesn't like the look of it, and wants to admit her to a hospital in Norwich. I explain she lives in Yorkshire, so he arranges for her to go to Bradford instead – better than Airedale (her nearest) for skin-grafts. She was due to go home today with friends of ours, but I feel it's up to me to get her there and see her settled. Outside, as I put her bags in the car, it's six below. Even the A1 is icy. But we make it by dusk – and by 8.30pm, after getting her registered, in bed and off to sleep, I'm told I might as well go home. My sister will be in to see her next morning. It's sleeting, and the M1 in Sheffield is down to one lane, but with no traffic around except grit lorries – who would be out on a night like this? – I have a clear run south. Midnight strikes just before I reach the Blackwall Tunnel. Home in three hours 40 minutes. I feel as triumphant as my father did, on one of his record-breaking journeys down to Abersoch.

Next day my mother's triumphant, too. The hospital decide against a skin-graft. My sister comes to collect her. Bandaged but cheerful, she goes home.

### 19.5.1997, Cromwell's

She's been here for over two months now. Is it wrong of us to have allowed it, when my father spent *his* last weeks at home? Impossible to say. But once we accepted what the GP told us, that a home was the only real option, there seemed no point in her being further afield. Cromwell's is friendly, well-run and ideally placed for visits from neighbours (handy for Gill too). Though the aspergillus is inexorable, in other ways she's prospering here: her mind has cleared and sharpened, and she chats all day with the nurses. She told me the other night: 'It's homelier than being at home.'

Today I find her sitting in a buttoned chair. The buttons, from what I can see, have disappeared, leaving the stringy elasticated bits that used to hold them. I imagine her body falling apart in the same way. But her mind's intact and racing, and after an hour I feel exhausted by her flow of talk. Is it the drugs? Does she save herself up for visits? Or is this what people are like when close to death? 'I'm glad you're here because I need the loo,' she says. I help her up, and she tries to walk alone, but her feet start to slide the minute they touch the floor and I end up half-dragging, half-lifting her there, no great effort, since she's only six stone. On the seat, she tilts to one side, and I worry she'll fall off. 'I'd better stay,' I say. 'Yes,' she says, not caring how unprecedented this is, me there in the room to hear the siss of urine and see the white toilet paper dabbed between her thighs. I carry her back to bed, no messing, her waist against mine, as though umbilically tied.

'By the way, I do *know*,' she says. 'You needn't worry, it doesn't scare me.' She means the aspergillus, and the fact she'll not get better. Her friend Margaret told her, my mother having asked ('And you must be honest') what the diagnosis was. It was I who told Margaret the other week. Yet I couldn't tell my mother – still can't address it, even now she's brought it up. How much of a failure is this? Have I built a wall between us? If I were braver and more candid, could we have deep talks about mortality? I doubt she wants that, yet feel I've let her down. She's wise, grown-up, a doctor. And here am I uselessly protecting her, from a truth she already knows.

# CHAPTER THIRTEEN

# One Day I'll Get the Call

ONE DAY I'LL get the call. It'll be Gill, my sister, at nine in the morning. She's just been phoned by Janice, at Cromwell's, the nursing home – my mother's suddenly worse, is 'very blue' in fact (a matter of blood supply not mood), and she, Gill, thinks I should come today. I'm sceptical: is it really necessary? (It's Kathy's birthday, and we've arranged to go out.) My mother has always had cold toes and fingers. Her being blue doesn't sound like the end, to me.

Distrustful, I'll call Janice, wanting it straight from her. She'll tell me my mother, first thing, asked to get dressed and sit in a chair, unusual for her – but then vomited, and there was blood in the vomit. It's difficult to say, she'll say. My mother's not in distress yet. She'd give her diamorphine if she were, but that would retard her breathing, which is already slower than it was. It's difficult to say, but if I can come I better had, today if possible, quickly, right away.

I'll put the phone down in the study, trembling. For months I'll have seen this coming, but now it has come unseen. I'll look out, beyond the roses framing the glass door, past the summer flowers on either side of the basement steps, to the bland sub-urban scene on the lawn beyond – hammock, folding chairs, badminton net – and it won't seem possible anyone could die on a day like this, death in all the books being a winter thing, death in my own small experience (my father, five years ago) meaning the short light of December and flurries of snow. I'll tell myself this, intending to hang on a couple of hours, no panic. There's work I need to do, things I'm meant to think about. But unable to work or think, I'll have a bag packed in fifteen minutes, leave a note for Kathy, and be gone.

I'll be in good time at King's Cross, early enough to walk the platform to the front of the train, where there's an all but empty carriage and a table to myself. I'll spread my books and papers out, but the two hours forty minutes to Leeds will be spent looking out the window, nothing written, nothing read. Out the window and into the past. I have done this journey so often lately, shuttling between my home and my mother's home, that the train is like a home, too. I'll work out that, at an average of a trip a month, though sometimes it's been once a week, and this is only counting *my* trips, not the holidays in Yorkshire *en famille*, I must have spent around £4,000 on these journeys in the past few years. Good-son behaviour. But bad-son to calculate the cost. The devil take me. But it's probably my mother I get it from. Didn't she hit the roof if ever I called her before six (when the cheaper rate begins) or if I came from London at times ineligible for a Supersaver? And sordid though the calculations are, they're meant to stop me thinking about the bigger thing – that I'm on my way to see my mother die.

The Skipton train is scheduled to depart from Leeds one minute after the London train arrives, an unguaranteed connection even if you sprint, but today we'll come in early, I'll make it easily, with three minutes to spare. It all goes so smoothly that a calm will descend, as if she cannot die today or will wait till we are with her, son and daughter, a replay of my father's death, in a home rather than at home, but otherwise straight from a Victorian novel, textbook-perfect, the family gathered round the bed. This sense of calm will last all the way to Shipley, where the train sits for twenty minutes before a platform loudspeaker apologises for the delay, 'due to an unidentified object being thrown onto the overhead line at Keighley.' Is the unidentified object a body? Has there been a suicide? Or is it a kids' game on the embankment gone wrong, a fatality of some kind blocking my way to another fatality, due to happen soon, perhaps having happened already?

I'll sit there at the little station as the minutes pass, and more and more people sigh, tut, collect their things, get off. How long can I hang on to the certainty I'll still make it or the resignation that if I don't I wasn't meant to, my mother being too far gone to care? The sun will spill its kindly light. There'll be school-children across the car park, excited, the last week of term. I'll have my handkerchief out and will snuffle in it, not tears of grief but hay fever. I'll wish I had a mobile phone, to check in with Cromwell's. After more delays, they'll announce a coach has been summoned and that when it comes, eventually, it will drop passengers at all stations, the names of which, in sequence, I've come to know by heart: Saltaire, Bingley, Crossflatts, Keighley, Steeton & Silsden, Cononley, Skipton. I'll have been wondering for ages about a taxi, and now I'll get off the train and go in search of one. Wandering the streets, I'll imagine my mother reproaching me when I reach her: 'A taxi? All the way from Shipley? How much did that set you back? What was the rush? You knew I'd be here.' Before I find a taxi, shouldn't I ring from a call-box and see how she is? If she's better, or dead already, a slow journey by coach won't matter. And yet it does matter. I start to panic at last: I want to get there fast.

There'll be four cabs parked in a row in the main square, all very local-looking. I'll stick my head in the window of the front one and the driver will pat the seat and say 'Please get in, sir'. When I try to ask him, first, can he take me to the other side of Skipton, twenty miles off at least, well beyond his usual circuit, he'll simply pat the seat again. I'll get in beside him, my two bags dumped behind us. He'll be big, friendly, Asian, his skin slightly pockmarked. So Skipton then, he'll say, pointing out that the cab is metered and also (paradoxically) that he needs my money now. I'll reassure him: I have the money, it's OK. Roughly how much will it be? He'll struggle with the sum, or the language, I'm not sure which. Sixty or seventy, he'll say, and I'll express incredulity, and make to get out, until he writes down 16/17 on a piece of paper, and I say fine, and reassure him once again I have the cash and explain about having to rush because my mother's very ill. We'll set off slowly. In the heavy traffic it's hard for him to make headway, but even when we have a clear stretch he'll drive at thirty, and I begin to wonder if he's got the point (though I say it twice more) that I'm in a rush because my mother's very ill. Most of the time he'll be jabbering into his mouthpiece at the end of its flex – he says something, then clicks a button, producing a hiss from the mouthpiece and a voice through it, also jabbering. 'My friend,' he'll explain, a big grin across him, and add that he himself is from Keighley, not Shipley, so knows the way to Skipton, it's OK. And I'll wonder if it is OK, if a man on the way to his mother's death doesn't deserve better service than this, from someone who'll be serious and dignified or at least get there in time.

Resignation ousting panic as we queue through Bingley, I'll ask him about his family. He has two sons, he'll say, aged three and five. And was he born here? Yes. What about his parents? They came in 1958. That's early, I'll say, thinking how rare brown faces were back then, how all the anti-Paki jokes began only as the influx grew, in the 1960s. Yes, he'll smile, very early, proud his parents were the first wave. But the Asian community in Yorkshire is big now, he'll say, 80,000 or 90,000. And we'll be driving along the valley past Keighley, spits of rain in the air, and I'll look at the wet hills and the meadows cradled in their U and the river Aire bisecting them, and I'll think how incongruous it is, people from a far hot country coming to settle here, how pleasing, too, the place back then having been so dull and monochrome. In Skipton, in the 1960s, there'd been just a couple of Asian families, pitched at the edge of town, as if ready to be run out of it. Now there are many more Asian families here, not all of them on the fringes, not all of them poor.

Have I ever been to Pakistan, he'll ask? Well, I've been to India, but no. His family is from Kashmir. When he went back to visit last year, it was jabber-jabber all the time. With Asians, wherever they are, it's always jabber-jabber. The English are so quiet, he finds. He'll ask where I live, and then how I like it in London, and don't I miss Yorkshire, which I do. My mother and sister are still here, I'll say (silent brackets: my mother only just). I often come to visit, but my children are London children and it's where I've lived for over twenty years. And his home? His home is Keighley, he'll say, he doesn't like London, it's a muck-hole, he visited it once but never again. So is the attraction here the countryside? I'll ask, nodding at a hay meadow or at some cowpat-heavy acre by the river. No, he prefers the towns, all the Asian people do. But in ,Pakistan, there must be many people who live off the land? Yes, he'll say, it's town we like, not understanding what I'm getting at or politely contradicting me. You work the land only if there's nothing else. Only white middle-class Europeans are romantic about fields.

It'll be drizzling steadily now, St Swithin's Day, too, which means rain for forty days and nights. But he'll be making progress none the less, reaching 50 on the Skipton bypass, though the steering wheel judders if he goes any faster, as he demonstrates – the car has remoulds, that's the reason. It's not his car, but rented from the boss, who runs it for Shipley Council. If it were private it'd be in better shape, but the council do things on the cheap, if I know what he means. Through all this, some part of me will be with my mother, will have gone ahead and sat down in the room, scanning her for signs of life, finding them one moment, losing them the next. Who's to say if she's still breathing? I can't know, locked here in the present, in a clapped-out car, with a driver who, to judge from his speed, would rather travel than arrive. But just for now, sitting by him, listening to him, past, present and future seem to dissolve. Calm again, I know she'll not let me down.

In ten minutes we're there, outside Cromwell's. He'll wait while I search my pockets for the fare, £26 it turns out, don't ask me why. By now he has taken in the kind of place this is, and can't help but see, as I do, an ancient face peering forlornly through the window. When he takes my money, not meeting my eyes, I'll sense he seriously disapproves of me putting my mother (as no Muslim would) in a home. I feel judged by him as he drives off: there's him, a local man with family values, and here's me, an alien from the wilds of London with no sense of kinship or blood.

Janice will be waiting to let me in, not the Janice I spoke to earlier but the smaller, blonder deputy who shares her name. I'll walk to the Byron room on my own. My mother will be there still – even if she were dead she'd be there, but she's alive, unconscious, her head propped on the pillow, not struggling to draw in air, not coughing either as she has these past few months, but breathing more easily, nearer death. Gill will be sitting beside her, will have been there all day, and we'll kiss each other on the cheek, perfunctorily, neither of us willing to be distracted. She'll say that Mum talked a little round lunchtime – a yes or no of acknowledgment, nothing more – but has uttered nothing since. I'll sit on the edge of the bed, and hold my mother's hands (which are warm now), and say I'm here. But her eyes will be three-quarter closed and she won't acknowledge me. There'll be occasional 'ums', little grunts of assent, but they'll come randomly, not in response to anything we've said. Janice, the original Janice not the Janice who let me in, will enter and say that's how it is with coma patients – they know you're there, and want to let you know they know, but can't respond appropriately. So too with the terminally ill: the hearing is the last sense to go. It's a thought I'll need, a consolation for not arriving in time to hear my mother speak. How far it's true is something else: she's partly deaf, and the good (left) ear is the one she's lying on. According to Janice, she will probably die tonight, but her breathing's easy so it may take longer.

At this point, reassured, Gill will leave to cross the road to her house: the kids are back from school, there's tea to make and her husband Wynn to contact, who she'd sent to meet me at the station and may still be waiting. I'll settle in for a long vigil. But five minutes after Gill leaves, my mother's eyes will suddenly widen, she'll stare me in the face, and my heart will lift, and I'll start to chatter, very quickly, very quietly, little nothings, comfortings, communication lines to reel her back in: Oh Mum, I'm here, I know you're not well today, you've had a bad day, but we'll soon have you better, we're all looking after you, I'm here now, Gill's been here all day, Janice's here too, I can see your eyes open, you can see me, can't you, oh Mum, I'm here, see, can you hear me, I'm here. I'll say all this but she'll just stare at me, and then her brow will wrinkle slightly, the trace of a frown, as if she's half-registered what I've said but doesn't agree or doesn't know what to make of it, and then she'll express a deeper puzzlement at something unprecedented happening, at which her face will cloud and her mouth clamp, and a little trickle of something will come from one corner of her lips, and then she'll open her mouth wider, awkwardly, as if to say something huge and definitive, to cough it out at last, to assert herself and make it plain, and the effort of this cough or assertion is so hard that her eyes will close, scrunch up and water with the effort (closed though they are, I see them water), and the silent cough will pass through her, and then again pass through her, and then a third time, and when her mouth opens and closes the third time there'll be no breath any more, only a tear in the corner of one eye. And the way both eyes widen and stare at the start of this will remind me exactly of my father, the last moment of his looking through me and the whole of life passing before his eyes. And it's this memory more than the lack of her breathing or moving that will make me realise my mother has just died.

A look at the clock: 6.05 pm, I got here just forty minutes ago. I'll be hyper, and trembly, and will put my face to hers like a mirror wanting to mist up. And because I've convinced myself she may be breathing still, or just anyway, I'll let go of her hand and call Gill from the bedside phone and tell her to come, now, fast, now. And it isn't imagination because I'll see the pulse in my mother's neck move, and lower in the neck another pulse, and then the doorbell will ring at the front of the home, and then (no one answering) ring again, and I'll rush to let Gill in, and race back, and we'll sit on either side of the bed leaning over the body we both came from, scanning it for life. At some point Gill will reach to feel if there's a pulse, but it'll be my wrist holding Mum's wrist that she holds instead, which we don't notice for a moment and are fooled by – life! hope! – until we laugh at the absurdity, because we know there can be no doubt now, she's dead. But we'll not fetch anyone else yet. We want this – her – for ourselves.

It will be peaceful sitting there: no need to fear the worst will happen, now it has happened, and for the best.

After five minutes or so, I'll go into the corridor and call for Janice, any Janice, and one of them will come in, a bit harassed, a bit taken aback and slightly nervous, as if we might feel shocked or cheated by the suddenness. She'll feel the nothing pulse and then ask us to give her ten minutes alone to 'tidy the poor darling up', which reluctantly we do. When we come back, our Mum will be lying flat, no props anymore, and there'll be a yellow flower between her hands, its petals resting on her chin. I'll hate that flower on principle, out of love and loyalty, knowing my mother would have hated it too. I'll want to touch her in sympathy for having to hold it, and for all she had to suffer before. But I'll feel inhibited from touching her, as I didn't with my father when he died: it feels invasive, an impropriety – Gill can do it but for me it would seem a transgression. I'll do no more than touch her hands, to test their warmth, and kiss her brow, as promised to Auntie Beaty (who we'll have called during the ten minutes outside, the first to know). Her face will have healed remarkably from the fall she had three weeks ago, just a bruise on the right temple. Impassive, high-cheekboned and with her hair drawn back, she will look beautiful. All has been shed now: warmth, flesh, stubbornness, life. She'll look like the lamb inside the sheared sheep. Almost a child. Agnes.

I'll cry a bit, less so when Gill's there, more when I go over to the empty house. It can't be my mother I'm crying for, who (so everyone says) is better off now, but myself. Among the items that will crack me up are her 80th birthday cards from three months ago, with their naff verses promising that the best years are all to come. I'll remove a bottle of whisky from her room, nine-tenths empty, and knock it back. I'll go over to my sister's and numb myself with telly. I'll feel great gasps of grief again as I re-enter my mother's house. But I'll sleep like a top in her bed, on the lumpy foam mattress she meanly persisted with despite her back problems. No ghosts. No nightmares. The two of us at peace.

Next day I'll wake at 7.30, feeling all right, doing OK. 16 July. I'm due to give a reading tonight at the Arvon Foundation, in Hebden Bridge, half an hour away: I arranged it months ago partly so I could see my mother *en route*. I'll go ahead with it, I think – tell no one what has happened and proceed as planned.

I'm tough, professional, I can do this, I'll tell myself for about ten minutes, until I see my mother again in her room at Cromwell's: after the fluffy fantasy of coping, the marble reality of her death. She'll look beautiful still, the lips a little tighter on her teeth, the mouth less slackly half-open. I'll sit beside her and cry, and wait for her to stir from her ice-posture to comfort me. I am crying like a child but she will not be a mother to me – has become this ex-mother, uncossetting, unreachable. I've sometimes thought she might have been warmer to me, more cuddly, when I was young. But my outrage at her not stirring will make me see this must be untrue – her unreactingness is painfully unfamiliar. I'll feel alone for the first time. Once or twice I thought I'd lost her before, to dementia, but she always came back. She doesn't now, nor ever will.

The day will stretch on and on.

At nine o'clock I'll read the newpapers. My mother's won't have been the only death. There'll be Gianni Versace, the fashion designer, gunned down outside his mansion in Miami. And Bernadette Martin, an eighteen-year-old Catholic girl who had fallen in love with a Protestant boy, Gordon Green, and was sleeping overnight at his house in Aghalee, Co. Antrim, with him and his sister, until shot through the head four times by a Loyalist gunman who entered the house and walked into the bedroom.

At ten, the undertaker will come. It'll be Malcolm, who did my dad too – the family undertaker we'll have to call him at this rate, though he has undertaken, so he'll inform us (he looked it up and counted), 248 funerals in between. Whereas he rolled up for my father with a coffin, with my mother he'll come with a little wooden trolley, inconspicuous in the back of his estate car. We'll fix a date for the funeral, next Tuesday, then I'll depart, not watching, but imagining every move, my mother lifted from bed, strapped to her trolley and then wheeled outside, half erect, as it were sitting up, for all the world like an elderly patient off to have a hospital check-up. I understand the trolley. Patients in Cromwell's like to watch what's going on outside the window, and a coffin would be bad for morale. But I doubt they're fooled that easily. Word will have got round. The lady doctor – Mrs

Morrison, remember, the one in the Byron room along the corridor, the one always chatting to the nurses, very sad, yesterday evening, poor soul.

At eleven, Dr Suleman will call, with a problem. It's he who certified my mother's death. But because he joined the practice just the day before, and didn't see my mother alive, the coroner won't let him sign the death certificate. The two doctors who could sign it, having seen her in the last fortnight, are both on holiday and won't be back till Monday, which makes things tight for the funeral, since the crematorium will need the green form from the coroner's office at least 24 hours ahead. The alternative is a post-mortem . . . I'll tell him we're going to think about it and that we'll call him back. But we don't want to even begin thinking about it: my mother has been slowly dying for months, everyone aware of the causes, and now to have to violate her body, dead as it is (the stomach slit open, the rib-cage cracked apart, the head sliced into), no, no, no, no, it's one indignity too many. The doctors will have to get their act together on Monday morning. I'll call Dr Suleman to tell him this, and he'll agree.

At midday, we'll clear the Byron room of my mother's things – the radio, the upright chair, the bedside cabinet, the little wooden table brought across from her house, to make her feel more at home. There'll be the uneaten boxes of chocolates, too, the unbroken-into gifts of soap and scent, the flowers, the pot plants, the clothes, the spangled labrador brooch, the cameo brooch, the 'Eighty Years Young' and 'Frankly My Dear I Don't Give a Damn' badges from her birthday party. We'll take them back to her house, hanging the coats and dresses in the wardrobe, filling her dressing table with tights and knickers, restoring the furniture to its rightful place, as if she could walk in and start over, or for ourselves to feel a sense of order again, or just to be armed against the pathos of seeing, on the windowsill, the brown plastic combs she wore in her hair.

At one o'clock, we'll check the contents of her handbag: three ten-pound notes, one fiver and a few pence change; a cheque card, signature barely legible; a phone card; nothing else.

At two, we'll eat a sandwich, and share the Tarte Au Citron

bar of chocolate we found in her room with 'Display until 15.7.97', yesterday's date, on its wrapper.

At three, the vicar will turn up, Trevor, nice and cheerful. He'd only just come to the parish when my father died but my mother he got to know quite well. She even had a spell of going to church, but then stopped, just like that. Did she think the C of E service somehow not real, he wonders? They often talked about religion. Two weeks ago he'd come to see her, but the nurses said they needed five minutes to change her, and twenty minutes later, still no sign of them finishing, he went. It will occur to me, as he's speaking, that my mother, for whatever reason (fear? guilt? Catholicism?), didn't want to see him and that the nurses helped her out. And yet she liked to spar with him. As to the funeral service, two hymns is normal, he'll say. Gill will choose 'Amazing Grace'. I'll take 'Abide with Me'.

At four, I'll drive to Skipton to arrange for memorial cards to be printed, to send to friends too old or far away to come to the funeral.

At five, I'll call those who can come, to give them the place and time. Auntie Edna will cry, Catherine Manby too. Two of the men will be awful, the tone all wrong, too bland, almost facetious.

At six, I'll start getting drunk for the evening with Gill and Wynn. Wynn says he can't bear the idea of corpses. Spending time with his cancer-ridden father-in-law (by his first marriage) was what did the damage: 'It put me off death for life.'

At eleven o'clock that night, I'll climb into her bed. The room will wear her scent still, as it always has. For how much longer will it stay? How bearable will life be when I've lost the last whiff of her?

And the day of the funeral will be summery but chaste, dark cloud respectfully covering the blue. Ragged robin and cow parsley will bloom in the untended garden, pink fuchsia by her front door. An old friend or two will cry off, but the church will be full. And after that, and after the crem, thirty or so guests will come back to my parents' house, as they've often done but never, as today, without the hosts. Outside, at the edge of the lawn, half a dozen children, sharing one club, will chip and drive golf balls down the meadow, until the last of the balls is lost.

And I'll worry was it wrong for an Irish Catholic to die in a place called Cromwell's.

And I'll wonder if the window of her room was open when she died (in legends the soul departs through the gateway of the teeth, and then, if there's a window open, out the house – otherwise the soul remains in purgatory). Did a shadow pass over? Was there an extra white cabbage butterfly dancing outside?

And afterwards, in the empty house, my sister, pissed, will say of course I know, don't I, that she, Mum, loved her, Gillian, more than she loved me.

And next morning five crows and four magpies will commandeer the lawn, moving in on the dead, swaggering about as if they owned the place.

And the morning after that, my last in Yorkshire, there'll be a blue, skimmed sky and mist in the valley bottom by the canal. And I'll remember the fog I drove through to visit my mother when I was up for the Bulger trial in Preston four years back. And I'll think of the white fog, the aspergillus, that filled the cavities of her lungs, and I'll wonder how far back it began, whether it was there then in 1993, or when my father died, or in my childhood, or when they met, its spores ready and waiting for the body to weaken so they (like those crows and magpies) could move in and make the place theirs.

And there'll be cuckoo-spit in the hedges: the froth of grief, the gobbed misery of the bereaved.

And before I go, I'll make an inventory, for no good reason, of her kitchen cupboard: 1 tin of Heinz mushroom soup; 1 packet of Bisto, gone lumpy and hard; 1 Saxa salt container; 1 Horlicks jar; 1 glass bottle with a ¼ inch of brown vinegar; 1 salt, pepper and mustard set (wooden), minus the lid of the mustard jar; 1 packet of dried onions; 1 tin of mandarin oranges, best before Dec. 96; 1 packet of Uncle Ben's long-grain rice; 1 jar of mango chutney; 1 packet of Davis gelatine, decades-old, price 10p; 1 Lea & Perrins bottle; 1 packet of bay leaves.

And her obituary will appear in the local paper next to a story about a children's author living in Earby, Melvyn Burgess, whose novel *Junk*, about heroin-addicted teenagers, has won a major prize.

And her friends will tell me my mother was 'deep'.

And back in London I'll not get used to the phone not ringing. At six-thirty part of me will be poised and braced still, an inner ear cocked for her evening call ('it's cheaper after six') and for the latest health bulletins. Now there is no latest. Now she is late.

And I'll think of the auburn plait, 18 inches long, I found in her wardrobe, and of how much else was cut off with it, including anger and selfhood.

And I'll wonder if the Mariolatry she was raised in helped her find a spiritual calm. And whether it was Roman Catholicism, or giving it up, that made her so long-suffering. And whether particles of her faith have blown invisibly, like seed-dust, into me.

And I'll lie back on the night grass and look upwards at the August sky, at shooting stars, the ash-fall of galaxies. So big tonight, not the usual little angled volleys, but flaring well-drops, vertical plummetings, with a stitch of silver left behind. Heart-stopping to watch. Such fire and elation. And I'll remember that when my mother almost died back in February, the Hale-Bopp comet looked on from one corner of the sky. Its flare was white and in slow-mo, like the fungus in her chest. Whereas the August light-show is celebratory: long lives passing before our eyes in an instant, lit snail-trails speeded up a million times. A nice way to think about the dead, that these could be their frolicking souls, each zip-trace a happy goodbye to us, as if to say: 'We're all right, let us go now – and don't grieve.'

And months later we'll spread her ashes among the roses where my father's were spread.

And we'll go back to Killorglin and climb Carrauntoohil, Ireland's highest mountain, losing ourselves on its summit and exhausting ourselves from damp and panic till we find a way down.

And red fuchsia will blood the hedges of Kerry.

And her anniversaries will pass. And others will follow her into the dark, among them Uncle Ron – and Beaty, writing and phoning me to the last.

And I'll meet more cousins – Peter and Kerry Kehoe (Eileen's sons), who work for DuPont; Peter and Alex Curtin (Kitty's), both of them in banking, though Alex's passion is fly-fishing and he has written a book about the mayfly; and then other cousins at the wedding of Marguerite's son, Ivor, to which I'm invited, an honorary O'Shea at last, if only for the day.

And among the things my cousins give me will be photos. Not one shows my mother younger than twenty, but several have her posing happily with her sisters, as though restoring her to youth and life.

And all these things will happen ahead, but part of me won't ever catch up, will still be in the car travelling towards them, alongside the driver whose parents, like my mother, came here from another country and learned to call it home. Every street we pass on the drive from Bingley to Cromwell's has such stories in it, tales of migration and sacrifice. The diaspora. The multitudes seeking an elsewhere. The lives they left behind.

These hills have seen it all before. The streams trickling down their face suggest they're saddened by it, as I've been, thinking of what my mother gave up. But it's not a tragedy, I see that now. It's not been for this driver and his parents, and it wasn't for her. Haven't I too made a life elsewhere? What's wrong with that? To give up what you've known is nothing, in exchange for love and freedom and work. Let me grieve for my mother, but let me not pity her. What did she say when I last saw her? 'It's been a good life.'

I'll begin to feel better, remembering that. I'll lean back in the seat of the cab as we inch towards Cromwell's through the summer light. 'Go on,' the driver will grin, 'make yourself comfortable.' Then the car will pick up speed, and long shadows will fly past, and he'll talk into his hissing mouthpiece like a medium calling up the dead.

# ACKNOWLEDGMENTS

SEVERAL PEOPLE offered support or made useful suggestions while I was writing this book. My thanks to, among others, Mikela Callary, John Cornwell, Alex Curtin, Hugh Eccles, Marguerite Falvey, Aisling Foster, Ian Jack, Liz Jobey, Pat Kavanagh, Kerry and Peter Kehoe, Margaret Melhuish, Susie Orbach, Bridie O'Shea, Janet Russell, Alison Samuel, John Walsh and Susanna White. The Loreto Abbey general archivist, Mary Blake, kindly answered several queries, as did Sister Cornelius and Sister Barbara O'Driscoll. I also had help from Mary Bredley and Suzanne O'Halloran at UCD, from Katy Lindfield at the Department of Health, and from the staff at the Wellcome Institute Library, London Library and British Library.

The epigraph from Auden's 'Twelve Songs: VIII' is reproduced by permission of Faber & Faber.

The lines from 'Let's Do It (Let's Fall In Love)' (words and music by Cole Porter, © 1920 Harms Inc, USA, Warner/Chappell Music Ltd, London W6 8BS) are reproduced by permission of International Music Publications Ltd.

The opening of Yeats's 'Never Give All the Heart' is reproduced by permission of A. P. Watt Ltd, on behalf of Michael B. Yeats.